MAKING CONNECTIONS

Reflecting on the Lives and Experiences of People with Learning Difficulties

A Reader

edited by

Ann Brechin and Jan Walmsley

at the Open University

Hodder & Stoughton

LONDON SYDNEY AUCKLAND TORONTO

in association with the Open University

SOUTH DEVON TECH COLLEGE

ACC 54475   CLASS 362. 3

This Reader forms part of the Open University course K668 *Mental Handicap: Changing Perspectives*. For further information on the course, write to Department of Health and Social Welfare (K668), North Spur Building, The Open University, Walton Hall, Milton Keynes MK7 6AA.

This reader is one part of an Open University integrated teaching system and the selection is therefore related to other material available to students. It is designed to evoke the critical understanding of students. Opinions expressed in it are not necessarily those of the course team or of the University.

British Library Cataloguing in Publication Data
Making connections: reflecting on the lives and
  experiences of people with learning difficulties: a
  reader
1. Learning disordered persons
I. Brechin, Ann   II. Walmsley, Jan
362.3

ISBN 0 340 51328 4

First published in Great Britain 1989

Selection and editorial material copyright © The Open University 1989

All rights reserved. No part of this publication may be reproduced or transmitted in any form or by any means, electronic or mechanical, including photocopy, recording, or any information storage and retrieval system, without permission in writing from the publisher or under licence from the Copyright Licensing Agency Limited. Details of such Licences (for reprographic reproduction) may be obtained from the Copyright Licensing Agency Limited of 33–34 Alfred Place, London WC1E 7DP.

Typeset by Wearside Tradespools, Fulwell, Sunderland
Printed in Great Britain for Hodder and Stoughton Educational, a division of Hodder and Stoughton Ltd, Mill Road, Dunton Green, Sevenoaks, Kent, by Richard Clay Ltd, Bungay, Suffolk

Contents

Acknowledgments   vi

Introduction   1

Section I   Roles and relationships   5

Introduction

1   'If you love him, let him go'   7
Ann Richardson

2   The social environment   13
Margaret Flynn

3   Do the professionals understand? Mothers' views of families'
service needs   24
*Mary MacLachlan, Pam Dennis, Hilary Lang, Sybil
Charnock and Jill Osman*

4   My own perspective and experience   29
Louisa Reynolds

5   Helping Bangladeshi families: Tower Hamlets Parent Adviser
Scheme   34
Hilton Davis and Prapti Ali Choudhury

6   Creating a 'working alliance' with people with learning
difficulties   42
Ann Brechin and John Swain

7   'Being there': evaluating life quality from feelings and daily
experience   54
Julie Wilkinson

8   Research interviews with people with mental handicaps   63
Dorothy Atkinson

Section II   Recognising oppression   73

Introduction

9   'What's in a name?'   76
Robert Bogdan and Steven J. Taylor

10   Learning to resist   82
Beverley Bryan, Stella Dadzie and Suzanne Scafe

11   A parent's diary   86
Anonymous

12   The new eugenics   89
     Michelle Stanworth

13   Sex and the mentally handicapped: a lawyer's view   94
     Mike Gunn

14   Barriers to adulthood: long-term unemployment and mental
     handicap compared   100
     Richard Jenkins

15   Learned helplessness theory and people with learning
     difficulties: the psychological price of powerlessness   109
     John Swain

Section III   Discovering a voice   119

Introduction

16   Locked away: life in an institution   121
     David Barron

17   A voice of our own   125
     Diane Amans and Christine Darbyshire

18   Day services: a users' account   130
     People First

19   The world of the congenitally deaf-blind: towards the grounds
     for achieving human understanding   133
     David A. Goode

20   Barry: a case study   140
     Valerie Sinason

21   Stigma and the self-concept of people with a mild mental
     handicap   147
     Andrew Jahoda, Ivana Markova and Martin Cattermole

Section IV   Support in the community   157

Introduction

22   Caring   159
     Pat Henton

23   A group home/landlady scheme   162
     Larraine Eastwood

24   Mary M . . .   167
     David Felce and Steven Toogood

25 Robert Griffiths   175
    Roger Blunden

26 Ageing in the community: a matter of choice   182
    Robert B. Edgerton

27 For better, for worse?   188
    Linda Ward

28 Community care: the ideal and the reality   199
    Gillian Dalley

Section V   Our common humanity   209

Introduction

29 A brief outline of the principle of normalisation   211
    Wolf Wolfensberger and Stephen Tullman

30 Setting the record straight: a critique of some frequent
    misconceptions of the normalisation principle   220
    Burt Perrin and Bengt Nirje

31 Whose community, whose care?   229
    Helen Smith and Hilary Brown

32 Parallels between the social role perception of people with
    learning difficulties and black and ethnic minority people   237
    Carol Baxter

33 Normalisation: the whole answer?   247
    Tim Robinson

34 Mental handicap and oppression   253
    Fiona Williams

35 How do we know what we think we know?   261
    Moyra Sidell

List of contributors   270

Index   276

Acknowledgments

We have been greatly assisted in our task as editors of this Reader by the support, encouragement and practical suggestions we have received from all members of the course team. While we must take final responsibility for the end result, we would like to extend our thanks for the time people gave willingly in offering constructive criticism and by helping us in the exciting but seemingly endless task of shaping and refining the selection and organisation of articles.

Thanks are due in particular to our colleagues on the course team, Dorothy Atkinson and Fiona Williams; reading members of the course team, Moyra Siddell and Alyson Peberdy; consultants on the course team, James Cummings (MENCAP), John Swain and Paul Williams; critical readers, Professor Oliver Russell, Zenobia Nadirshaw and Tariq Hussein; and external assessor, Professor Chris Kiernan. We are also grateful to Peter Lee and Giles Clark of the Open University Publishing Division for their valuable editorial advice, and to Christine Love, whose patient typing and photocopying helped us through every crisis calmly and efficiently.

The publishers would like to thank the following for permission to reproduce material in this volume:

The American Association on Mental Retardation for 'Ageing in the community: a matter of choice' by R. B. Edgerton from the *American Journal on Mental Retardation*, 1988, 92; the American Psychological Society for 'Barry: a case study' by V. Sinason originally published as 'Secondary mental handicap and its relationship to trauma' in *Psychoanalytic Psychotherapy* Vol. 2, No. 2, 1986; The Australian Group for the Scientific Study of Mental Deficiency for 'Setting the record straight: a critique of some frequent misconceptions of the normalisation principle' by B. Perrin and B. Nirje (abridged) from *Australia and New Zealand Journal of Development Disabilities* Vol. 11, No. 2; Basil Blackwell for 'If you love him, let him go' by A. Richardson from *LSE Quarterly* September 1987 and 'The new eugenics' from *Reproductive Technologies: Gender, Motherhood and Medicine* by M. Stanworth (ed.) (1987); BIMH Publications for 'Do the professionals understand?' by M. MacLachlan, P. Dennis, H. Lang, S. Charnock and J. Osman (1987) and 'Helping Bangladeshi families' by H. Davis and P. A. Choudhury (1988) both from *Mental Handicap* and for 'Mary M' from *Close to home: a local housing service and its impact on the lives of nine adults with severe and profound mental handicap* by D. Felce and S. Toogood (1988); Blackwell Scientific for 'Stigma and the self-concept of people with a mild mental handicap' by A. Jahoda, I. Markova and M. Cattermole from *Journal of Mental Deficiency Research* No. 32, 1988; The British Institute of Mental Handicap for 'Research interviews with people with mental handicaps' by D. Atkinson from *Mental Handicap Research* 1, 1, 1988; Carfax Publishing Company for 'Creating a "working alliance" with people with learning difficulties' by A. Brechin and J. Swain (1988) and 'Whose community, whose care?' by Hilary Brown and Helen Smith (1989) rewritten from 'Whose ordinary life is it any way – a feminist critique of the normalisation principle' by the same authors, both from *Disability, Handicap and Society*; Cassell for 'The social environment' from *Independent Living for Adults with Mental Handicap: A Place of My Own* by M. Flynn (1989); *Community Living* for 'Locked away' by D. Barron (July 1987); Croom Helm for 'A group home/landlady scheme' by L. Eastwood from *Reassessing Community Care* by N. Malin (ed.) (1987); The Free Press for 'The world of the congenitally deaf-blind' by D. Goode from *Qualitative Sociology: A Method to the Madness* by H. Schwarz and J. Jacobs (1979); King Edward's Hospital Fund for London for 'Robert Griffiths' by R. Blunden from *Lifelines* by S. Humphreys, G. Evan and S. Todd (1987); The Open University for 'My own perspective and experience' by Louisa Reynolds, 'Being there' by J. Wilkinson, 'Barriers to adulthood' by R. Jenkins, 'Learned helplessness' by J. Swain, 'For better, for worse? by L. Ward, 'Community care' by G. Dalley, 'Parallels between the social role . . .' by C. Baxter, 'Mental handicap and oppression' by F. Williams and 'How do we know what we think we know?' by M. Siddell (all specially commissioned); *Rehabilitation Psychology* for 'A brief outline of the principle of normalisation' by W. Wolfensberger and S. Tullman, Vol. 27, No. 3, 1982; Routledge for the extract by P. Henton from *Caring* by A. Briggs and J. Oliver (eds) (1985); Springer Verlag for 'Sex and the mentally handicapped: a lawyer's view' by M. Gunn from *Medicine and the Law* 5, 1986; University of Toronto Press for the extract 'What's in a name?' from *Inside Out: The Social Meaning of Retardation* by R. Bogdan and S. J. Taylor (1982); Virago Press for the extract 'Learning to resist' from *The Heart of the Race* by B. Bryan, S. Dazie and S. Scafe (1985); Tim Robinson for his article 'Normalisation: the whole answer?'.

Every effort has been made to trace and acknowledge ownership of copyright, the publishers will be glad to make suitable arrangements with any copyright holder whom it has not been possible to contact.

Introduction

This Reader should be of interest to anyone involved with or concerned about the lives and experiences of people with learning difficulties in Britain today. It has been developed as part of an Open University course, *Mental Handicap: Changing Perspectives*, a follow-up to the successful introductory course, *Mental Handicap: Patterns for Living*.

The book aims to develop further our knowledge and understanding of the lives and experiences of people with learning difficulties. This is a wide-ranging ambition which leads us into many different areas. It therefore creates the opportunity for us to 'make connections' between different sets of ideas. There are four ways in which we hope this can happen.

The first and most important kind of connection the book highlights is the connection which arises out of a sense of common humanity: the recognition that 'people are people first'. The experiences encountered, therefore, by those labelled 'mentally handicapped' are looked at in the light of all human experience. We can ask ourselves, 'How would I feel?' or 'Why do such things happen?' and may come to have a different way of thinking about the nature of the problem.

In taking this approach, it may sometimes seem that the nature and severity of some complex impairments is almost disguised. This Reader does include accounts of people with profound handicaps and others with extremely challenging behaviour, but they are presented in a way which allows us to identify with them as people. The risk, if it is a risk, of seeming to play down the role of 'impairment' in defining people's lives and experiences was outweighed, we felt, by the importance of 'making connections' with people as people.

Secondly, we have tried to adopt a wide frame of reference in selecting articles to include. You will find yourself considering a discussion of the concept of adulthood as well as a detailed account of a psychotherapy session; or moving from a parent's account of her first encounters with professionals to an analysis of shared experiences of oppression. Ideas from many sources thus find their way into this book and begin to feed into each other. An opportunity is provided for new connections to be made as more conventional divisions into different subject areas are set aside.

Thirdly, we have included different styles of account: for example, personal, experiential accounts, professional accounts, researchers' accounts, and more abstract analytic accounts. Because of this, inevitably, some will have a less polished writing style than others. They may also have the advantage sometimes of being easier to understand! All seemed to us to be relevant and important as sources of information to help us towards a better understanding of the lives and experiences of people with learning difficulties. Setting them alongside each other, and seeing what is being said from different perspectives, helps to draw our attention to connections which we might otherwise miss.

Finally, we have tried to draw in material which helps us to understand the process of acquiring and developing knowledge and understanding. This naturally includes research accounts, but the struggle to understand and influence the world and those around us is not something that only researchers are involved in. It is an experience we all share: we all try to 'make connections' as part of the process of making sense of ourselves and our world. We have tried to include articles which clarify rather than mystify this process. Thus research is not presented as something separate to be conducted only by an élite of researchers, but as part of a struggle to understand better, a struggle in which we are all involved – another example of 'our common humanity'.

This book sits alongside another course volume, *Know Me As I Am*,[1] and complements it. In that book, the focus is on people with learning difficulties as they talk about their experiences, their lives and their views of the world. They 'tell' their stories in whatever way suits them best: through poems, pictures and stories, and by dictation, sign language, interview or their own hand, and they do so as individuals with human concerns and personal feelings.

Know Me As I Am thus reflects the importance of listening to people at first hand, of coming to hear about and understand their lives and feelings from their point of view, of creating opportunities for communication when talking or writing is difficult, or investing time and care in 'getting to know' and 'getting alongside' people. Their 'accounts' represent the direct experiences and perspectives of people with learning difficulties.

This Reader shares the perspective that people's experiences are central. It takes a wider look at the development of knowledge and understanding in relation to people with learning difficulties. It brings together articles, some existing and some specially commissioned, which reflect the 'struggle to understand' from a wide range of starting points. It extends the spectrum of perspectives from people with learning difficulties to include parents and professionals, researchers and philosophers.

The book is divided into five sections. Section I, 'Roles and relationships', provides the starting point for the book by looking at the ways in which our roles and relationships in life are bound up with each other, profoundly affecting the way we feel about and come to understand each other. In particular it includes articles which explore the roles of parents, professionals and researchers in relation to people with learning difficulties.

Section II, 'Recognising oppression', draws our attention to the oppressive nature of some of those relationships. Often with the best of intentions, policies and practices can operate against people's best interests and may do more harm than good. In trying to understand people's circumstances and the enormous problems they sometimes face, however, explanations tend to start with the individual and the nature of any impairment. We felt it was important to focus our attention on the other side of the story, and recognise forms of oppression which can damage and restrict people's lives.

Section III, 'Discovering a voice', builds on that sense of recognising the other side of the story. People are not passive. There is a growing appreciation that there is a voice to be heard from a perspective which is often ignored. People with learning difficulties can speak out for themselves, can be heard, and can have important things to say. Different approaches may work in parallel, all helping to uncover the individual's view of the world. Such 'discoveries' will continue to grow as we become more effective and attentive listeners.

Section IV, 'Support in the community', looks at some of the related struggles to create more effective, flexible and individually responsive means of support in the community, often in the context of dwindling resources. We hear about stresses and strains alongside the positive achievements and possibilities. The stakes are high and the sense that these are people's lives we are talking about comes through strongly. The range of articles includes accounts of individual experiences alongside evaluations of the concept and practice of community care.

Section V, 'Our common humanity', is the final section. This juxtaposes a range of theoretical perspectives which can help in trying to understand better the lives and experiences of people with learning difficulties. There is a shared starting point throughout these approaches in the acknowledgement of common humanity; an emphasis on 'sameness' rather than 'differentness'. Interpretations, however, may diverge, adopting different emphases and perspectives, and suggesting sometimes different implications for practice. Such variations are an essential part of any process of developing our knowledge and understanding, and we need to give attention to them all as we try to develop our own understanding of the issues.

Note

1   Atkinson, D. and Williams, F. (1989) *Know Me As I Am: An Anthology of Prose, Poetry and Art by People with Learning Difficulties*, Sevenoaks, Hodder and Stoughton.

Section I Roles and relationships

Introduction

We start here with roles and relationships, which are central features in all our lives. The focus is on the way in which particular pressures and assumptions may affect roles and relationships involving people with learning difficulties. Roles become defined: parents, professionals or researchers on the one hand and sons or daughters, patients or clients, on the other. These roles may then influence the patterns of relationships which develop and, in turn, the expectations and life experiences of all those involved.

The emphasis is essentially on the struggle involved in those processes; the struggle, very often, not to become trapped by the constraints of such roles and relationships. Most of the articles reflect and consider the efforts which can be made to create more flexible relationships, to break down some of the barriers which tend to exist and to develop relationships which allow people to grow and develop. Often this involves taking risks, making a stand and, inevitably, exploring new and unknown territory.

The first article is about a mother's relationship with her son. The interview with her was recorded as part of a research study conducted by Ann Richardson, but the extracts here simply allow us to hear the mother talking. She describes, with a great deal of insight, the difficult process and feelings she went through as the time came for her son to move away from home. It seems an appropriate starting point for this Reader as it reflects very effectively, and without oversimplification, an important aim which is widely shared at this point in time: the aim of becoming a person in your own right.

We move next to an extract from a book by Margaret Flynn. Her study of people living in the community in various settings provides a rich and valuable source of information about the detail and quality of their lives. The extracts we have selected here focus on accounts of particular roles and relationships, as people talk about partners and children and about contact with their own families. Although these are people who have often spent many years in institutions, their lives now vary widely, reflecting a range of positive and negative experiences of relationships.

The next two articles shift the emphasis on to relationships with professionals. First we hear from a group of parents, MacLachlan *et al.*, who write about their experiences as parents of severely handicapped children when they formed a group to begin to share and explore their concerns together. It is unusual to find a description of a support group written by the parents involved, and this account succeeds well in presenting the parents' perspective on what was happening. Support from key professionals was important, but they also reflect the complexity of trying to build relationships of trust and support. And there is a sting in the tail.

The second of these two contributions comes from a professional, Louisa Reynolds. She was writing to a friend, largely to get things off her chest, about a series of events and experiences which happened to people with whom she worked. She reflects, with some vehemence, some of the anger and frustration that can be felt by professionals on behalf of people suffering at the hands of unfair systems and power relations. It seemed to her that the nature of professional roles, and the assumptions being made about client roles, was making it possible for people's individuality and essential humanity to be not only ignored but almost dismissed, as if it were of no importance.

We move next to a more positive account of professional support. Davis and Choudhury describe a support service and a relationship which seemed to transcend the difficulties of more traditional approaches. It is a most heart-warming account of helping a Bangladeshi mother to rediscover and re-establish her own strength against enormous odds. The concern was to reach out to families for whom conventional services seem inadequate or inappropriate. In particular the authors wanted to meet the needs of black families for whom language and cultural barriers, as well as experiences of overt racism, can mean that support is non-existent.

In the Brechin and Swain article a more analytic framework is offered. This attempts to explore what lies behind some of the negative experiences of professional–client relationships. It examines the potential contribution of normalisation, explores some common misinterpretations and offers a framework, drawing on concepts of self-advocacy, for describing and developing more appropriate approaches to professional–client relationships.

Finally, we offer two researchers' accounts of relationship aspects of their research studies. Wilkinson, in her article, reveals some of the personal feelings involved in being a researcher. Her research reflects an attempt to escape from the usual constraints of researcher–subject relationships, by living the same day by day, minute by minute experiences as the people she was studying.

Atkinson provides a thoughtful account of the research interviews she conducted. This is an all too rare description of what the research actually felt like. Real people were involved here, not just a researcher and subjects. They opened their doors, switched off their televisions, dressed up for the occasion and created the relationship as they wanted it. The researcher too had feelings and anxieties, and made judgements and occasionally misjudgements about her relationship with those she was seeing. What makes these accounts special is that they take notice of the relationships involved in research on people. By choosing not to ignore the importance of these relationships, they push us to recognise that they must always be there, influencing the process and outcomes of research.

1 'If you love him, let him go'

Ann Richardson

This extract presents a single interview from a research study. A mother, aged 65, is talking about her feelings when her son, Martin, moved from home to a hostel two years before.

I: Could I just ask you first to tell me a bit about Martin?

M: Martin is now 24. He's Down's syndrome and a quiet boy, no trouble at all. He was hyperactive as a child, but he's very easy to get on with, you know. A quiet boy, gentle boy. He loves his food, likes his glass of wine . . .

I: And before he left home, was he able to do things for himself, dressing and bathing?

M: He's quite capable. For years he's been going to the toilet on his own; he's dressed himself in the mornings. With a little bit of supervision, you know, if things are put on inside out. He could put his coat on and feed himself.

I: And shaving?

M: No, I shaved him. I think that was asking just a little bit too much.

I: Can you tell me, before he went away this last time, had he stayed away from home at all?

M: Oh, he's been away. I used to let him go away for a fortnight almost every year . . . That was good for him, it was a leading up over the years. And giving my husband and me a much needed break. [. . .]

I: And how did Martin take to going away?

M: Martin loved it . . . He loves clubs and, although he's a quiet boy . . . he likes company. He's a social lad in a quietish way.

I: Was it difficult for you to let him go away for those spells?

M: No, no trouble at all. I was sad at times taking him there. But when I got him there I used to think, thank God, I'm going to have a break. It was lovely . . . Even my husband enjoyed the break.

I: Was he always well looked after when he was away?

M: Oh, no. No. There was one occasion, after my husband died – I realised then eventually Martin would have to go into care. He went to a home . . . and when we went to collect him, I cried all the way home. I despaired, because I thought, what's going to happen to my child when I go? He was unkempt, the clothes I had sent I knew had never been worn. I was so desolate . . . I'm not suicidal – I'm not that type – but that was as near as I ever felt. I thought, God, I would rather take my child's life – I really mean this, I felt so strongly – than let him go into a place like that.

So, then when I heard about this place being built, the hostel he's in now. My social worker said . . . it sounds as if it would be right for Martin . . . And one night I went to a meeting – I don't know what came over me. I said, 'This place, do you think you could put Martin's name down for it?' . . . I said 'I don't mean now, I mean in about five years' time.' Then she said there was a very large waiting list (and) I suddenly burned my bridges. I said, 'Look, if you can get him in, put his name down for now.' I went home and cried my eyes out, didn't I! I'd done something on the spur of the moment, but which was really in the back of my mind for years.

Then, from the time I had made up my mind to let him go until I knew he'd been accepted, it was months and months. One part of me was hoping they wouldn't accept him and another part was saying, God, what shall I do if they don't accept him? . . . You've got this guilt. This helpless child – because he is a child, isn't he, mentally – and there is this feeling that, well, I'd know where he is and he would be able to identify which he does now . . . So when I go eventually – and, I mean, we're all going to go, aren't we – he'll miss me, I know he will, he would be inhuman if he didn't, but it won't be so traumatic for him as his father's death was . . . If you have a child you have to let go, don't you? It's very tough if you can't. A measure of your love if you let them go, but it isn't easy. Believe you me, it isn't. It's very difficult.

I: Could I just ask you to tell me briefly what sort of place he is in?

M: Well, there are 24 places, altogether, and I think they have 20 residents now. I was very disappointed in some respects. When Martin went in, they took them in groups of eight, which was ideal. It was nicely done. The chief officer, he had us all eight parents over to tea with the kids and we met each other and it was lovely . . . (Later) they've had people in there that have real behaviour problems and that has upset Martin terribly. [. . .] Now, can you imagine how I felt about this? Here's a happy boy, he was so happy, he settled in so I had no worries . . .

Well, the staff, I can't speak highly enough. They wouldn't do that job if they weren't totally dedicated, they couldn't do it. No, they are lovely (and) they are hard working . . .

I: So, how often are you able to visit him?

M: Oh, every week, every week. And I have him home every month for three or four days. Oh, yes, he loves that.

I: You've talked earlier about – You said you'd thought for quite a long time that you would have to let him go.

M: Oh, yes. Well, it was on the cards, wasn't it, that he would have to go eventually.

I: When do you think you first thought seriously about it, living away for good?

M: Well I thought it. I put it to the back of my mind. We all do. It's something you don't want to think about . . . But from childhood, from babyhood, you think about it. But it's not pressing, is it? You know – well at least you think – that you have a long lease of life. You don't! But my husband, the shock of his death, I began to realise then, you know, that it could happen.

      Oh, another thing. One of the mothers dicd, a widow like myself living alone with her handicapped son, on the Friday. And it was Monday before she was found and that handicapped boy was with her. I used to go to bed at night – I still suffer from insomnia, I'm sure it's from then – and I'd think, supposing I had a stroke or die? [. . .]

I: To what extent were you able to talk it over with people, when you were thinking about it?

M: Oh, my daughter agreed and my sister . . . They thought, yes, Martin should go. But you see I resented that. Because Martin's *my* child. There's a part of you which says, who do they think they are? Would they do it to their own children?

      You are at war all the time . . . There is the emotional side of you which loves your child dearly and you don't want to part with him. There is the other side, common sense, which says now is the time. If you love him let him go. You are doing it for him. But there's a selfish side, too, can I manage on my own? I am going to be so lonely . . . And financially, I had more for Martin than my pension now. But that didn't come into it for me.

I: You said there was the selfish angle. Was that facing your own loneliness?

M: That's right. It's a hard thing to face. I mean I've always been a very gregarious person. I'm one of five, I've never been on my own in my life. [. . .]

      Actually I needed Martin more, to be honest. I only realised it later. I could see that I needed Martin more than he needed me. And if you are honest about it, you do as you get older. You need someone. I'm a touching person, I missed contact. I could cuddle Martin. He didn't like it much but I'd kiss the back of his neck. So I missed this very vital thing for me – the touch . . .

I: You said an interesting thing – a lot of parents have said the same – that you needed him more than he needed you.

M: You know that's rather a shock when you realise. You've had a handicapped child for years and you feel they've taken over your life, you know. I think you suddenly come to realise you need that child. You need that person.

I: Can you tell me in what way you needed him?

M: I needed . . . someone to relate to. I needed to have a pattern to my life. I've always had a pattern and most of it with a handicapped child. [. . .]
       And I needed him first of all because he was my child and I loved him dearly. And he was a helpless child . . . Martin needs me and every day it's a sort of complement with someone. It makes you feel good. You rarely guessed it, because your life was so boxed in, but there's a debit and credit in every walk of life. The debit side of a handicapped child is that you are really tied for life. But the credit side is that there is somebody who loves you and it's a lovely form of love. There's no ifs or buts about it. It's a pure love and it's lovely, you know. So you lose all this. And it's very shattering. It really is shattering.

I: Did anybody help you and support you at that time? To what extent did your social worker give you support?

M: Well, unfortunately, I gave the impression of being very capable. I'm not saying this in a big-headed way. And my social worker told me himself that he didn't know anything about it. I think I was the first mother of a handicapped son he had known. He was very good . . . He called and would ring me up. Oh, yes, he was helpful.
       My daughter was very sympathetic . . . A very kind girl. If I cry, she will cry with me, you know. But you don't upset your family. So you hide a lot, don't you? You pretend, you know, because they have their lives and you can't be sad all the time, can you?

I: Was it something you were able to discuss with Martin himself, that he was going away?

M: Oh, yes. I made it sound exciting, as I used to do with my daughter when she went to school. I used to say 'A lovely room, Martin, won't it be lovely?' and he would say, 'Yes', oh bless his heart.
       I mean I was happy about it, you know . . . I had no qualms about it. It was *myself* I was sorry for. [. . .] It was my grief. It's not grief for the other person, is it? . . . And if we are honest about things, you come to terms with yourself. Until you come to terms with yourself, no one will accept anything. [. . .]

I: How were you preparing yourself for it?

M: I didn't want to think about it. I didn't. I was very emotional. Sadness, with a capital S, very sad. I didn't show it to Martin. I mean, I was normal about the house. But I ached, I really ached.

I: I know from what you said already that you needed him and, of course, you loved him. What did you feel were the implications? What was making you feel so sad?

M: Losing him. I was losing a child. He was like my other self, in a way. [. . .]

I: How do you feel when you think about Martin now?

M: I'm happy for him. Except for the little hiccups, you know . . . And I like my relationship with the staff. I can go in there and say 'Is it all right to make a cup of coffee?' or they'll make me one. If a button's missing from Martin's shirt, I can get it, I know where things are. This is lovely. This is very important, that their parents should feel part of the child's life . . .

And I feel I'm in Martin's *home*; they make me feel that. I feel I am going in my son's home. Another thing they do which I didn't do. I never knocked on Martin's bedroom door. They are giving him dignity. Even I didn't give him that dignity. Well, he was only my little boy, wasn't he? It's made me realise that I didn't really treat him as an adult. They are showing me . . .

I: Most parents say that they don't really see their handicapped sons and daughters as adults. Do you think this makes it harder to let them go?

M: No, no. Oh, there's a part of you, you know, that wants to keep them as children . . . They've been children for so long that it's second nature to you to treat them as children. (But) that sadness would have been there – just as if you have a daughter gets married, you are sad.

I: The same sadness?

M: No, no. Because they are going to lead a normal life and they are going to be capable of looking after themself and you are entrusting your child into the hands of somebody else who does care. So there's that difference . . . Think about it this way. Martin mentally is probably six. Now think of putting an ordinary child of six into the care of someone else. Any mother would feel this way.

I: When Martin first went away, was it a difficult period just to begin with or did you have a sense of having done the right thing? Tell me about the actual day, first of all.

M: Oh, desperate. I just wanted to cry, but I couldn't. I couldn't let Martin see me unhappy. This was it. So there was all this bottled up. Martin's very sharp that way. He could tell by my stance with my back to him if I was miserable or feeling unhappy. He is very sensitive to moods. And that day, that day, oh it was awful. I was so full of grief . . . I think I was dreading it, it had built up. It's like going to a funeral, you are wishing it was all over and done with. But I was so relieved . . . It's so final, isn't it. This is the thing. The finality of it all. [. . .]

I: How long did it take you to adapt to Martin not being here?

M: Not very long, actually. Well, you see there was this reward, the credit side, Martin was happy . . .

I: So, how did your life change?

M: Well, I'm much more relaxed; I don't have pressure. I can come in and if I want to eat, I eat, you know. It may sound a small detail, but it's – I'm much more relaxed. I can go out any time I want. I meet friends. I go to meetings. I have no pressure at all. There's no rushing home, no seeing to Martin . . . I can go away. You know, my life is quite full in a way, because I'm older. Had I been a younger woman, it might have been different. I'm adapting to the fact that I'm 65 now. I'm comfortable to be sitting in front of the fire at night, if there's something good on TV, or read, you know . . .

I: What was it in particular that helped you to adapt to not having him here?

M: Realising how lucky I was to get him in . . . The relief of knowing that if anything happens to me, Martin is all right. And that's worth all the grief, all the tears, all the sadness. [. . .]

I: And what, from Martin's point of view, are you happiest about?

M: He has a social life now, which he didn't have with me. He goes out, they go to the pub sometimes. And he goes down to his club . . . They'll go shopping, they'll go to the local town on the bus. They are giving an Easter party and they have meetings and they are consulted. And when Martin asked for a meeting – I mean, I can't believe it, my child, my son, saying 'Meeting, please'. Well, this is incredible, isn't it. I didn't ask him things. Martin is a more rounded person now. He is a personality now. He wasn't, he was my little boy here. [. . .]

Acknowledgment

Particular thanks must be given to the mother whose interview is used in this chapter and to Mrs Kit Ward, who carried out that interview.

2 The social environment

Margaret Flynn

The extracts published here focus on only two aspects of the social environment, partners and children, and families. In the original chapter Margaret Flynn also discusses living arrangements, the experience of living alone, co-residents and neighbours. The information is based on a research study which looked at the lives of eighty-eight people living independently in North-West England. Most of the people who took part in the study are former residents of hospitals and hostels, currently living in their own homes.

2.1 Social networks and socialisation

There is a vast body of research regarding the value and benefits of support from our social networks. These are regarded as a resource which helps us to cope with stress and overcome its debilitating effects. Social support has been reported to protect against depression (for example, Brown and Harris, 1978; Surtees, 1980; Billings and Moos, 1981) and against mental illness and psychological distress (for example, Miller and Ingham, 1976; Williams, Ware and Donald, 1981; Lin and Dean, 1984; Gottlieb, 1985); it is reported to reduce stress in work and unemployment (for example, Gore, 1978; House, 1981); and generally to alleviate illness (for example, Lin *et al.*, 1979; Asher, 1984). While there are methodological problems in the literature regarding social support (Starker, 1986), the conclusion that it is critical to well-being is unavoidable. In brief, the present state of knowledge suggests that social support moderates the damaging effects of stressful life events and is related to good health.

Without question, in times of need, our personal networks (that is, the web of social ties that surround us) and social activities can be important sources of support, information and material assistance, regardless of how we are labelled. For people with mental handicap, however, difficulties may arise as a result of a limited grasp of the skills necessary for social behaviour and social relationships. By definition, a person with mental handicap is impaired in the effectiveness with which she/he 'meets the standards of personal independence and social responsibility expected of his/her age and cultural group' (Grossman, 1975).

Nobody is born with an understanding of appropriate behaviour. This is culturally determined and passed on. People with mental handicap are denied many of the socialising experiences to which non-mentally-handicapped people are exposed. Edgerton (1975) illuminates this fact with the description of a man who was labelled as having a mental handicap at the age of four. At the age of eighteen years, the man was discovered to have an IQ of 104. He was ill-prepared for an independent life and in his own words observed that it was 'much easier to be retarded'. This sobering case study prompted Koegel (1978) to report, 'it would appear that the socialization process undergone by mentally retarded people leaves even a normal individual ill-equipped for participation in normal networks' (p. 8).

At this point, it is timely to reflect upon the implications of normalisation for association with others. Perhaps it is 'culturally normative' to encourage association with non-mentally-handicapped people and discourage association with other devalued individuals. It appears misguided, however, to hope that friendships can develop with non-mentally-handicapped people and to aspire to this for everybody. Friendships have a longitudinal perspective and social, attitude and value similarity affect friendship formation (Baker, 1983). It is to be expected that people who have spent vast periods of their lives associating with people with mental handicap will form friendships with them. Discouraging these friendships implies that we do not value them. [. . .]

Information about people's social environments was derived from social workers' observations and those of their clients. [. . .] The resulting picture is difficult to interpret as the information gathered from the two sources is not directly equivalent. [. . .] Ostensibly, however, it appears that most people have regular contact with individuals who may be described as friends. However, we must not lose sight of the fact that a number of people experience loneliness and isolation. According to social workers, four people had no contact with friends and eleven only had intermittent contact. In the interviews eighteen people did not mention contact with others. As the recipient of two marriage invitations and many requests for further contact with the people I met, I have to conclude that some people's networks are wanting. [. . .]

2.2   Partners and children

[. . .] A powerful argument in suppressing close friendships amongst people with mental handicap is that they may lead to sexual relationships, and an active sexual life requires a degree of responsibility and maturity beyond these people. But attitudes and policies are changing, there are ever-increasing numbers of people living in community settings and the negative features of strict control in institutional settings are being replaced by attempts to foster more socially appropriate behaviour (Pitceathly and Chapman, 1985). Whittemore and Koegel (1978) observe that leading as normal a life as possible must result in acceptance of the tenet that healthy social and sexual relationships are basic to a person's adaptation to community life.

Marriage and parenthood enter people into new social relationships and a few studies have looked at people with mental handicap in these roles. Of marriage, researchers have indicated its importance in enhancing self-esteem, providing companionship and enabling couples to be more independent and self-sufficient than they could manage living separately (Mattinson, 1970; McCarver and Craig, 1974; Floor, Baxter and Zisfain, 1975; Craft and Craft, 1979). There are three married couples in the population of eighty-eight and a further six couples are living together. One such couple is described in Flynn (1987), and another in Flynn (1989). One couple were expecting a baby at the time of interview and one man is a single parent. A single woman had an abortion several years ago.

Research regarding people with mental handicap as parents produces a rather clouded picture. Their abilities to provide appropriate environmental stimulation for their children's development, to perceive their children's needs and deal effectively with misbehaviour for example, are concerns. Mattinson (1970) noted that when parenting problems arose, these tended to be due to factors other than IQ, such as family size and socioeconomic status. In a study of two families, Winik (1982) found that parents experienced difficulties in coping once their child became verbal and active; they tended not to be aware of problems, and sorting out daily concerns was as much as they could manage. She concluded that people need an extensive amount of support to facilitate parenting. In contrast, Johnson (1969) proposed that the rights of a child should be paramount and wonders whether parenthood is the 'automatic right of all human beings'. Mindful of the possibility of non-mentally-handicapped children becoming precociously competent, O'Neill (1985) underlined the importance of 'the presence, duration and quality of the parents' social support. School and social agency supportive contacts with retarded parents are encouraged because these people are at risk from adjustment problems' (p. 267).

The experience of being married/having a partner and being a parent must be gathered from the following accounts and observations. In the study, no attempt was made to assess the quality of people's relationships or the adequacy of parenting skills. Information was gleaned from contact with social workers, case records and the interviews themselves.

For example, Mr and Mrs Heaton are desperately unhappy with their flat and neighbourhood as they have been exposed to physical and verbal abuse. They go to their neighbours in time of distress and keep in contact with both of their families. They are both unemployed. Mrs Heaton reflected on their lives together and the roles they have:

> He gives me the housekeeping money . . . he takes me out. If I haven't got any money left, he'll take me out for a packet of ciggies or a drink . . . He used to help me with the shopping a lot, because I got cataracts on me eyes, I can't see. I can't see across the road now. He's got to come with me and take

me everywhere . . . I can manage round in the house, do the washing and that
. . . I don't like asking a man to wring me underclothes, but he wrings all me
other stuff out like sheets . . . I do me work, tidy up here and just put the telly
on and watch it . . . If I do the bedroom; he'll do in here for me you know;
brush up and wash around . . . He decorated this, he helps, he's a good fella
. . . if he wasn't happy with me he wouldn't come back . . . Are you married?
Take my advice, don't!

Mr Bowland and Miss O'Brien are looking forward to the birth of their
first child. They see Miss O'Brien's family regularly and are gradually
meeting people in their own locality. Miss O'Brien is trying to overcome
her shyness with the help of her partner and social worker. Both
unemployed, Mr Bowland shares all the household tasks. He said:

I've made the tables, they taught me how to make things like that at the
centre (for people with epilepsy). I also do the decorating. I've done all of
this flat . . . We're going to the hospital once a week to the antenatal clinic.
There's a launderette nearby and we take the washing at weekends . . . We
were both at the centre and they teach you how to do lots of things there,
that's men and women. So while we can both cook, I do it mostly, especially
now that Joan's having a baby.

Mr Rangecroft and Miss Watson share their flat with two lodgers. They
have few contacts with people outside their flat. They are both unemployed
and share many of the household tasks.

We do the cooking, cleaning and laundry together. Do shopping on
Saturdays once a fortnight. We both go to the shops. We do washing
(laundry) in the bath. I don't know how long we've been together, on and
off. We met at the hostel . . .

Mr Walker and Miss Cooke are anxious to leave their flat. They are
unemployed and bored with being at home most days. They have had
arguments with their friends and now have no friends on whom they can
call. Mr Walker has strong views about his partner's appearance. He also
regrets her sterilisation:

It's only bloody right that women should dress up. I mean bloody men just
stick anything on. It's only right you dress up . . . See we want a child. I've
got nephews and that and they say if we're on the bus, 'Look Uncle Ben,
look . . . !' Well it's not the same as 'Look dad, look . . . !' She's going to see
if she can have the operation reversed.

Mr Longton and Miss Madoc live in an attractive flat on a modern estate.
They have busy social lives and enjoy meeting friends at the local pub.
They are both in full-time employment and share the housework. Miss
Madoc said:

I like living with Joe. I can get to work easily and get home and it's near for
Joe. I look after Joe. I mean, we fall out, but we all do it don't we? But we
get along all right . . . We like it here don't we Joe? He likes mending watches
. . . He likes mending them, it gets on my nerves . . .

Mr and Mrs Sewell live in a small terraced house. They are unemployed
and share the shopping. They no longer meet people from the hostel in

which they lived and their social worker is concerned about their over-dependence on her. Mrs Sewell said:

> I do the cooking in the kitchen and the washing . . . and cleaning and all that
> . . . I learned in a flat in the hostel . . .

Mr Sewell said:

> We go out shopping . . . I love her you know. She spoils me. She brought me
> these boots and this watch. Boots for the snow . . .

Miss Greaves is soon to marry Mr Harlow, a man she has been living with since her mother died. They share all of the household tasks. They have few contacts with people other than their families. He gave up his place at the ATC as she did not like his daily absence. She said:

> I spoils him . . . I bought him a new suit and then I gives him money for
> spending money, then I buys him cigs . . . then if he's short I gives him money
> . . . I never used to share you know, I used to keep it to meself. I didn't share
> . . . I know now I have to now as I'm getting married . . . I follows him . . . I
> gets terrified in case he might be with somebody else and leave me on me own
> again you know . . . (Friends at her former place of work) keep saying to me
> . . . if he likes you, he'll not go. I said, 'But I don't trust him.' . . . Nobody
> (visits) really, I falls out with them me, that's why I don't have nobody me
> because I falls out with them . . . I'm cruel, I'm cruel at times, and then I
> makes friends . . . but I always falls out with them.

These insights into people's close relationships demonstrate that the companionship of a partner is valued and important. It seems possible that the preparation of adults for independent living blurs the traditional male and female household roles. It was evident that, with the exception of Mr Sewell, all the men I met involved themselves in routine household tasks. Unemployment may also play a part in involving male partners in the running of households. However, the Central Statistical Office (1983) shows that a smaller number of males than females involve themselves in household tasks. While having a partner is not a guarantee against loneliness and isolation, with the exception of one couple, social workers were very positive about their married and cohabiting clients' achievements.

Only one man has the custody of his child. Mr Taylor's daughter is six, and since his wife left him he has kept a full-time job and immersed himself in his daughter's upbringing. With the assistance of a home help and a home carer (known as Aunty Rita), a social worker, and a foster mother who looks after his daughter until Mr Taylor gets home from work, Mr Taylor's accomplishments are a tremendous source of pride to his social services department.

Two women have had children but no longer have the custody of them. This includes Mrs Ellis who looked after her children until they went to school, at which time her husband left her and he and his new partner acquired custody.

> I see my children at my sister-in-law's. Since the divorce I've told my husband, if I go round to our home, it was in my name, I'll beat the woman that broke us up. My husband had a child by her when she was only thirteen. He was taken to courts but he still has the children. Most weekends I see the children. When I was married I stayed in the house. My husband was always out with his cousin, I was always in with the children. He'd never take me out. When I was in I sometimes had as many as ten (epileptic) fits in a day. It was hard . . .

Miss Jordan looked after her daughter for seven months, unsupported before she was fostered. She makes infrequent visits to see her daughter and the experience has become especially difficult since her daughter reached adolescence. Miss Jordan's social worker always accompanies her and chats to the daughter more comfortably than her client can. The social worker is concerned that Miss Jordan is distressed by the visits, but as her client does not want them to cease, dealing with these is a feature of the support. During one visit Miss Jordan's daughter was overheard as she said to her foster mother, 'I wish they'd go. I don't like Marjorie, she's thick.' As a result of this, the social worker does the talking and Miss Jordan, having primed her social worker with questions beforehand, remains silent.

Parenthood for one woman in her early teens resulted in incarceration in a hospital for people with mental handicap. The extent of contact she had with her family during her many years of institutionalisation is unknown. At seventy-nine she is the oldest person in the study. She has been living in a co-residency with two other women for three years. It is noteworthy that in addition to help from her social worker, this woman is also supported by her son and his family. She delights in her lately endowed independence but is somewhat confused by her status:

> Me son comes. I have a son. He's got a son married and the other one works. I'm not a grandmother yet. Who'd make me a grandmother? I don't think anybody would. Oh yes, I am a grandmother. [. . .]

2.3 Families

Families have always had an important role in the care of their members with mental handicap and they remain the major care-takers in this country. Arguably the families who involve themselves in the lives of people in this study did not anticipate that the populations of hospitals and hostels would ever be encouraged to decline. Studies report that families are sceptical of community alternatives to institutions. They believed that they offered a permanent home (Payne, 1976; Meyer, 1980).

This section touches on a range of experiences and indicates some of the difficulties experienced by some people in relation to their families. Although we know that families applaud deinstitutionalisation, normalisation and integration in the abstract, they resist this for their sons/daughters/ brothers/sisters (Card, 1983; Ferrara, 1979). As Byrne and Cunningham (1985) observe, 'These views are perhaps explicable when one considers parents' factually based perception that community attitudes towards mentally handicapped people are relatively negative' (p. 856). [. . .]

Some of the younger people I met referred to their visits to their families:

> Me mum and dad live near. They come occasionally. I always go at weekends.

> Sometimes me mum and dad come. I went there on Sunday. Sometimes I go during the week.

> My sisters come a lot and I go to my parents. I see my family a lot.

Two people spoke angrily of their parents:

> Fourteen bloody years since I last seen my mam. She couldn't care less. I just get down half the time, get cheesed off, fed up.

> I've been very hurt. I haven't had a very good life with me parents . . . If me dad sees me in the pub he says, 'What the bloody hell are you doing here?' and he sends me out. He doesn't like me going in pubs. Now look at me, I'm twenty-seven and they still treat me like a two-year-old. I can't make it out at all.

Of the sibling relationship, Powell and Ogle (1985) observe:

> Siblings play a critical role in our lives. Brothers and sisters know us like no one else. They have been with us during the good times and the bad. Siblings constitute our first social network, and their early influence affects us throughout our lives. Our sibling relationships are typically the longest relationship we will have in life. (p. xiii)

Siblings are closely involved in the lives of eleven people in total; in other words, they visit and/or are visited regularly by and maintain contact with their brother's/sister's social worker. One way of approaching the relationships people have with their siblings is to examine a range of people's descriptions of these. In spite of people's independence in terms of their living arrangements, it will be seen that some siblings do have expectations of their handicapped brothers and sisters that cannot be realised. This is powerfully illustrated by a man who lives alone:

> I like to come home, have me telly on and done me hobbies like that, and me brother doesn't approve of all that. Me brother says I should go in the garden (gardening) . . . I'm not very keen on it. This house is rented . . . (the rent) I give to me brother and he takes it to the place and he pays it . . . without him I'd be lost . . . See me brother's always looked after me mum and he's looked after the family . . . he used to look after me and we used to have terrible rows . . . He's just the opposite to what I am. He rows with everybody . . . Trouble is, he doesn't like the way I eat. I can't help it. I just like chips you see. Trouble is it makes me fat and I can't get into me clothes properly and he gets upset about that . . . I just like to come in and enjoy meself doing pictures. He doesn't approve of that . . . Me sister's coming this Sunday, I give me washing to her . . . They phone up, see how I'm getting on, see if I'm all right . . . I don't have any friends at all. Only friends I have is me brother.

This man's position is shared to a lesser extent by that of a woman who lives with her boyfriend. She said of her sister, 'Sometimes she interferes but I think she's only doing it, thinking of me like, you know.' Another man who is regularly visited by his brother was critical and despondent when talking about his brother:

> Now and again he comes down on a Saturday to see me. I've not never been (to his house). He doesn't like me most of the time. I don't know why because I am his flesh and blood when all's said and done . . . He wanted me put away he did . . .

One woman has ceased to see her family as a result of her changed living circumstances and dislike of their expectations:

> My sister doesn't come. None of my family come . . . I've got a twin sister and older sister and she's finished with me altogether since I moved in here, because I was living with her at the time . . . I only get criticised when I go. She criticises me and it upsets me. She doesn't like Alan and Alan don't like her . . . She said, 'You're no sister of mine. Where's your glasses? You look a state, you look ill, you look a tramp.' Then she just walked away.

In the main, shared activities with families include preparing and sharing meals, going shopping, going drinking and going on day excursions. One woman has decorated her elderly mother's flat. One man and his sister regularly visit children's homes as they were brought up in one and they remember what it was like not having any visitors. This appeared to be the most satisfying sibling relationship that was described. Two social workers expressed concern that their clients are too generously disposed towards their siblings and regularly give them money from their meagre incomes. Another social worker believes that his client is sexually abused by her brother, but he has no evidence to support this. He also believes that she has become a prostitute.

Reading letters and helping people to sort out their money are frequent points of contact with siblings. One woman described her routine:

> What I generally do, I generally leave me money with me sister-in-law. I generally take it every week and she sorts me money out for me. And like, if a bill comes, I generally take it to me sister-in-law's.

During the course of the study I met one person's sibling. He interpreted his brother's speech and signing as these are so idiosyncratic. He is concerned about his brother's drinking problem and has reservations about his ability to manage independently:

> (Tapping his forehead) I've had it up to here. I preferred it when he was in the hostel. He drinks his money and he's round at our place for meals. I've had him all me life.

Regardless of the anguished relationships some people have with their families, the interviews suggested that forty-eight people are in the habit of visiting their families regularly and thirty-nine are visited by them. The frequency of visits to and by families is not known. This information was not sought in the interview because of the difficulties many people experience regarding time, dates and frequency (see Flynn, 1986):

> Go at Christmas as well as Mondays. They take me home night time.

> When it's fine I go to me sister's in Dene Road.

> I see my family when they come and me other brother comes.

> I see Eveline my sister. She lives in hostel. She used to live at hospital, my sister. I don't smoke, me. She does, I don't.

Some people expressed regret at the absence of contact with their families and recalled their bereavements:

> My mum lives in Manchester. I don't see her. I got brothers and I don't see them much. I wish I did see them more.

> I've got an Aunty in Wiltshire and she's 94 . . Then I've got a brother but he doesn't bother with me.

> Me mum died just before last Christmas. I used to go round there every day and help her cook. She's dead now though and that really upset me mostly. I've got no parents now. I've got a dad but I don't know where he is. I've got sisters of course but I never bother with them. They don't bother with me so I don't bother with them. [. . .]

References

ASHER, C. C. (1984) 'The impact of social support networks on mental health', *Medical Care*, **22**, 349–59.

BAKER, P. M. (1983) 'The friendship process: a developmental model of interpersonal attraction', *Sociological Spectrum*, **3**, 263–77.

BILLINGS, A. G. and MOOS, R. H. (1981) 'The role of coping responses and social resources in attenuating the stress of life events', *Journal of Behavioural Medicine*, **4**, 139–57.

BROWN, G. W. and HARRIS, T. (1978) *Social Origins of Depression*, London, Tavistock.

BYRNE, E. A. and CUNNINGHAM, C. C. (1985) 'The effects of mentally handicapped children on families: a conceptual review', *Journal of Child Psychology and Psychiatry*, **26**, 847–66.

CARD, H. (1983) 'What will happen when we've gone?' *Community Care*, **28**, 20–1.

CENTRAL STATISTICAL OFFICE (1983) *Social Trends 14*: A publication of the Government Statistical Service, London, HMSO.

CRAFT, A. and CRAFT, M. (1979) *Handicapped Married Couples*, London, Routledge and Kegan Paul.

EDGERTON, R. B. (1975) 'Issues relating to the quality of life among mentally retarded persons', in M. J. Begab and S. A. Richardson (eds) *The Mentally Retarded and Society: A Social Science Perspective*, Baltimore, University Park Press.

FERRARA, D. M. (1979) 'Attitudes of parents of mentally retarded children toward normalization activities', *American Journal of Mental Deficiency*, **84**, 145–51.

FLOOR, L. D., BAXTER, M. R. and ZISFAIN, L. (1975) 'A survey of marriages among previously institutionalized retardates', *Mental Retardation*, **13**, 33–7.

FLYNN, M. C. (1986) 'Adults who are mentally handicapped as consumers: issues and guidelines for interviewing', *Journal of Mental Deficiency Research*, **30**, 369–77.

FLYNN, M. C. (1987) 'Independent living arrangements for adults who are mentally handicapped', in N. Malin (ed.) *Reassessing Community Care: with Particular Reference to Provision for People with Mental Handicap and for People with Mental Illness*, London, Croom Helm.

FLYNN, M. C. (1989) *Independent Living for Adults with Mental Handicap: A Place of My Own*, London, Cassell.

GORE, S. (1978) 'The effect of social support in moderating the health consequences of unemployment', *Journal of Health and Social Behaviour*, **19**, 157–65.

GOTTLIEB, B. H. (1985) 'Assessing and strengthening the impact of social support on mental health'. *Social Work*, **July–August**, 293–300.

GROSSMAN, H. (1975) *A Manual on Classification*, Washington DC, American Association on Mental Deficiency.

HOUSE, J. S. (1981) *Work Stress and Social Support*, Reading, Mass., Addison-Wesley.

JOHNSON, W. R. (1969) 'Sex education and the mentally retarded', *Journal of Sex Research*, **5**, 179–85.

KOEGEL, P. (1978) *The creation of incompetence: socialisation and mildly retarded persons*, Working Paper No. 6, Socio-Behavioral Group, University of California.

LIN, N. and DEAN, A. (1984) 'Social support and depression', *Social Psychiatry*, **19**, 83–91.

LIN, N., SIMEONE, R. S., ENSEL, W. M. and KUO, W. (1979) 'Social support, stressful life events and illness: a model and empirical test, *Journal of Health and Social Behaviour*, **20**, 108–19.

MATTINSON, J. (1970) *Marriage and Mental Handicap*, London, Duckworth.

McCARVER, R. B. and CRAIG, E. M. (1974) 'Placement of the retarded in the community: prognosis and outcome', in N. R. Ellis (ed.) *International Review of Research in Mental Retardation*, New York, Academic Press.

MEYER, R. J. (1980) 'Attitudes of parents of institutionalized mentally retarded individuals toward deinstitutionalization', *American Journal of Mental Deficiency*, **85**, 184–7.

MILLER, P. M. and INGHAM, J. G. (1976) 'Friends, confidants and symptoms', *Social Psychiatry*, **11**, 51–8.

O'NEILL, A. M. (1985) 'Normal and bright children of mentally retarded parents: the Huck Finn syndrome', *Child Psychiatry and Human Development*, **15**, 255–68.

PAYNE, J. E. (1976) 'The deinstitutionalization backlash', *Mental Retardation*, **3**, 43–5.

PITCEATHLY, A. S. and CHAPMAN, J. W. (1985) 'Sexuality, marriage and parenthood of mentally retarded people', *International Journal for the Advancement of Counselling*, **8**, 173–81.

POWELL, T. H. and OGLE, P. A. (1985) *Brothers and Sisters – A Special Part of Exceptional Families*, Baltimore, Paul Brooks Publishing Co.

STARKER, J. (1986) 'Methodological and conceptual issues in research on social support', *Hospital and Community Psychiatry*, **37**, 485–90.

SURTEES, P. G. (1980) 'Social support, residual adversity and depressive outcome', *Social Psychiatry*, **15**, 71–80.

WHITTEMORE, R. D. and KOEGEL, P. (1978) *Loving alone is not helpful: Sexuality and social context among the mildly retarded, Working Paper No. 7*, Socio-Behavioral Group, University of California.

WILLIAMS A., WARE, J. E. and DONALD, C. A. (1981) 'A model of mental health, life events and social supports applicable to general populations', *Journal of Health and Social Behavior*, **22**, 324–36.

WINIK, L. (1982) *Mildly retarded adults as parents: a description of the parenting practices of two mildly retarded couples, Working Paper No. 22*, Socio-Behavioral Group, University of California.

3 Do the professionals understand? Mothers' views of families' service needs

Mary MacLachlan, Pam Dennis, Hilary Lang, Sybil Charnock and Jill Osman

3.1 Background

In July 1984 a letter was sent from the Community Care Team and the staff of the South Devon Social Services Department's Special Development Centre in Paignton, asking for help from the parents and families of young adults with severe mental and physical handicaps. As a result, our group was formed – five mothers of young adults ranging in age from nineteen to twenty-eight years, with varying disabilities including cerebral palsy, epilepsy and partial vision, as well as severe mental handicap. Two 'professionals' were also included – the Supervisor of the Special Development Centre and the Senior Clinical Psychologist from the Community Mental Handicap Team.

Initially we agreed to meet for five sessions. It was not easy. We were required to relive the early days with our children, and things that we had long stored away out of sight and mind were brought to the front again. We all experienced deep and sad emotional feelings, to the extent that the group was in danger of breaking up. One of the six original members felt unable to continue; another felt likewise but later returned to the group and has remained with it ever since. It is to the credit of the professionals that by their careful, tactful understanding, the group held together and has grown in confidence. We now feel that we should share some of our thoughts with others in an endeavour to encourage a better service for people with mental handicaps and their families.

3.2 Learning to cope

During the early years we, as mothers, all spent much time with our children, trying to make them appear normal. Most of us had not been told that they were mentally handicapped and we were left to discover this over a period of years. When realisation finally came, we tended to avoid anything and anyone to do with mental handicap and had tremendous difficulty in accepting the inevitable. Most of us admitted feeling guilty about having produced a child who was handicapped. [. . .]

However, whilst our children were young they were accepted more easily by other families with 'normal' children. We did not feel as isolated and embarrassed then as we do now they are adults. In the early years we all developed a necessarily strong mutual bond with our children and it became increasingly difficult for us to contemplate accepting short-term care when it eventually became available. None of us had been able to release our child to permanent residential care, even though we live with a constant dread of what will happen to them when we are no longer able, or here, to look after them.

During our discussions of this point we did a role reversal, three mothers playing the parts of professionals advising the parents of a child with mental handicap, played by the Supervisor and Senior Clinical Psychologist, to allow their child a weekend away in short-term care. It was interesting to see how hard we tried to persuade them to relinquish their child, a true case of 'do as I say, not as I do'.

We felt, with only one exception whose husband truly shared the load, that responsibility for our handicapped children was ours, and that it was our task to keep the family together and make sure that their presence did not influence the normal life of the family.

3.3   Our view of the professionals

In the early years the professional who gave the most help was the one with whom we had built up a situation of trust. It varied from family to family who that person was. In some cases the family struggled on alone.

We feel that the medical profession does not understand the impact on a family of having a child who is mentally handicapped, and the needs of that child and the family within which it lives. While the child is young there is fairly good paediatric care in all fields, but once adult the support ceases. There is often no responsible medical consultant available and very scanty control exists over physical health and medication. We wish that a yearly physical examination by an interested and caring practitioner was routine, and not something which *might* happen if we request it. This is so essential, both for the good of our grown-up children and for our own peace of mind.

We all expressed grave concern over the standard of nursing care given to our children in general hospitals. Each of us has found that we are expected to fulfil the role of nurse if our child is admitted to hospital, both during the night and day, *not* just for our own peace of mind but because the nursing staff seem unable to cope with the needs of people with severe mental handicaps. Is sufficient training given to general nurses who may have to cope with someone who is mentally handicapped in acute illness? Should there, perhaps, be specially qualified nurses, trained to cope with such situations, on call in every general hospital?

With a few exceptions we feel that we receive scant help from social workers and community nurses, social workers coming rather lower in our estimation than community nurses. Some of us have had no help from social workers or other key workers for two years. We have all gone for long periods without help from anyone; and if someone is allotted, the support provided is not maintained for any length of time, so no feelings of trust can be established. We all loathe the use of 'answering machines' by the people who are supposed to help us. What use are these machines in an emergency? We feel that they deter confidentiality, which is a difficult and tenuous thing at the best of times.

We were shocked to find that some of us were unaware of the allowances to which we and our children with mental handicaps are entitled. None of the professionals had enlightened us.

3.4   Looking to the future

Having completed our first five meetings we decided to continue, in an effort to find a more positive way forward following the disturbing look back. This time discussions were based mainly on the fact that one day our sons and daughters would have to go into permanent care. We spent one session thinking how we had ourselves felt about leaving home, and how leaving home usually occurs within a family. As a result we formed definite views.

We feel that short-term care is absolutely essential, to give the mother and other relatives some chance to be a 'normal' family and also to give the person who is handicapped a gentle experience of being away from home and learning to communicate within new situations. We know that short-term care is now much more readily available than it was when our children were young and we wondered what this would lead to when today's young children reach their twenties. Will their parents opt out altogether?

Continuity of care is important. People who are handicapped should not be shunted around to whichever establishment will have them; they should have a chance to know and be known at one constant place of care. For the same reason intervals between short-term care should not be too long and should allow for gentle adjustment. Every one of us felt most strongly that, as parents, responsibility for children with handicaps lay with us while we were here; but we all felt that it would be unfair to burden our other children with that responsibility.

We know that the time for permanent care will come, and that it will leave a strangeness and emptiness within us. We in no way wish to relinquish totally our responsibility and would like to retain some control both from the medical and caring points of view. We believe that residential care must be provided within the community and not in the 'wilds'. In this way people with handicaps can continue to be part of the community, and local residents can perhaps in some way monitor what happens to them. Care must be taken to see that things remain familiar, consistent and, above all, comfortable and cheerful.

3.5 In retrospect

We know that our own family lives have been to a great degree controlled by our children who are handicapped. Some of the difficulties we have had to live with are:

- husbands' jobs have been influenced, and in some cases promotion has been blocked, by the inability to move around the country freely;
- housing has needed special consideration;
- 'time off' for going out in the evenings or with our other children has had to be planned around the availability of 'minders' which has become increasingly difficult to arrange and more expensive as the years have passed by;
- we, both as family members and as individuals, have missed out on opportunities to develop our own interests;
- holidays have never been easy to plan and we have had to rely on the availability of short-term care, hoping for the good health at the right time of the child who is handicapped;
- some of us have had to consider carefully the type and size of car purchased in order to accommodate a large wheelchair and be easy enough to get our child in and out of.

3.6 To conclude

We are all well aware of families which have broken up because of the strain imposed by caring for a child who is handicapped, particularly whilst the parents have been young. Have we been taken advantage of by Social Services because our happy marriages have enabled us to continue to care for our children, who are now adults?

Throughout their lives we have always tried to meet the needs of our children and we all agree that they should live as normal a life as possible, surrounded by people who can provide security, personal care and, above all, love. If our children with mental handicaps are healthy and content, the reduction of strain on the rest of the family is abundantly apparent.

We have put down these thoughts in this article in the hope that they may help to stimulate a better service for families of people who are handicapped and bring about a greater understanding between the professionals and the parents. We found as our meetings progressed that our trust in each other increased, and that included our two 'professionals'. It seems that the way forward is becoming more positive and, with a little time and thought, services all round could be better.

3.7   Postscript

Since compiling our article two of us (one widowed) have received letters from our key worker (a social worker) stating that she is receiving so many referrals now that it is more and more difficult for her to give adequate help to each individual. Consequently, as her recent involvement with us has been minimal, she is closing our cases.

We wonder if we are correct, after all, in saying that 'the way forward is becoming more positive'!

4 My own perspective and experience

Louisa Reynolds

This account reflects one person's feelings and experiences. It was written originally in the form of a series of letters to a friend, expressing the anger and frustration she was feeling. We have chosen to retain the informality of the style as this reflects most directly and honestly the emotions wrapped up in the communication. The name of the contributor has been changed to protect her identity as she is currently employed in a relevant post with a Local Education Authority.

I've been working with adults labelled mentally handicapped for six years. I'm a teacher interested in how people learn and in how to find the creative source in students and encourage its growth. I've worked with all ages and 'types' of people. Mostly now in the area of art and creative writing. I don't think art and creative writing belong to a select few but to everyone. Also that the ability to express oneself in whatever way one chooses enhances the quality of life in a real way. I think there are aspects of the society in which we live that crush individual expression in the service of an élite, of market forces and of a smooth-running bureaucracy. I have seen this nowhere more clearly than in the area of people who have been labelled mentally handicapped. They are, more than any other group I have come across, reduced to the level of passive consumers. At the same time lip-service is paid to consultation. Over the years I have come to see this issue as being on the level of human rights. There have been times when I have had the feeling of living in the middle of a Dickens novel. The gloss of material comfort is not enough when you can't speak and be heard, when you can't act and be seen.

I think one of the best ways of sorting out how to work with mentally handicapped people is to put yourself in their shoes. There has long been a climate in which workers make a very clear dividing line between them and us and I think this is responsible for much of the abuse of rights that occurs. It is also very dangerous in another way. By this I mean that from the idea that mentally handicapped people are different from the rest of us it can be a short journey to thinking that they do not feel like the rest of us and can therefore be treated differently.

(It also doesn't do to forget that this facility is what made it possible for the Nazis to gas millions of people, those labelled mentally handicapped being among the first to go, and this only forty years ago.)

Jan Shorter was one of my students who went out into the community, into a house. Soon after, the staff at college were advised that she was to undergo a behaviour-modification plan. I can see why the idea came about as Jan was a handful at the best of times. Obsessed with food, she was quite capable of begging ice-cream off toddlers. Taking her round the outdoor market was an expedition that required great ingenuity. She is also very affectionate. She also at that time masturbated quite a lot without regard to where she was or who she was with. So the idea had naturally come about that if she was to live in the community she would have to learn other ways of behaving. The first I heard of this was when I was presented with a page of responses to be made to Jan in various situations, e.g. I was not to allow her to come into the room in her usual way saying 'Helloooooo!' and giving me a hug. I'm not sure of the exact details but it was on the lines of saying 'Good morning' firmly and maybe shaking her hand. I wish I'd asked for a copy of the sheet but at the time I refused to have anything to do with it. Everyone who was part of Jan's life was to respond on these lines. Saying these same words to her in response. It occurred to me that a case could be made out for this being a subtle form of torture. How would I feel if everyone I came into contact with suddenly changed their many and varied responses to me and all said the same things? And if I was further told that this was how it was normal to behave and I was not to be released from this situation until I also conformed to this pattern of response? I think I'd phone Ray Bradbury and ask for 50 per cent of any profits he made on the story. Or go mad.

In my first job with mentally handicapped people I was part of a team of two providing house experience with a craft bias, for people living in a local hospital.

I'd thought of making patchwork cushions and had lots of different material cut up ready in squares. They filled a table. Ivan was the first to choose. All I'd asked was that each of them choose two pieces that they liked. Ivan was young, funny, extrovert.

He couldn't do it. He kept saying, 'No, you.' I kept explaining that, if I chose, it would be what I liked and not what he liked. He still couldn't do it. 'No, you.' I was worried that I had made the first task too difficult or that I hadn't managed to get across what I wanted. I tried to make it simpler by holding different pieces and saying 'Do you like this one?' and talking about the different colours. Eventually he did choose and carried on to make a patchwork cushion that incorporated many such choices. I thought of this again two years later when we were making something else. Curtains I think it must have been. Ivan was adamant that he chose the material. He insisted that we went to the local material shop so that his choice was larger than the pieces we already had. He chose and paid for the material by himself and carried it proudly back to the house. Ivan was the first person to teach me that living in an institution is about *not* making choices. I believe the initial choice was difficult for him because he feared he might get it wrong and be told off. He wasn't sure that it wasn't a trap of some sort. But if you are not actively encouraged to make choices it must be a fearsome thing to be faced with. And this is not something felt only by people in institutions. Artists have that feeling sometimes when faced with the bare canvas. Each mark involves choice. Shape, colour, where to put it. And each mark made becomes a limitation of sorts, because when it has been made the other possibilities are excluded. And each mark builds up into more and more of an irremediably personal statement that can be seen by others. Choice is difficult but has to be encouraged as much as possible because it involves saying 'I'. 'I like this', 'I want this', 'I don't like', etc. It is possible to institutionalise areas of choice but never the choices themselves. This is an area of freedom that we can encourage as much as possible.

With the same class part of our weekly routine was to go shopping in the open market, usually for tea, coffee, biscuits, etc. One afternoon we looked on a second-hand stall. I suggested that we could buy something for the house. One of our group liked a painting, another chose a pair of wooden candlesticks to be used on special occasions like birthdays. We bought them and took them back to the house. One of the group found the hammer and a nail. We decided where the painting should hang. I thought this a good, all-round individual and group experience. Anyway it felt good. Later that week I had a phone call from my own boss to say that she was having trouble with the hospital. What we had done, with my encouragement, was not seen as normal. Normalisation was just coming into fashion.

I was even being suspected of wanting to take the pictures and candlesticks for myself at a later date. We rode this storm. I wrote one of my long letters with lots of long words in explanation. A meeting was held and we carried on going to the second-hand stall, occasionally.

At the same time as this, a day room had been completely kitted out with a new fitted carpet and a new velvet three-piece suite, with the result that for four months all outings of any sort were stopped for the residents because the funds were exhausted.

I see this as being a conflict between what certain sections of the community see as being normal and therefore OK in accordance with normalisation, and what is sensible.

Thomas was one of the people who came to the above group. He was articulate, could write letters. He was fine in our group though very reluctant to actually do anything, especially if it meant doing something for other people. But he was having problems at the hospital. The first we knew of this was when he came one day, sat and said nothing. I tried to talk with him but his speech was blurred and, worst of all, when I looked at his eyes I realised that the Thomas I knew wasn't there anymore. I got in touch with my boss and she found out from the hospital that Thomas had been prescribed something known colloquially among the medical profession as the 'Zombie Drug'. I protested because I couldn't see any point in rendering Thomas unfit for anything let alone learning. The dose was lessened on Wednesdays. The drug apparently has side-effects. The first I knew of this was when we were all on a bus on an outing. Thomas lunged suddenly at a woman sitting at the back of the bus. He grabbed her breasts and wouldn't let go. He kept saying that he wanted them, that he wanted to be a woman. The next thing that happened was that we heard he had gone shopping on his own one Saturday and had gone into a hairdresser's where an apprentice was on her own. He had gone up to her and kissed her. She'd screamed and the police were called. He'd been taken back to the hospital and a few weeks later been removed permanently to a secure unit. There was no trial.

It would seem that those labelled mentally handicapped are not governed by normal laws. None of these behaviour traits were in evidence before this drug was used. I know I'm not alone in believing in the sanctity of each individual human life. What I saw here amounts to someone having their life taken from them while their body carries on breathing.

Another of our students was a woman of middle years called Miriam. She was again one of the more assertive and articulate of the group. She had in the past been an 'outsider', with a husband and house of her own. She was unhappy at the hospital and let everyone know it, with the result that she had the reputation of being a moaner. For a year she complained of stomach ache. She seemed more tired than usual and gradually more apathetic. Then she caught a cold. It got worse and, the hospital doctor being away at the time, a local GP was called in. He diagnosed pneumonia and sent her to hospital. She died there a few days later. There had to be an autopsy and it was discovered that she had in fact died of stomach cancer. I will never forget her funeral. There were two nurses representing the hospital, her mother, her aunt and me. The priest wore plimsolls under his cassock, and squirted holy water on to her coffin from a plastic squeegee thing. It was all over in minutes. Her mother kept asking the nurses whether she had left any money behind.

Miriam was a victim of not being listened to. What she needed was to be treated as someone with worth. She didn't even get this at her funeral.

An advocacy group had been set up in a local hostel after a group of residents had requested it. Records of the meetings were kept. They are mostly about who is responsible for feeding the cat. The last one was discovered by one of the staff at the hostel. In it Albert brought up the subject of his girlfriend. They both attended the local Adult Training Centre (ATC). Winnie seemed to spend an enormous amount of time in the toilet and the supervisor was punishing her by stopping the first course of her dinner. Albert's objection was that they paid for the dinners and nobody had the right to stop them eating them. This sheet of paper found its way on to the table of the head of social services and a message went back down the line that the group was to be stopped unless a member of staff was included. So they stopped. As Albert said, there wasn't any point having them if staff were included.

Albert was one of the people who had asked for sex education. At the hostel he is not allowed to have Winnie in his room for so much as a cup of coffee. I went to one of his reviews in which his social worker, the head of the ATC and the head of his hostel all referred to his personality problem.

This turned out to be that he still objected if anyone 'reasonably chastised' his girlfriend.

I brought this up some time later with the head of the ATC and said that I thought it was very normal behaviour. 'No, you don't understand,' he said. 'This is different.'

'Why is it different?'

'Because he gets angry.'

'But I'd get angry, you'd get angry, if you thought someone was abusing a person you care about. Anyone would.'

To which he made no reply.

Normalisation is now the officially recognised approach. Two-day courses have been running on it. I went to one of the early ones. There were about a hundred people there. Two were parents. None was labelled mentally handicapped.

It was an odd experience for me personally as I came out feeling quite alien after all the talk of what is normal.

My favourite example was the lecture on appearance. A social worker came before us dressed sort of like a punk. She asked for our opinion of her appearance. The woman sat next to me called out, 'I think you look rather wonderful!' To which she replied, 'Yes, but what would a normal person feel about it?' The woman next to me muttered 'I thought I was normal!' We weren't consulted again.

5 Helping Bangladeshi families: Tower Hamlets Parent Adviser Scheme

Hilton Davis and Prapti Ali Choudhury

Families of children with mental handicaps are provided with inadequate help (Hannam, 1980). In the UK help is virtually non-existent for families who do not speak English. Powell and Perkins (1984) found that Asian families had limited understanding of their child's handicap and inadequate knowledge of available services. A similar situation exists in the East End of London, where a very large Bangladeshi population makes heavy demands upon the child health services (Watson, 1984). Gulliford (1984) found that Bangladeshi families of children with severe mental handicaps were more deprived and more socially isolated and lacking in social support than white families. Again, they showed less knowledge of the child's handicap and were less likely to perceive their needs as being met by the services.

Superficially services are available to all members of the community. However, communication and other difficulties inhibit the uptake of services by Asian families (Horn, 1982) and prevent the provision of help that cares for the psychological and developmental needs of children and families as a whole. The difficulties of working through an interpreter are documented by Gulliford (1984). She, like Powell and Perkins (1984), stresses the need for workers who speak the language of the family. The purpose of this chapter is to illustrate the plight of such families and to demonstrate how appropriate help can be provided.

To provide general help for all families of children with special needs, the Tower Hamlets Child Development Team instituted the Parent Adviser Scheme (Davis, 1985a and b). Trained counsellors (parent advisers) work with families on an on-going and regular basis. Trained health visitors, physiotherapists, social service personnel and teachers visit families at home and work in partnership with them. Essentially they respect the families as a whole, listen to them and negotiate all actions with them (Cunningham and Davis, 1985).

Having established a mutually trusting relationship, parent advisers attempt to be useful in ways determined by the families. They support them, whilst helping them to explore their situation, set goals, formulate and carry out plans, and evaluate the results. The intention is to facilitate the development of parental self-confidence and to foster the family resources in order to enable them, in the long term, to help themselves and their children. A focus of the work is the behaviour and development of children with special needs, but only within the context of the needs and wishes of the families as a whole.

This kind of work is impossible if parent advisers do not speak the same language as the families. As experience had shown that working through interpreters was not viable, one of the authors, Prapti Ali Choudhury, from the Bangladeshi community itself, was employed as a full-time parent adviser. She had no professional qualifications and her only relevant experience had been eighteen months spent as an interpreter for health visitors. She spent three months in training, focusing on counselling skills. Then, closely supervised, she began by seeing one family. Gradually she took on more families, most of whom had desperate problems. In virtually all of them the changes associated with having a parent adviser have been remarkable and fundamentally related to increased parental confidence and self-respect. The following description is of one typical family. A research evaluation of the work will be available towards the end of 1989.

5.1   The family

The family lived in a fourth-floor council flat where the lift was frequently broken. The area was intimidating, as is often the case in inner cities. Mrs B. was forty-five years old and had two sons (aged twelve and sixteen years) and a daughter with Down's syndrome (aged eleven months) living with her. On first meeting, Mrs B. appeared bewildered, lonely, distraught and unable to cope with the problems facing her, including: the recent sudden death of her husband; her daughter's Down's syndrome; her own ill-health; her inability to speak English; her fear of leaving the flat; her enforced separation from her other children in Bangladesh; the absence of a support system (family or friends); and extreme poverty.

5.2   The help provided

November to December 1985

Mrs B. agreed to see the parent adviser, who began visiting weekly. At first, Mrs B. cried constantly and described many of the problems listed earlier. She had had no one with whom to share the shock of her husband's death. She felt isolated, and her feelings flooded out when she met the parent adviser. She was aware that her daughter, Nipa, was different from other children, yet she had no idea of the diagnosis and she did not know how to help her or what to expect in the future. She acknowledged support and help from an excellent social worker, but this was greatly impeded by the language barrier.

   Slowly, Mrs B. began to trust the parent adviser and to talk to her more openly, treating her 'like a friend'. She discussed her inability to leave the flat on her own. Her husband had done everything for her; now she depended totally on her sons. Although she desperately needed practical and emotional help, she had not been able to go to the 'Wednesday Club', a nursery group for mothers and children with special needs. Therefore, as the first practical help, the parent adviser accompanied Mrs B. to the 'Club' each week with a view to her eventually making the trip on her own. Much time was also spent in discussing feeding problems, since Nipa would only take a bottle and would eat nothing solid. The parent adviser also began to involve appropriate service personnel, acting as an interpreter to overcome the communication difficulties.

January to March 1986

Within a month of first attending the 'Wednesday Club', Mrs B. made the trip on her own. It was a terrifying step for her, but it was greeted with joy by the parent adviser, awaiting her at the nursery. This event alone significantly increased Mrs B.'s self-confidence. Her difficulty in leaving the flat was further decreased by the physiotherapist's provision of a push-chair, something which she had never had before. Other professional involvement facilitated by the parent adviser was further demonstrated by joint visits with the family's health visitor who was enabled to communicate with Mrs B. for the first time.

Another agreed plan was for the parent adviser to accompany Mrs B. to the post office and to help her draw her Benefit money. She had never experienced financial dealings before, but subsequently she gradually became able to shop on her own and to take responsibility for the family's finances away from her son, whose honesty she doubted. The elation associated with the first trip to the post office was accompanied by Mrs B.'s spontaneous and emotional declaration of how much better she felt generally and how important the parent adviser was to her. Although the parent adviser allowed Mrs B. to talk about whatever she wished during her weekly visits, a recurrent issue was Nipa's feeding difficulties. Consequently, advised by the Child Development Team, she began to help Mrs B. to experiment with different foods, prepared and presented in different ways.

Mrs B. began to express concern about her elder son, whom she regarded as not caring about the family. He constantly stayed away from home and gave what appeared to his mother to be false explanations. The parent adviser arranged to meet him. By listening respectfully she was able to establish a sufficiently strong relationship with him to enable him to discuss the family situation openly. He shared some of his grief for his father's death, and became able to discuss his feelings with his mother, which enhanced her self-esteem. Mrs B. was also encouraged by at last succeeding in feeding Nipa solid food on a spoon. Her increasing competence was illustrated by the fact that her financial understanding had improved to such an extent that she asked the parent adviser to help her to open a bank account.

April to June 1986

The parent adviser continued listening, helping Mrs B. to clarify her ideas, understand her feelings and make plans. Liaison between the family, the parent adviser and the health visitor enabled the acquisition of a liquidiser for preparing Nipa's food and the completion of an application for a day nursery place. A major task in this period was to support Mrs B. whilst she nursed her daughter through a severe viral infection. Subsequently, for the first time in their relationship, Mrs B. and the parent adviser were able to discuss her developmental progress. No toys were available, partly because Mrs B. could not afford them, but mainly because she had little conception of the role of play in child development. The parent adviser supplied some toys from a stock kept by the Child Development Team. Together, they explored the functions and types of play, focusing upon Nipa's reluctance to concentrate or to play with anything for any length of time. Mrs B. began to play with and stimulate her.

It was only because of the parent adviser that Mrs B. learned the contents of a letter from her younger son's headmaster, informing her that he had been truanting. The letter was, of course, in English. As a result the parent adviser was able to liaise successfully between the family, the Social Services and the school. Further contact with Social Services brought about the provision of a refrigerator, bought by money from a local hospital charity.

Another aim during this period was to attempt to introduce Mrs B. to another family with whom the parent adviser worked. The intention was to help both families to increase their own support systems and to reduce their social isolation. This, however, was only partially successful because of the reluctance and dominance of the husband in the other family.

Mrs B. and the parent adviser continued to explore ways of facilitating Nipa's developmental progress. In particular, it was noticed that Mrs B. rarely talked to her daughter, instead using non-verbal vocalisations. Her explanation for this was that Nipa would not understand if she spoke to her properly. After discussing this observation at some length, Mrs B. began to talk to her daughter, slowly and simply, in an effort to help her learn to speak.

July to September 1986

The interest in developing her daughter's language was reflected in Mrs B.'s own desire to learn English. She decided that many of her difficulties could be reduced by speaking English. By liaising with the social worker, the parent adviser was able to help Mrs B. to begin classes at an Asian Study Centre. Unfortunately her attendance was soon disrupted by a series of events, including illness. Nevertheless, Mrs B.'s confidence was further boosted at this time by her success in doing all her shopping completely on her own for the very first time. She described it with excitement, as an adventure. At this point, as at many others, the role of the parent adviser was to help Mrs B. to evaluate herself, and help her to attribute success to her own courage, resourcefulness and ability.

It was during this period that Mrs B. began to take proper care of her home. She had begun to neglect it when her husband died, and had cared little about it since. Now she began to clean the house and keep it tidy, and to wash the family's clothes regularly. The Child Development Team supplied some children's clothes, and Mrs B. began to organise appropriate storage on hangers under cover. She continued to shop on her own and became more able to manage money matters. Her confidence and happiness increased and was manifested in dealing more warmly with the children. A joint visit with the social worker was productive in enabling Mrs B. to apply for Attendance Allowance and for assistance from the Family Fund.

Visits by the parent adviser were an obvious source of pleasure for Mrs B. She continued to talk openly about herself and her situation. She continued also to pine for her children in Bangladesh.

The parent adviser provided further practical help by being with her when she was seen by a doctor to evaluate her claim for Attendance Allowance and when the Family Fund social worker visited. She also accompanied Mrs B. on visits to various clinics. Certainly, her presence enhanced the benefit derived from visits to the Child Development Team. Mrs B. described how different she felt now compared with how she felt before having a parent adviser, when nobody seemed to listen, understand or help. This is not to say that nobody tried; various professionals had visited her, but she was unaware of who they were and what they were doing. She perceived her own needs as having been totally unmet. The problem was not just of language, but a failure to understand her feelings, her culture and her situation.

October to December 1986

When Nipa was admitted to hospital for three days for the insertion of grommets to aid recovery from a middle-ear infection, Mrs B. required the support of the parent adviser and the social worker. Nevertheless, her ability to manage the family was increasing all the time. More toys and clothes were provided by the parent adviser, and some time during each visit was spent playing with Nipa on her return home.

The process of respectful listening, discussion and support continued. The parent adviser helped Mrs B. arrange to see an optician, who prescribed badly-needed spectacles. A nursery place for Nipa was eventually obtained, and the parent adviser visited the day nursery with her. Mrs B.'s delight in the nursery was offset by the Social Services Under-5s Section's usual failure to provide transport. Transport was eventually arranged because of the parent adviser's intervention. Despite this, on her own initiative Mrs B. began to learn her way to the day nursery and was eventually able to make the journey alone.

Christmas presents for the family were a washing machine and a telephone provided by the Family Fund. Mrs B. needed considerable instruction from the parent adviser before she could use either.

5.3   Sequel

The parent adviser continues to visit, but Mrs B. is more independent. She is able to leave the flat, to visit the nursery and to do the shopping unaided. She has also begun to make friends and is more able to communicate with professionals generally, when they listen. Not only has Mrs B. progressed but the family has become more of a unit, with the sons taking an active role in the affairs of the family. Nipa is making enormous strides in health, happiness and psychological development generally.

5.4   Conclusions

The description has been of one family out of many who are now visited by parent advisers. It illustrates the adversity faced by Asian families, documented in previous work (Gulliford, 1984; Powell and Perkins, 1984). Apart from difficulties of communication, a major and compounding difficulty is the disrespectful and self-fulfilling assumption made by many professionals that families are unable to cope once they have fallen down the scale of deprivation. On the contrary, this story illustrates the way in which people can be helped to help themselves, given attention and respect. The suggestion made by Powell and Perkins (1984) that such 'families desperately need a named person who speaks their own language' (p. 52) is fully validated by our work. The help given by the parent adviser included providing the mother with: someone to talk to, who would listen; social and psychological support; information; someone to accompany her out of the house; child management and developmental advice; referral to other professionals; and social contacts outside the family. The parent adviser also facilitated other professionals' work with the family by interpreting and explaining on their behalf, and she mediated between family members.

Such help has brought about enormous change in the family described and in many other families. Changes observed include, for example:

- improved parental confidence, mood and feelings of receiving support;
- improved ability to cope in many areas, such as managing and

organising the home, financial management, child care, communicating by learning English and general independence;

- improved general quality of life;
- increased family cohesion;
- improved social support;
- improved developmental progress and decreased behaviour problems with the children;
- improved service provision to the family as a whole.

It is our belief that these changes arise because of respecting the family, having time to listen to them and communicating well with them (that is, counselling them). As this study shows, the need for specialist medical, social, therapeutic and educational skills is very much secondary to the need to facilitate people's own resources, provide them with general support and treat them with respect. Mrs B. and her family remain deprived and disadvantaged in comparison with the majority of families in this country. Nevertheless, since being in contact with the parent adviser their happiness and quality of life has been enhanced beyond anything made available by the helping professions, and they are now more able to cope independently.

Acknowledgments

This work has only been made possible by the generous funding of the Mental Health Foundation and the co-operation of the Tower Hamlets Child Development Team.

References

CUNNINGHAM, C. and DAVIS, H. (1985) *Working with Parents: Frameworks for Collaboration*, Milton Keynes, Open University Press.

DAVIS, H. (1985a) 'Developing the role of parent adviser in the child health service', in Pugh, G. and De'Ath, E. (eds) *Working Together with Children with Special Needs*, London, National Children's Bureau.

DAVIS, H. (1985b) 'Counselling parents of children who have intellectual disabilities', *Early Child Development and Care*, Vol. 22, pp. 19–35.

GULLIFORD, F. (1984) 'A comparison study of the experiences and service needs of Bangladeshi and white families with severely mentally handicapped children', unpubl. dissertation for Diploma in Clinical Psychology, Leicester, British Psychological Society.

HANNAM, C. (1980) *Parents and Mentally Handicapped Children*, Harmondsworth, Penguin.

HORN, E. (1982) 'A survey of referrals from Asian families to four social services area offices in Bradford', in Cheetham, J. (ed.), *Social Work and Ethnicity*, London, Allen & Unwin.

POWELL, M. and PERKINS, E. (1984) 'Asian families with a pre-school handicapped child – a study', *Mental Handicap*, Vol. 12, pp. 50–2.

WATSON, E. (1984) 'Health of infants and use of health services by mothers of different ethnic groups in East London', *Community Medicine*, Vol. 6, pp. 127–35.

6 Creating a 'working alliance' with people with learning difficulties

Ann Brechin and John Swain

6.1 Introduction

Relationships between professionals and people labelled as having a mental handicap have their origins in past and present social structures and attitudes. Within this broad context of changing patterns of social organisation, social and professional constructions of mental handicap have led to particular attitudes and practices being adopted. In the Western world, two approaches have come to dominate in the course of the past fifty years: a medical approach and an educational approach. The growing consumer movement, reflected in this instance by the burgeoning of self-advocacy, and the advent of the normalisation movement has impinged very little as yet on these strongly established professional traditions. Reactions to change have tended to involve attempts to encompass new approaches within existing frameworks of practice and thinking.

Yet the concept of self-advocacy and the parallel emergence of normalisation demand a radical revision of professional roles and approaches. Assumptions about the nature of the professional–client relationship will have to change significantly if professionals are going to keep pace with the changes which are coming increasingly from sources beyond their control.

In this chapter, we shall be exploring the nature and implications of existing professional approaches, and the growing awareness of the importance of professional–client relationships. We shall be considering how new styles of relationship might be defined and generated; relationships which would be more in tune with the increasingly influential changes in philosophy and policy, and which can support, in turn, the development of new professional attitudes and practices. [. . .]

6.2 The medical approach

From the medical perspective, the problem, if it is a 'problem', is seen as located in the individual, its origin lying in an innate physiological disorder which brings it into the realm of medical jurisdiction. Thinking and practice impose what has been called the 'sick role' (Tuckett, 1976) on people with learning difficulties.

The assumptions and implications of this have been exhaustively written about (for example, Mittler, 1979; Ryan and Thomas, 1987) in relation to mental handicap and, on a broader front, to medicalisation in general (Illich, 1977; McKnight, 1977; Kennedy, 1981). In essence the effect of medically conceived interpretations and solutions has been to provide institutional care settings and services, often taking over pre-existing custodial arrangements, in which basic nursing care, supervision and protection have been provided, with drug therapy as the major planned 'intervention' or treatment. Decisions about management, life-styles and living arrangements, even about educational capacity, have been taken by doctors, with a consequent decrease in the power of individuals and their families to plan and control their lives. The impact of such approaches on relationships has been essentially to increase dependency with stereotyped perceptions leading to self-fulfilling prophecies (Edgerton, 1976; Ryan and Thomas, 1980). People labelled as 'mentally handicapped' have been perceived as sick and incurable, as dependent, and as ineducable. In return they have, not surprisingly, behaved in ways which confirmed these perceptions.

Essentially the medical approach has painted a pessimistic picture. Retarded development, disturbed patterns of behaviour and inability to form relationships or to be self-sufficient have been seen as resulting from disease or physiological abnormality. Yet, although this defines the individual in a 'sick role', no cure is available. A counsel of despair was offered for many years, which in effect said 'put them away and forget them'. Against such a background of hopelessness, compounded by living circumstances which were at best dreary and unstimulating for patients and staff alike, and at worst a contravention of basic human rights and dignity, individuals had no opportunity to develop any other picture of themselves. The picture was provided for them in terms of medical explanations, with patterns of behaviour, development and any personal or emotional problems accounted for by their medical condition. Diagnosis and treatment were in the hands of the medical experts who held the franchise on knowledge. Professional–client relationships were thus inevitably one-sided, with all the power and knowledge (at least that which was perceived as relevant) resting with the medical profession. At best the relationship was paternalistic; at worst it was authoritarian and dehumanising.

6.3 The educational approach

A second major influence which has had a dramatic effect in the second half of the century has been the educational approach. Interestingly, though, the close ties with and influence of medicine have meant that only recently has an educational approach begun to emerge which is freed from the decision-making power of the medical profession, and from the diagnostic and treatment framework. With improvements in educational technologies, more detailed understanding of how behaviour is controlled and developed, and a greater focus on curriculum planning has come a flood of new opportunities for people with learning difficulties. The recognition that, given appropriate opportunities, time and carefully devised teaching strategies, even people with very severe learning difficulties can make progress, has led to a new commitment. The aim of this approach is not so much to offer care and protection as to help people to reach their 'full potential'.

While this has only relatively recently become widely influential, affecting policies and services across the board and not just in the formal educational sphere, Ryan and Thomas (1987) point out its longer history. They quote Seguin, for example, saying as far back as 1846, 'While waiting for medicine to cure idiots, I have undertaken to see that they participate in the benefit of education.' [. . .]

The opening up of educational strategies and opportunities has had to include, of course, a broadening of the more traditional educational curriculum, with a recognition that the development of basic social skills, including methods of communication, may be the important focus.

Such new developments have led inevitably to new kinds of relationship. Not only in school contexts, but in hospitals and day centres and at home, the new relationship has become a teacher–pupil one.

Successful teaching requires that learning should take place. This provides a valuable feedback loop, in one sense, which forces the 'teacher' to seek more appropriate methods or goals if the first strategies are not successful. In another sense, though, it also puts an onus on the individual with learning difficulties to accept the role of learner in the relationship – perhaps for life (Tomlinson, 1985). Opportunities for continuing education in adulthood are increasingly recognised as desirable, but when people are put in a position of having an obligation to learn with no prospect of ever quite passing the test and graduating to full citizenship, this may not be so desirable.

There are some within education who quarrel with an approach which, with an emphasis on objectives and skill development, appears to require little more than continuing compliance from pupils. Goddard (1983), for instance, argues that education should involve setting in motion a 'process' of active development which can enable 'the individual child to unfold his or her unique personality'. [. . .]

Unfortunately in the realm of education, particularly for people with learning difficulties, attitudes and practices mitigate against this happening. In general it seems that the greater the learning difficulties, the more didactic is the approach and the more controlling the relationship. The aims, the curriculum and the methods used are predicated upon, on the one hand, assumptions of incapacity and unsatisfactoriness, and, on the other hand, assumptions that the only worthwhile goal is 'independence'. This is then defined in a normative sense which must therefore inevitably exclude these pupils from its attainment. [. . .]

Such contradictions are integral to educational relationships with other adults also. Under the tutelage very often of the psychologist, nurses, care staff, ATC instructors and parents acquire the new educational methodologies which enable them to develop a more effective teaching role. What this usually means in practice, however, is that they can more effectively control and manipulate the behaviour of their 'pupil'.

6.4 Parallels between the medical and educational approaches

In one sense the educational approach is the polar opposite of the medical one, in directing attention to the possibilities of improvement and change, rather than to the physiological account of permanent impairment. In another sense, however, the approaches stand alongside each other. Both assume that existing social constructions of normality define the goal to which people with learning difficulties must aspire; both define and understand the 'problems of mentally handicapped' people in such a way as to indicate clearly the impossibility of ever achieving that goal (the best hope being to build up patterns of skills which approximate to 'normal' behaviour); and both create a professional–client relationship which enshrines the professional in a world of exclusive and privileged knowledge, and consequently entombs the individual with learning difficulties in a fundamentally dependent role.

6.5 Self-advocacy and normalisation: impact and implications

[. . .] The two developments [self-advocacy and normalisation] have emerged in parallel, developing separately, but inevitably influencing and interacting with each other. It will be argued here that their aims can and should converge. Self-advocacy is in essence about a process of self-actualisation. It is about people coming to identify and express personal feelings, wishes and circumstances and coming to understand what contributes to the positives and negatives of their existence. It is about opening up ideas about the range of choices which could and should be available to them.

Any professional approach that does not concern itself with supporting and facilitating these same processes of growth for people with learning difficulties must be seriously open to question. Similarly, approaches which seem to imply a pre-knowledge of the aims and goals of other people's lives, and lack the willingness to retain an open mind, to live with uncertainties, possibilities and transitions – these too must be seen as professional approaches with little to recommend them.

When we look at the normalisation movement we can see that it has implications for professional approaches, but it will be argued that the concept itself has been open to more than one interpretation, leading to differential impact on professional practice. These interpretations can be reviewed and considered in the light of the aims of the self-advocacy movement, with the question being posed – does this interpretation of normalisation and the implications for professional practice appear to support and facilitate the open-ended processes of growth emerging from the advocacy movements? We are suggesting, in effect, that this can be used as a kind of litmus test of appropriateness against which professional approaches can be measured.

The early voices expounding and refining the idea of normalisation and its implications came from Denmark, Sweden and the United States (for example, Nirje, 1969, 1980; Bank-Mikklesen, 1969; Wolfensberger and Glenn, 1973; Wolfensberger, 1980). These were quickly taken up and written about in the British context (for example, Thomas *et al.*, 1978; O'Brien and Tyne, 1981).

One of the earliest definitions of normalisation at an international symposium saw it as 'making available to the mentally retarded patterns of everyday life which are as close as possible to the patterns of the mainstream of society' (Nirje, 1969). Nirje's more detailed definition included reference to the importance of normal rhythms of life, daily, weekly and yearly; normal developmental experiences such as leaving home in adulthood; and normal respect and understanding (Nirje, 1980).

Wolfensberger in the United States has focused attention specifically on the implications for service delivery and has developed an assessment procedure aimed not at individuals, but at the quality of services. PASS (Programme Analysis of Service Systems; Wolfensberger and Glenn, 1973) evaluates services in terms of how far they comply with appearances, practices and settings which would be valued by the rest of society. Again, this has been taken up in this country with workshops on 'PASS' and 'PASSING' being widely networked largely through the energies of Campaign Community and Mental Handicap Education and Research Association (CMHERA).

Within the movement, definitions have shifted over time. A critical account of such shifts (Baldwin, 1985) suggests that this has made evaluation of the concept particularly difficult to achieve.

We are suggesting here that normalisation, over and above these many attempts to define it coherently and carefully, is open to different interpretations in practice. In our view two common interpretations of the term are unfortunate and probably unintended by at least some of the protagonists of the concept. The third interpretation seems to us to be the one which is in line with the philosophy of valuing and supporting each individual, reflected in the growing advocacy movement.

The first and perhaps commonest interpretation of the term is the one which takes it to be about normalising people, i.e. making people as close an approximation of normal as possible. A clear example of this was presented in the recent critique by Sinha (1986) of the goals of psychology. Contrasting practices of differentiation, 'preserving the "normal" through the exclusion of the deviant', and the newer approach of normalisation, he sees normalisation as 'predicated upon the changing of the subject so classified, towards normality'. Moreover he suggests that 'the predominant model for the implementation of normalisation practices utilises behavioural pedagogies and objectives-based curricula'. Sadly, he may well be right. Professionals do tend to see normalisation in terms of practices designed to change the individual.

It is perhaps not surprising that such an interpretation should come to the fore in the implementation of normalisation. It is precisely in line with the common professional assumptions outlined earlier and fits comfortably within the existing style of professional–client relationships. [. . .]

The second kind of interpretation is perhaps the extreme of the position that Wolfensberger espouses. Seeking to ensure that people are seen to live in pleasant, ordinary homes, are seen to drive in ordinary vehicles (not Sunshine buses, for example), go on ordinary holidays (not with large groups of other people who also have handicaps), wear attractive clothes, have attractive hairstyles, receive the same kind of support services as other people, and now, with social role valorisation (Wolfensberger, 1983) be seen to have appropriate, valued roles in society; seeking all this, begins to sound dangerously close to a marketing strategy. The product, i.e. the person in this case, becomes secondary to the packaging and to the image that is projected and promoted.

In the midst of this sales hype, what rights does the individual retain to be as he/she wishes to be? Must the individual bend to comply with (usually) middle-class value systems in order to achieve some kind of acceptance? Normalisation in this sense begins to sound like superimposing a currently fashionable veneer without any attention to the detail of what lies underneath.

In terms of the professional–client relationship, how easily this translates into the professional working to make the individual with learning difficulties socially acceptable – again on other people's terms.

Both these interpretations of normalisation seem to be in danger of losing sight of the individual at the centre of things. The relationship which is implied between professional and client by these assumptions still tallies with the traditional relationship. It remains inherently dependent from the client's point of view. Behaviour, development, appearance, social role, etc. are still judged against a 'given' of social norms accepted as appropriate goals by the professional and the task is to bring the 'deviant' individual into line as far as possible, by modifying or repackaging or both. 'Success' inevitably remains elusive by definition unless the individual escapes the label altogether.

This account sounds extremely critical of professional practice, and it should perhaps be made clear that such approaches have, paradoxically, contributed to considerable progress. Finklestein (1980) described this same paradox in relation to people with physical impairments. In the field of mental handicap the growth of the self-advocacy movement, reflects the ability of a spirit of self-determination to emerge in the face of *and* (paradoxically) with the help of, an oppressive and dependency-inducing style of professional help.

Many professionals, of course, struggle to escape from this difficulty. Others fail to recognise its existence. [. . .]

6.6   A preferred interpretation of normalisation

We have referred earlier to a third interpretation of normalisation which we see as being in line with the spirit of much that has been written, particularly in the earlier days. More recent summaries of these earlier statements are available (Bank-Mikklesson, 1980; Nirje, 1980). This account of normalisation focuses on opening up a range of life-style opportunities which are available to the rest of the population but which have tended to be closed to people with learning difficulties.

Some inherent problems remain in a concept premised on the desirability of normality, in whatever sense it is interpreted. If it is used, however, to highlight commonly experienced deprivations and restrictions, and stimulate a move away from those towards a range of service provisions and life-styles which would normally be seen as more adequate, more acceptable, and even more desirable – which would, in short, be valued by most of that society – then normalisation must offer some hope of a breakthrough.

Such an emphasis shifts the focus away from modifying or repackaging the individual, on to a concern to minimise the restrictiveness of opportunities. As such, it is not at odds with the 'litmus test' of self-advocacy, seeming to support a view of people as potentially autonomous and with a right to self-determination within a less restrictive social milieu.

What it does not do, of course, is to prescribe an appropriate style of professional practice. The principles of normalisation relate to a style of living towards which people with learning difficulties and their supporters can aspire. It does not suggest how their relationships with each other may have to change as part of the process. The tendency is, then, for professional–client relationships to continue in the existing model – even, as suggested earlier, pushing their interpretation of normalisation principles into line with their established practice in order to reduce the dissonance they might otherwise experience. It seems essential to look explicitly at the implications of this interpretation of normalisation for professional styles of working.

6.7 Towards a working alliance

What are the alternatives to the more traditional professional–client relationship? Are there alternatives to the modifying or repackaging strategies which aim to reduce deviance? What measures of success might there be if the goal of changing client behaviour in some way is no longer centre stage?

It is too simplistic to suggest that, by offering improved opportunities in a less restrictive setting, individuals with often severe learning difficulties, frequently additional disabilities, and histories of damaging experiences, will thereby have *access* to improved, more satisfying life-styles. Access requires more than just the existence of possibilities. Professional roles in offering support both directly and indirectly through other helpers will remain important in facilitating this process of accessing opportunities. But how can this role be described?

It has been suggested that the self-advocacy movement offers a model of growth and development against which professional assumptions and approaches can be tested. This is not to argue that professionals should try to replicate the process of supporting self-advocacy, but it is to suggest that the aims, mode of operation and nature of the professional–client working relationship should, at the very least, not be in conflict with the emergence of self-advocacy.

Williams and Shoultz (1982) set out their view of some of the processes at work in self-advocacy, and the following account is built around their observations.

Gains from self-advocacy	*Features of support offered*
1 Growth and confidence	Enhancing mastery and control
2 Trust	Learning to be on their side in seeing problems
3 Self valuing/pride	Learning to enjoy and know people
4 Identity	Believing in people
5 Determination	Commitment
6 Responsibility	Accentuating positive qualities
7 Ability and knowledge	Sharing skills and information
8 Sensitivity to others	Monitoring own communication
9 Developing a voice	Learning to assist without control or power
	From Brechin and Swain (1987)

Such skills as are implicated in those two lists are essentially relationship skills and are arguably as relevant to individual professional–client relationships as they are to work with self-advocacy groups.

In exploring what this may mean for professional practice, it may be helpful to look at other attempts to reconstrue the nature of professional activity. Models do exist which move away from the tendency to pathologise the individual.

Perhaps the most useful body of literature and experience to look at is that which addresses approaches to counselling. Stemming largely from the work of Carl Rogers (for example, Rogers, 1951, 1978), a school of thought has grown up emphasising both the centrality of the relationship between professional and client and the concept of personal growth – a growth which is essentially self-defined and personally experienced. Others such as Maslow (1973) had proferred similar views about the potential of human development given appropriate nurturing opportunities for growth.

Such ideas have been extended and broadened (see, for example, Egan, 1986; Murgatroyd and Woolfe, 1982) to encompass the notion of 'helping skills' or even 'human relationship skills' (Nelson-Jones, 1986). The term 'working alliance' (Deffenbacher, 1985) also seems to lay an appropriate emphasis on the concept of partnership.

Though they seem to have great relevance here, approaches to 'counselling' have tended to emerge and operate mostly in the context of more able, verbal and reflective groups in society. Working with people whose verbal skills and ability to conceptualise may be limited or sometimes non-existent offers a particular challenge. [. . .]

Shared Action Planning (Brechin and Swain, 1986, 1987) is an attempt to take up this challenge. A method or approach to working together has been devised with the explicit intention of creating a relationship and setting in motion a process which supports the moves towards normalisation whilst still tallying with the emergence of self-advocacy. The process which is generated becomes in effect an end in itself, creating as it does a working alliance within which both partners develop a shared approach to identifying and tackling goals and problems. [. . .]

A radical approach to shared assessment, which emphasises the importance of getting to know and understand each other, the identification of aims in terms of what people would like to see happening, and a process of considering plans for action which recognises the existence of different perspectives, moves the focus away from the ual concern with the individual and how he/she should change, to focus instead on the role of other people and wider circumstances. The professional as mediator is frequently the picture which emerges. But, whatever the plan for action arrived at, it is the process of travelling, and the nature of relationships generated on the journey, which is of prime concern in Shared Action Planning. Interestingly, Egan's discussion of the concept of a working alliance makes a similar point (Egan, 1986). He cites Deffenbacher (1985) as suggesting that many of the outcomes of the helping process, such as the development of goals and plans, happen inadvertently, with the most important focus being the client–helper relationship.

6.8   Drawing out principles of professional practice

We have been concerned here with the need for consistency in the principles underlying different movements, attitudes and approaches. The assumption tends to be made that principles of normalisation, the self-advocacy movement and professional–client relationships will somehow remain in tune with each other. The reality seems to be somewhat different. Interpretations of normalisation are too easily made to fit with long-established assumptions and practice. [. . .]

Out of this, we can arrive perhaps at some principles of practice which can be seen to be both compatible with normalisation (in our preferred sense) and supportive of self-advocacy.

6.9   Six principles of practice

We would suggest that *from the perspective of people with learning difficulties*, a working alliance with professionals should seem:

1   to be an entitlement rather than an imposition;
2   to promote self-realisation rather than compliance;
3   to open up choices rather than replace one option with another;
4   to develop opportunities, relationships and patterns of living, in line with their individual wishes rather than rule-of-thumb normality;
5   to enhance their decision-making control of their own lives;
6   to allow them to move at their own pace.

Such principles of professional practice, measured as they are in terms of the client's perspective on the relationship, are, on the face of it, clear and straightforward. Abiding by them, indeed trying to find ways of moving towards them, is however, infinitely more problematic.

This chapter has explored some of the issues and challenges involved in helping such a process of change to take place.

References

BALDWIN, S. (1985) 'Sheep in Wolf's clothing: impact of normalisation teaching on human services and service providers', *International Journal of Rehabilitation Research*, Vol. 8, pp. 131–42.

BANK-MIKKLESEN, N. E. (1969) *Changing Patterns in Residential Services for the Mentally Retarded*, Washington, DC, President's Committee on Mental Retardation.

BANK-MIKKLESEN, N. E. (1980) 'Denmark', in Flynn, R. J. and Nitsch, K. E. *Normalisation, Social Integration, and Community Services*, Baltimore, University Park Press.

BRECHIN, A. and SWAIN, J. (1986) 'Shared Action Planning: a skills workbook', in *Mental Handicap: Patterns for Living*, P555, Milton Keynes, Open University Press.

BRECHIN, A. and SWAIN, J. (1987) *Changing Relationships: Shared Action Planning with People with a Mental Handicap*, London, Harper & Row.

DEFFENBACHER J. L. (1985) 'A cognitive–behavioural response and a modest proposal', *Counselling Psychologist*, Vol. 13, pp. 261–9.

EDGERTON, R. B. (1976) 'The cloak of competence: years later', *American Journal of Mental Deficiency*, Vol. 80, pp. 485–97.

EGAN G. (1986) *The Skilled Helper: A Systematic Approach to Effective Helping*, 3rd edn, California, Brooks Cole.

FINKLESTEIN, V. (1980) *Attitudes and Disabled People*, Monograph 5, New York, World Rehabilitation Fund.

GODDARD, A. (1983) 'Processes in Special Education', in Blenkin, G. and Kelly, A. (eds) *Primary Curriculum in Action*, London, Harper & Row.

ILLICH, I. (1977) *Disabling Professions*, London, Marion Boyars.

KENNEDY, I. (1981) *The Unmasking of Medicine*, London, Allen & Unwin.

MASLOW, A. (1973) *The Farther Reaches of Human Nature*, London, Penguin.

McKNIGHT, J. (1977) 'Professionalised service and disabling help', in Illich (1977).

MITTLER, P. (1979) *People Not Patients: Problems and Policies in Mental Handicap*, London, Methuen.

MURGATROYD, S. and WOOLFE, R. (1982) *Coping with Crisis: Understanding and Helping People in Need*, London, Harper & Row.

NELSON-JONES, R. (1986) *Human Relationships Skills*, Eastbourne, Holt, Rinehart & Winston.

NIRJE, B. (1969) 'Towards independence', in 11th World Congress of the International Society for Rehabilitation of the Disabled, Dublin.

NIRJE, B. (1980) 'The normalisation principle', in Flynn, J. and Nitsch, K. (eds) *Normalisation, Social Integration and Community Services*, Baltimore, University Park Press.

O'BRIEN, J. and TYNE, A. (1981) *The Principle of Normalisation: A Foundation for Effective Services*, London, Campaign for Mentally Handicapped People.

ROGERS, C. (1951) *Client Centred Therapy*, London, Constable.

ROGERS, C. (1978) *Carl Rogers on Personal Power*, London, Constable.

RYAN, J. and THOMAS, F. (1980) *The Politics of Mental Handicap*, Harmondsworth, Penguin.

RYAN, J. and THOMAS, F. (1987) *The Politics of Mental Handicap*, revd edn, London, Free Association Books.

SINHA, C. (1986) 'Psychology, Education and the Ghost of Kaspar Hauser', *Disability, Handicap and Society*, Vol. 1, No. 3, pp. 245–59.

THOMAS, D. *et al.* (1978) *Encor: A Way Ahead*, CMH Enquiry Paper 6, London, Campaign for Mentally Handicapped People.

TOMLINSON, S. (1985) 'The expansion of special education', *Oxford Review of Education*, Vol. II, No. 2, pp. 157–165.

TUCKETT, D. (ed.) (1976) *An Introduction to Medical Sociology*, London, Tavistock.

WILLIAMS, P. and SCHOULTZ, B. (1982) *We Can Speak for Ourselves*, London, Souvenir Press.

WOLFENSBERGER, W. (1980) 'Overview of normalisation', in Flynn, J. and Nitsch, K. (eds) *Normalisation, Social Integration and Community Services*, Baltimore, University Park Press.

WOLFENSBERGER, W. (1983) 'Social role valorisation: a proposed new term for the principle of normalisation', *Mental Retardation*, Vol. 21, pp. 234–9.

WOLFENSBERGER, W. and GLENN, L. (1973) *Program Analysis of Service Systems: A Method for the Quantitative Evaluation of Human Services, Vol. 1, Handbook*, 2nd edn, Toronto, National Institute on Mental Retardation.

7 'Being there': evaluating life quality from feelings and daily experience

Julie Wilkinson

> Beware that you do not lose the substance by grasping at the shadow.
>
> Aesop, 550 BC

7.1 Introduction

Research has shown that generally the life quality of people with learning difficulties improves when individuals move from hospitals to the community (see, for example, Felce *et al.*, 1986). In order to avoid complacency once 'resettlement' has occurred, rigorous evaluations are needed which look at what *actually* happens in the community, and what service users *feel* about their lives when they get there.

Gallant attempts are being made along these lines. In relation to user opinion Flynn (1986, 1987), Flynn and Saleem (1986) has conducted pioneering work on interviewing people with learning difficulties, and similarly Cattermole and Jahoda (1985) have been committed to understanding the lives of people with learning difficulties through interviews and consultation. Sugg (1987) used informal, open-ended interview schedules to find out about people's previous hospital lives and their current life-styles, and Atkinson (1985) and Atkinson and Ward (1987) interviewed people to investigate their feelings about aspects of community living.

It is slowly being accepted that to evaluate life quality you have to use *different* methods from those established, if you really want to listen to people and get a user-centred picture of their lives (for example, Bolton Community Health Council, 1987). The approach described here is one such method: beginning from the position of the service user, and referring to the individual's experience and feelings as the starting point in the evaluation of life quality. The purpose of this paper is to describe the nature of the method as opposed to actual outcomes; data is used for illustrative purposes only. (A full report, including a discussion of outcomes, is in preparation.)

7.2   The Oaklands Housing Project and the people living there

The Oaklands Housing Project is a community service based on the 'ordinary life' principles (King's Fund Centre, 1980). Oaklands has been monitored since its implementation and an important focus of the evaluation has been the quality of life available to those living in its first two staffed houses. These are adjacent, three-bedroomed, semi-detached dwellings, each home for three men in their late thirties and early forties. The six inhabitants have all been described as having severe learning difficulties, with only one person able to speak in a way that would be readily amenable to an ordinary interview situation.

In order to attempt to see life from the point of view of the men, the ultimate goal for the researcher was to try to put herself into their shoes: to see life from their perspective rather than to 'look down' from above. A decision was made to be with each man in all walks of his life, while attempting to dismiss any privileges and trappings of the researcher role that would set her aside from her companion. The researcher wanted to experience as far as possible life as an Oaklands inhabitant. Hence the development of the 'being there' role.

7.3   The 'being there' approach

With just six people making up the research group the opportunity arose to look at their life-style in detail. The overall research aim was to implement a 'bottom-up' type of evaluation, beginning with a structured documentation of the service users' lives and their response to different people and places. The life-style generated by the service was then to be compared with ideals and guidelines seen to be vital in the pursuit of a good quality of life.

The major guidelines used with the evaluation data were the 'Five Accomplishments' described by O'Brien in his paper, 'A guide to personal futures planning' (1987). Specific interests within the evaluation concerned the relationships in each person's life, and the extent to which they were involved in their local neighbourhood.

Getting to know one another

At the beginning of the eighteen-month research period, time was spent getting to know the inhabitants, staff and routine of the two houses. After becoming acquainted, staff – in discussion with service users – produced an outline of each man's typical week.

This acted as a directory of people with whom the men were likely to be in contact during the subsequent 'being there' phase of the research. The researcher sought their permission to 'be with' each man in all settings and gave explanations of the research intentions.

Devising a structure for being around

During the 'being there' phase – which spread over nine months and covered the equivalent of one week for each man – days were divided into three blocks: 8 a.m. until 1 p.m., 1 p.m. until 5 p.m. and 5 p.m. until 10 p.m. The observation of house routines had indicated that the fourteen hours included in the time blocks covered each person's average waking day. The researcher was with one service user for one of these time blocks for five days a week. Flexible 'days' were worked to cover evenings and weekends, and the rest of the working day was spent writing up the observations.

The 'being there' periods were organised in a rotating manner, so that individuals got to know the researcher well – and vice versa – at a roughly equal rate. This also allowed for a levelling out of the obvious seasonal influences that might distort 'normal' patterns of activity, such as Adult Training Centre (ATC) holidays and extremes of weather conditions. The planning of the 'being there' sessions occurred on a week-in-advance basis, checking out with service users and respective contacts that the proposed periods of being with a user would not be problematic. This worked well for everybody concerned.

The research role

The nature of the relationship that the researcher had with the men at Oaklands was most akin to the participant observation described by Edgerton *et al.* (1984): 'All of these persons were visited at their residences . . . and otherwise accompanied as they went about many of their everyday activities.' The main difference was that during the 'being there' phase the researcher attempted to avoid *directing* the content of the user's life-style in order to collect information. Edgerton, by contrast, describes how research cohort members would be invited to restaurants so that informal talks could occur around specific topics. The researcher evaluating life quality at the Oakland houses aimed to talk with people in naturally occurring situations about the things they were doing and the people they were with. This had the added bonus of offering service users with severe communication difficulties the chance to be more expressive in the *actual* circumstances about which they were attempting to converse.

It was believed that, if lengthy periods of time were to be spent with an individual, the researcher should aim to be of neutral influence but should respond to conversation if this was initiated by her companion. It was not possible or desirable to remain an objective outsider when the men were getting to know and trust her. Rather than frame this as an unresolvable problem, use was made of the conversations that invariably occurred between the researcher and her companions, and this proved to be a valuable and initially unexpected source of user-orientated data. Throwaway statements made by a couple of the men, for example 'Why don't they say what's happening; what do they think we are?' (in reference to a much-delayed homeward journey on the ATC coach), gave useful insight into the person's views.

The immediacy of events and people, who featured regularly within the experience of users, acted as a memory-aid to prompt the answers to the questions asked by the researcher. With the man who did not speak or sign at all, the chance to observe his differing facial expressions and body posture when exposed to different people and places offered a great deal of insight into how he was feeling. These experiences were noted in diaries that were used to document each person's experiences and reactions.

The 'being there' role enabled the researcher to make a valiant effort to see life from the point of view of Oakland service users. Formal interviews – piloted at the start of the research – had been unsuccessful in terms of collecting relaxed, informal and natural data from the users, whereas 'being there' allowed information to be gleaned along the way. The role also permitted the avoidance of a total dependence on indirect information gathering. However, this was recognised as having its own strength and was included in the scheme of things in the form of semi-structured interviews with people who emerged as key figures in the men's lives. The 'being there' role allowed for the emergence of an evaluational backcloth, made up of the continuous flow of the individual's experience, comment and expression. Against this, more specific questions regarding life quality could be addressed.

Recording the data

The observations yielded by the 'being there' role were initially recorded on a dictaphone in any *private* place offered by the setting in hand. This was normally a lavatory, cloakroom or unused work room. When recording the data, time divisions of fifteen minutes were used to aid the transcribing of the tape content into the diary format. Each man had his own set of diaries. The right-hand pages were divided into four columns – 'Time', 'Place', 'Activity' and 'Who With' – and recorded data were transcribed into these four divisions. An example of such data is shown in Figure 7.1.

The left-hand pages were headed 'Miscellaneous Comments' and were *carte blanche* for *any* other information that was not direct observation. This included user's and staff's comments, descriptions of social settings, researcher comment and feelings, and the documentation of research dilemmas. It provided a complementary dimension to the structured and objective recording of behaviours on the adjacent sheet.

Time	Place	Activity	Who With
8.15 a.m.	Kitchen	Roger came into the kitchen – dressed smartly for the ATC. John asked him would he like breakfast. Roger smiled and John set about making him a bowl of porridge. Roger tidied up around the room; putting away drained dishes into cupboards. He went and sat at the table, poured himself a cup of tea from the pot (already made) and waited for his breakfast. John worked silently and Roger looked out of the window.	John (staff)

Figure 7.1   Observations recorded in a diary

The inside of the front cover of each diary contained a time/day grid for the individual concerned. When a specified observation had been completed and transcribed it would be filled in on the grid, complete with the source of the transcription, as indicated by the volume and page number of the diary concerned. This organised and cross-referenced the 'being there' data, and also gave visual guidelines for the rotations of who was 'due' for an observation session in the plan for the following week. In other words, it ensured the random nature of the 'being there' timetable.

The back cover of each diary contained a second coding grid, this time recording the *content* of the miscellaneous comments page. Its coding categories were entirely dependent on the material generated by 'being there' with each person. The diary contents were thus semi-structured, cross-referenced and partially coded as they were being transcribed. This provided a sound base for the next stage – data analysis.

The analysis methods used

The initial content analysis on the diary data was conducted along the lines described by Taylor and Bogdan (1984). The diaries were read through several times and three lists made: all of the *settings* experienced by the men; all of the *people with whom contact had occurred*; and all of the *things that they had done*. Clear divisions were immediately apparent between places/people/activities that had an association with 'learning difficulty' and those that were of an 'ordinary' nature.

For the purpose of the quantitative analysis a coding framework was devised, with the days of the week on the vertical axis and the fifteen-minute time blocks (covering the fourteen hours of a waking day) on the horizontal. Each day 'row' was divided into three to indicate the predominant place, person/s and activity recorded during that fifteen minutes. From the coded content of each diary it was then possible to say what percentage of each person's time was spent in which activities, where and with whom. It was at this point that the 'learning difficulty'/'ordinary' distinction became interesting: looking at which situations, with which people, offered most choice, respect, community presence, community participation and competence, with reference to the 'Five Accomplishments' (O'Brien, 1987). In this way a quantitative framework was erected within what was essentially a qualitative study. The content analysis of the 'key people's' interview data offered an historical and biographical backcloth against which to view the 'here and now' data yielded from 'being there'.

7.4 'Being there': a discussion of issues arising

The impact on the researcher

The 'being there' phase of the evaluation lasted a total of 588 hours, and stretched over approximately 126 sessions, implemented over a nine-month period. The impact on the researcher was disturbing. After a month or so the powerlessness that seemed to be experienced by her companions, and therefore indirectly by herself, induced feelings of frustration and occasionally anger.

It seems that everyone experiences lack of control in certain situations, such as waiting for a delayed train or in the work place. The difference for the men from Oaklands was that most settings exerted control over them rather than vice versa. This would seem to be inevitable to some extent as they depended largely on paid others for their welfare. However, the incipient build-up of powerlessness was disturbing and something the researcher found hard to handle. She recorded her reactions within the diaries. Statements like 'I was very bored and furious; people should not have the right to waste other people's time' reflected the strength of her feelings.

It should also be said that occasionally the researcher felt joy and excitement as her companion mastered a novel task, participated in an evening class or quite simply was satisfied to be at home.

At times it was difficult for the researcher to remain in a role that offered minimum control and maximum opportunity to be misunderstood. Overall, the accumulation of such feelings during the eight months of 'being there' left her pessimistic, lethargic and having to fight very much against the access to 'escape routes', such as the ATC staff room. The respite gained from two breaks – each of one week – taken during the 'being there' phase was much needed by the researcher, giving her a chance to take stock of the research process and to re-enter the 'being there' phase with renewed energy. Conducting the research proved to be an exhausting and draining experience.

The advice given by Patton (1980) to workers using participant observation techniques was supportive at the times of stress: 'At times the evaluator may become totally immersed in the program experience. These periods of immersion may be followed by times of withdrawal and distance (for personal as well as methodological reasons), to be followed still later by new experiences of immersion in and intimacy with the program.' After a break the researcher was able to return to 'being there', having regathered thoughts and energy, to continue with the task in hand. The guidelines within the literature on participant observation reminded her that in order to fulfil the research goals she needed to be aware of her own position in the scheme of things. These would seem to be valuable lessons for any worker choosing to conduct research in this way.

Comments about the role

Overall, the aim during the 'being there' phase was to be present but not to direct; to be around but not to influence. Generally it was felt that this aim was fulfilled. On a couple of occasions it was deliberately overlooked, for example when one man who had been recently bereaved of both parents became inconsolably upset at the ATC. The researcher had the opportunity to comfort him and take him home, either of which may or may not have happened had she not been around. When incidents like this interrupted the ideal role behaviour they were documented and a note made of the reasons for the researcher taking the action she did. In general when significant disruptions occurred the welfare of the individual was put before a rigid adherence to the research aims.

The research role was not without its difficulties for the researcher, not least in attempting to explain to very helpful ATC staff that she did not wish to use the staff room or office, but rather wanted to spend tea, coffee and lunch breaks with her companion. It was also interesting, again within the Centre, to see how the status of the service user within the trainee 'pecking-order' increased due to the presence of the researcher, who was appearing – and was often introduced – as his 'friend'. This also upset what was assumed to be the naturally occurring state of affairs, as many trainees surrounded the researcher and her companion for the first few visits. However, the dilemma soon diffused as it became clear to everyone that the 'friend' was (choosing to be) as powerless as they were with regard to access to the staff room and so on. 'Choosing to be' is bracketed here as the vital difference between the researcher and her companion. At times it was difficult to imagine the frustration that would have been experienced had that 'choice' to leave the ATC after four hours not been present. Comments from an Oaklands inhabitant on one occasion – about wanting to go home – indicated that he too felt desperate about having to remain there for a whole day.

The way ahead

The research method described here hopefully produced an account of life-styles as near as possible to the viewpoint of the men who experienced them. Every effort was made in the pursuit of an understanding of how life looks – and feels – as an Oaklands Housing Project inhabitant. The battle for researchers must be in favour of methods that encourage the emergence of user opinion, and against any complacency after the initial setting up of community living situations. The 'being there' approach recognised the importance of putting 'subjects' at the centre of research and striving to give them a voice in a way parallel to the internal empowerment being belatedly offered by self and citizen advocacy movements.

The purpose of this chapter is not to suggest total replication of the 'being there' method, as it is recognised that this would be a time-consuming operation, but rather to give insight into the potential of this kind of approach. Abbreviated versions of 'being there' could well be used, based on the same underlying desire: to catch a glimpse of life from the position of a consumer of the service in question. The fundamentals of 'being there' may well guide managers in the sharing of service experiences with clients, suggesting ways in which the shared experiences could be documented as well as carried out. Similarly, a specified period of 'being there' may provide an insightful backcloth against which to place and view other types of methodology. The time spent with people in this way would act as an anchor, reminding the researcher who the research is about and who the outcomes are ultimately for.

Hopefully, a main concern conveyed is the need to redress the balance of research, recognising the importance of 'bottom-up' as opposed to 'top-down' monitoring of services, with the focus being on user opinion and experience. Information of this nature can then begin to offer meaningful answers to questions relating to the difficult notion of 'quality of life'.

Acknowledgments

The research on which this chapter is based was funded by the Joseph Rowntree Memorial Trust. Thanks are due to Linda Ward for her comments and Linda Holley for her typing.

References

AESOP (550 BC) 'The dog and the shadow', in Cohen, J. M. and Cohen, M. J. (1960) *The Penguin Dictionary of Quotations*, Harmondsworth, Penguin.

ATKINSON, D. (1985) 'With time to spare: the leisure pursuits of people with mental handicaps', *Mental Handicap*, Vol. 13, pp. 139–40.

ATKINSON, D. and WARD, L. (1987) 'Friends and neighbours: relationships and opportunities in the community for people with a mental handicap', in Malin, N. (ed.) *Re-assessing Community Care*, London, Croom Helm.

BOLTON COMMUNITY HEALTH COUNCIL (1987) *Living in Bolton: A Study of the Lives of Mentally Handicapped People Supported by the Bolton Neighbourhood Network Scheme*, Bolton Community Health Council, Andomac Chambers, Arndale Centre, Hotel Street, Bolton, BL1 1DA.

CATTERMOLE, M. and JAHODA, A. (1985) 'Understanding the lives of people with a mental handicap', paper presented at the British Psychological Society Conference, Cambridge, September.

EDGERTON, R. B., BOLLINGER, M. and HERR, B. (1984) 'The cloak of competence: after two decades', *American Journal of Mental Deficiency*, Vol. 88, pp. 345–51.

FELCE, D., de KOCK, U. and REPP, A. (1986) 'An eco-behavioural analysis of small community-based houses and traditional large hospitals for severely and profoundly mentally handicapped adults', *Applied Research in Mental Retardation*, Vol. 7, pp. 393–408.

FLYNN, M. C. (1986) 'Adults who are mentally handicapped as consumers: issues and guidelines for interviewing', *Journal of Mental Deficiency Research*, Vol. 30, pp. 369–77.

FLYNN, M. and SALEEM, J. (1986) 'Adults who are mentally handicapped and living with their parents: satisfaction and perceptions regarding their lives and circumstances', *Journal of Mental Deficiency Research*, Vol. 30, pp. 379–87.

FLYNN, M. (1987) 'Independent living arrangements for adults who are mentally handicapped', in Malin, N. (ed.) *Reassessing Community Care*, London, Croom Helm.

KING'S FUND CENTRE (1980) *An Ordinary Life*, London, King's Fund Centre.

O'BRIEN, J. (1987) 'A guide to personal futures planning', in Bellamy, G. T. and Wilcox, B. (eds) *A Comprehensive Guide to the Activities Catalogue: An Alternative Curriculum for Youth and Adults with Severe Disabilities*, Baltimore, Paul Brookes.

PATTON, MICHAEL QUINN (1980) *Qualitative Evaluation Methods*, Beverley Hills, Sage Publications.

SUGG, B. (1987) 'Community care: the consumer's point of view', *Community Care*, 22 January, pp. 6–7.

TAYLOR, S. J. and BOGDAN, R. (1984) *Introduction to qualitative research methods: the search for meanings*, 2nd edn, Chichester, John Wiley & Sons.

8 Research interviews with people with mental handicaps

Dorothy Atkinson

8.1 Introduction

[. . .] The opinions of people with mental handicaps are increasingly being sought by planners and practitioners (Sigelman *et al.*, 1981a, 1982), and individuals are at the same time being encouraged to speak for themselves (Sigelman *et al.*, 1981b). In recent years, researchers have begun to recognise the value of including the views of people with mental handicaps in areas of research which directly touch their lives. (See, for example, Edgerton, 1967; Edgerton and Bercovici, 1976; Edgerton *et al.*, 1984; Malin, 1983; Faire, 1985.) The challenge remains, however, for reseachers to involve individuals effectively, so that not only are people enabled to express their point of view, but their viewpoint is faithfully and accurately represented in subsequent research projects. [. . .]

The decision to involve people with mental handicaps in the research design, and actively to seek their viewpoints and personal experiences, is easy to justify. They are, after all, best placed to describe their own social situation, their personal experience of it, and their feelings about it (Wyngaarden, 1981). [. . .]

8.2 Specific issues of research design

[. . .] This chapter looks at the methodology of a research project which included the perspective, and viewpoints, of people with mental handicaps. Their view, as consumers, was considered paramount. The research aimed to look at people's everyday lives in the community; their friendships, support networks, and the pattern of their days. The project's primary aim was to look at the lives and life-styles of people with mental handicaps through their eyes, and through the eyes of people who knew them well, in order to add to the growing understanding of what 'life in the community' is like for people moving out of long-stay hospitals.

The desired outcome from the project was a full and rich picture of people's lives, described as far as possible by the people themselves, and supplemented by accounts from social workers. The aim and desired outcome determined the research design. Interviews with people with mental handicaps themselves and their social workers would be necessary;

interviews which would provide time and space for people to talk about, and reflect upon, their day-to-day experiences of community living.

The issues of research design, as outlined above, had to be addressed and dealt with in order to set up interviews which 'worked' for respondents and researcher alike. The aim was for people to have an opportunity to talk about themselves and their lives to someone with time to listen; and for the 'listener', or researcher, to have an opportunity to hear the fullest possible account of people's experiences. [. . .]

The research interview: anticipated areas of difficulty

Four main areas of likely difficulty were identified at the outset, and these influenced the final design of the project:

- the respondents – their possible characteristics;
- the respondents' perception of the research;
- the need for feedback;
- the respondents' perception of the researcher.

The respondents

The respondents had all previously lived in mental handicap hospitals. Therefore, the following possible difficulties had to be allowed for:

1 Institutional background Respondents' background of institutional care could inhibit them in interviews, possibly in two ways. They could, through relatively limited experience of ordinary life, have little to say. Or, they could be inhibited by fear of failure resulting in return to the hospital.

2 Limited understanding It was assumed that the people being interviewed had some intellectual limitations. Some, therefore, might have difficulty in understanding the purpose of the research and in understanding the questions asked. They might also find it difficult to convey their own experiences and conceptualise, generalise, recall events and names of people, and generally communicate their ideas to another person.

3 Trying to please It was anticipated that some respondents might try hard to please the interviewer. They might try to establish what ideas the interviewer had in mind and then produce answers along the lines of their perception. It was likely that great care would be needed, therefore, to help people express their ideas without influencing their choice of words and mode of expression.

4 Communication problems It was possible that some respondents would have speech or hearing problems, and that it might prove difficult for interviewer and respondents to communicate.

Respondents' perception of the research

It was anticipated that the negative experiences of respondents, as people who had been segregated and stigmatised, might influence their perception of the research. In particular, they might harbour fears about the purpose of the research, for instance that it was designed to check on them, to test them, or to catch them out.

The research had to take account of these factors as they could lead some people to refuse to participate at all, and others to feel obliged to do so. In addition, there might be a reluctance to talk about problem areas, attempts to cover up difficulties by putting on a brave face, and worries about confidentiality.

Need for feedback

Respondents' worries about the nature and purpose of the research project could possibly be allayed by the promise of early feedback. An assurance that an interview would later be followed by a report of the findings, and that these findings might help people in other parts of the country, was thought essential in this context.

The research problem was how to put this assurance into practice. Time had to be built into the schedule after the completion of interviews for the design and production of a suitable, easy-to-understand, written account of actual findings, with illustrations, which could be distributed to all respondents (Atkinson, 1983).

Respondents' perception of the researcher

1 Respondents who knew the researcher as a social worker Nine respondents were 'clients' of the researcher. Some of the others, though not 'clients', lived locally and perceived the researcher primarily in the role of social worker. It was possible, therefore, that client respondents and local respondents might query the motives of the social worker-researcher. They might also have difficulty in relating to the social worker as a researcher, and to discussing matters in a more formal manner than usual. [. . .]

2 Respondents who did not know the researcher Most respondents did not know the researcher prior to the project. To take account of this fact and of all the possible fears and other difficulties outlined above, a personal introduction seemed necessary.

The people best placed to make such introductions were the respondents' visiting social workers. They would, in any case, be asking their clients if they would participate in the research interviews and a personal introduction seemed to be a logical consequence of this request. It might also help to alleviate some of the possible fears about the purposes of the research project. It should be acknowledged, however, that such personal introductions could lead people to identify the researcher as a colleague of their social worker, and that they would tailor their replies accordingly. Again, the researcher would have to watch for this tendency.

8.3 Research design

The research problems identified above all relate to interviews with people with mental handicaps. Clearly, to *base* the research on interviews which could contain so many pitfalls would be to run a high risk of eliciting inaccurate information. Respondent interviews were thus conducted during the later stages of the fieldwork; they were to be final checks on data collected by other means.

The project was based on a *battery* of methods, the aim being to construct a 'fail-safe' system of gathering information. As the material sought could prove elusive, safeguards were built into the research design at each stage. The safeguards were established through the interlocking design, which allowed for the cross-checking and cross-referencing of material.

The battery of methods comprised:

● the study of individual (and group) files from Social Services area offices;

● a three-part interview with social workers;

● interviews with respondents;

● a diary kept by respondents for one week after their interview.

8.4 Method

[. . .] Each interview commenced with a simple explanation of the research aims. Respondents were told that the research aimed: to look at the experiences and achievements of people living in the community; to record those experiences in a report or a book; and to circulate the findings in order to help people in other areas to share similar opportunities of community living. Respondents appeared to grasp the idea and appreciate the potential value to others of their personal experiences. Many people were keen to receive early results of the research, and they were assured of this outcome.

The research aimed to set a friendly and informal tone to the interviews. A gift of flowers, cake or chocolates was taken to respondents' homes as a way of saying 'Thank you' in advance for their time and trouble in taking part. The gifts also helped to set an easy, informal atmosphere. Time on arrival was spent in preliminary chatting to establish rapport, and pets, photographs, pictures and ornaments were admired and commented on.

The actual interviews commenced with a warm invitation to talk about the preceding day with the question: 'Can you tell me what you did yesterday?' Respondents started with when they got up, and continued through their day until bedtime. This quickly got the conversation flowing, and events were recalled in detail. The structure of the whole week followed easily from this starting point. The interviews were meant to elicit information on people, places and activities; areas of life that respondents seemed happy to discuss in detail. No attempt was made to probe any area of very private concern, such as personal problems or previous hospital histories. Interviews usually ended on a light-hearted note as talk was turned to pets and favourite television programmes.

The researcher accepted cues given by respondents. Thus, in most instances, certain words such as 'handicap' were avoided by mutual consent; previous unhappy experiences, perhaps in a group home, were regarded as closed chapters; and the few references made to hospitals were initiated by respondents, not by the researcher.

8.5 Issues arising from the research project

Detailed fieldnotes of all the follow-up interviews were kept by the researcher. These notes were written immediately afterwards, and provided full commentaries on the dynamics of the interviews, and the interactions between researcher and respondents. They filled in gaps when the recorder was not switched on, and they contain observations and quotes not recorded elsewhere.

A content analysis of the complete set of fieldnotes has highlighted some areas of interest which emerged during the interviews:

- the researcher's perception of the respondents;
- the respondents' perception of the research (and the researcher);
- the interaction between respondents and researcher;
- the relationship between respondents and researcher;
- roles and relationships within households.

These points will be covered briefly in this chapter. A discussion of the interview process itself, and of the dynamics of the interaction between researchers and respondents, is rarely attempted in the research literature (Oakley, 1981). Yet the dynamics of an interview, and the relationship between its central participants, are influential in determining the quality and richness of its outcome.

The extracts which follow are taken directly from the fieldnotes. They are the researcher's own descriptive account of the interviews and what happened, as well as being a personal interpretation of interactions between people. They are a behind-the-scenes look at research interviews, albeit from the researcher's point of view.

The researcher's perception of the respondents

Interview with Joan Woods, Mabel West and Vera Bainbridge:

> I wore my old clothes because I expected the place to be extremely grim. I knocked. The window was open (for the cat) and there was much muttering and shuffling from within. I called out 'Hello!' and eventually a woman asked, 'Did I hear a knock?' I was allowed to let myself in by Joan Woods: 'You can save my legs those few yards.' Although I was in my old clothes, they were all looking smart. The room itself was cluttered, but nothing out of the ordinary. Had they cleaned up specially?

Interview with Keith and Beryl Gill:

> They were very welcoming, and were calling out to me long before I reached their door. They both looked very smart. They both looked as if they had dressed up for the occasion, and they seemed to be wearing *new* shoes.
>
> We sat down. They seemed relaxed and very happy to talk about themselves. Perhaps they were glad of the company.

The respondents' perception of the research (and the researcher)

Interview with Laura Vickers:

> Laura was not at her best. Was she worried about this interview? Had Ralph and Enid made her nervous? She had a dry mouth; was it nervousness? She commented on this herself.
>
> I got a little irritable about the hearing aid not working properly, and she may have added that irritation to the semi-formality of the occasion. She remained a little ill-at-ease throughout. The one positive outcome, from Laura's point of view, was that I stayed longer than usual.

Interview with Charles Deacon, Fiona Appleby and Roger Boland:

> Dominic (social worker) warned me that Charles had already heard on the grapevine about my impending visit, and was alarmed about the use of a tape recorder. I arrived with a cake, and Dominic in tow. Fiona was unsure how to respond and what to do; she only has the use of one hand, and she found it awkward getting herself, and cake, into the kitchen. She returned and sat on the settee. Charles remained sitting. The atmosphere was tense. No one asked us to sit down. The spare bit of settee was covered in papers and magazines, the foot stool likewise. Dominic sat on the floor. Eventually Charles moved the papers from the footstool and let me sit there.
>
> I asked about using the tape recorder. Roger didn't mind. Charles said he wasn't sure, and asked Fiona if she minded. She said 'no' but it was not clear whether that meant 'no, she didn't mind' or 'no she didn't want it on'. Charles asked her again. She was looking away, half turned, flicking through a magazine saying nothing but making it clear what she really felt. I agreed not to use it.

Interview with Edgar Carter, Robert Harper and Norma Jones:

> Everyone seemed composed during the interview. The only time they lost their composure was when the diary was introduced, and they had to admit they couldn't write.
>
> No one mentioned 'handicap' or knowing 'handicapped people'. Their Gateway Club was identified by its clientele, and references to 'groups'. I was expected to read the clues and know what they meant. They asked about Maurice Deacon who had left his group home to live in a caravan: 'He is still free, isn't he?', and commented about Glenda Whiting who had left her group home for a hostel: 'Oh no! That's not nice, moving her.' Fiona asked if I knew their hospital, but Edgar interjected: 'I'm trying to forget that place. She's bringing the past up. I want to forget that place. We're free aren't we? It's better now.'

Descriptive comments about the researcher

Alice Wise (in an aside to her social worker): 'She's very nice, isn't she? I thought she'd be strict and horrible.'

Joyce Hardcastle: 'Are you an important Social Services person? Are you very high up? Edgar said you were.'

Edward Hayes (in an aside to his social worker): 'She must be very important, asking us all those questions.'

The interaction between respondents and researcher

Interview with Denise Parker:

> Conversation was difficult, because she is very deaf and not forthcoming; not a great conversationalist. Communication was difficult because I had to shout at her. I found the asking of questions very trying as I began to feel more and more like an interrogator.

Interview with Philip Grey, Douglas Field and Melanie Saunders:

> We sat around the table. Philip made a pot of tea and poured. My cup and saucer were different from theirs, from their best set. They were being polite; they didn't touch their tea and seemed to be waiting until I'd gone to have theirs.
>
> There was a nice atmosphere. They helped one another. Philip had a lot to say, but was unable to make me understand. His best friend, Douglas, translated for him. Everyone seemed to enjoy the conversation and thanked me profusely afterwards.

The relationship between respondents and researcher

Interview with Joan Woods, Mabel West and Vera Bainbridge:

> They all hoped I'd call again. It was a very positive visit, ending with pleasantries, smiles and warmth. They have no real confidante and they seemed sorry about this. They get only practical advice from the area office. They have a nice home help, but not someone to sit and talk things over with. My visit actually met a social, and emotional, need; someone just to sit and listen, and take them seriously. I felt sad. [. . .]

Roles and relationships within households

Interview with Ralph and Enid Walker:

> Ralph and Enid referred to each other as 'my wife' and 'my husband'. Enid sat on the settee, while Ralph and I sat in armchairs by the open fire. Ralph offered me coffee, and Enid went off to get it. She didn't sit down immediately, she hovered and began to wander in and out of the kitchen getting lunch ready. They took up their roles in the interview; Ralph in expansive mood sitting by the fire talking to the visitor whilst Enid made coffee and kept an eye on lunch.

Interview with Doreen Gilmore, Joyce Hardcastle, Arthur Stott and Nigel Short:

> I was obviously interrupting their routine. Arthur was told off for repeatedly looking at his watch; he wanted to get his tea ready and get off to his club. Joyce became anxious about missing *Crossroads* and Doreen told her off too.
> Doreen was obviously in charge. She had an authoritarian manner, told people off, kept order and made sure they answered. There was some overt hostility between Doreen and Arthur, encouraged by Joyce. Nigel didn't like it and tried to smoothe it over – 'He's not that bad.' Poor Arthur just stood there and took it. It's not a united group. They talked about their separate holidays and activities. As I left, Arthur was already dishing up food for himself to eat alone.

8.6   The research interviews: some implications

The sequence of interviews confirmed the pertinence of points made in the rehabilitation research literature. It is essential to find ways of including people with mental handicaps in research which focuses on their lives and experiences.

Open-ended questions, a friendly and informal atmosphere, and a conversational format all helped the respondents to talk freely about their lives. Three additional factors were included in this research project, and these also seemed to contribute to the outcome:

● social workers, as knowledgeable informants, were interviewed first – the researcher was thus forewarned of important people and events to listen for during respondents' conversations;

● respondents who shared a home were seen together – this meant that roles and relationships and everyday household dynamics were demonstrated in the interview itself;

● the interviews began with a gift from the researcher, seen and received as a token of recognition of the respondents as people with valuable time to give and worthwhile experiences to share.

It should be acknowledged that each of these factors could have had a negative outcome. Firstly, the researcher could have been *biased* in her views through having access to prior information from social workers. It could be argued that the respondents were approached with a mind at least partially made up. Secondly, joint interviewing can actually *cause* difficulties. People's anxieties about secrets may be allayed, but others may be evoked: there is no confidentiality in a group interview; there may be few opportunities for some people to maintain a personal, treasured viewpoint in the face of group pressure; and the situation could be used to bring 'dissident' group members into line. The group interview is a public forum where people can be ridiculed and humiliated. Thirdly, the researcher's gifts could be seen as *bribes*. Could anyone refuse to co-operate after having been seduced by flowers and a smile?

Throughout the course of the fieldwork, some trends emerged. These are summarised as follows:

● the researcher was seen sometimes as a *threat* (recreating a 'test' situation and causing anxiety); sometimes as a *helper* (answering benefit queries and helping write letters); and often as a *friend* ('Do come again');

● interviews often seemed to leave respondents feeling *valued*; time was spent with them and they were listened to; the preceding gift, and the later feedback, also helped in this;

● respondents saw the interviews as important occasions; they dressed up for them, tidied the house, and offered hospitality.

8.7   Conclusions

People with mental handicaps can, and do, contribute to research projects which focus on their lives and life-styles. There are challenges in achieving their full and active involvement, and it is up to researchers to find innovative and imaginative ways of meeting these challenges. It is hoped that this chapter is a small step in that direction.

The interpersonal dynamics of interviews are important. They are elusive, however, and are felt or experienced, rather than observed. Feelings, expectations and perceptions of researchers and respondents alike are in operation, and these colour the interactions between them. In joint interviews, feelings between peers add to the complexity of the interpersonal dynamics. The challenge is to understand these processes; a first step towards acquiring such understanding is to describe them. This chapter has offered some descriptive passages from fieldnotes in an attempt to highlight the importance of the interpersonal dynamics of research interviews.

Acknowledgments

Thanks are due to the people who took part in this project, who gave their time so generously. This applies especially to those whose homes were visited, but also includes their visiting social workers who talked so long, and with such warmth, about the people they knew. Thanks are due, too, to other colleagues in Somerset, both in the Social Services Department and in the Health Authority, for their interest and active support of this project.

References

EDGERTON, R. B. (1967) *The Cloak of Competence: Stigma in the Lives of the Mentally Retarded*, Berkeley, University of California Press.

EDGERTON, R. B. and BERCOVICI, S. M. (1976) 'The cloak of competence: years later', *American Journal of Mental Deficiency*, Vol. 80, pp. 485–97.

EDGERTON, R. B., BOLLINGER, M. and HERR, B. (1984) 'The cloak of competence: after two decades', *American Journal of Mental Deficiency*, Vol. 88, pp. 345–51.

FAIRE, C. (1985) *It's Never Too Late: An Evaluation of Bath District Health Authority's 'An Ordinary Life' Project for Elderly People with a Mental Handicap*, Bath, Bath DHA.

MALIN, N. (1983) *Group Homes for the Mentally Handicapped*, London, HMSO.

OAKLEY, A (1981) 'Interviewing women: a contradiction in terms', in Roberts, H. (ed.) *Doing Feminist Research*, London, Routledge & Kegan Paul.

SIGELMAN, C. K., BUDD, E. C., SPANHEL, C. L. and SCHOENROCK, C. J. (1981a) 'Asking questions of retarded persons: a comparison of yes–no and either–or formats', *Applied Research in Mental Retardation*, Vol. 2, pp. 347–57.

SIGELMAN, C. E., BUDD, E. C., SPANHEL, C. L. and SCHOENROCK, C. J. (1981b) 'When in doubt, say yes: acquiescence in interviews with mentally retarded persons', *Mental Retardation*, Vol. 19, pp. 53–8.

SIGELMAN, C. K., BUDD, E. C., WINER, J. L., SCHOENROCK, C. J. and MARTIN, R. W. (1982) 'Evaluating alternative techniques of questioning mentally retarded persons', *American Journal of Mental Deficiency*, Vol. 86, pp. 511–18.

WYNGAARDEN, M. (1981) 'Interviewing mentally retarded persons: issues and strategies', in Bruininks, R. H., Meyers, C. E., Sigford, E. B. and Lakin, K. C. (eds) *Deinstitutionalization and Community Adjustments of Mentally Retarded People*, Monograph 4, Washington DC, American Association on Mental Deficiency.

Section II Recognising oppression

Introduction

The theme of this section of the Reader is 'recognising oppression'. Rather than reviewing definitions of 'mental handicap' we have chosen to examine from a range of perspectives how being so labelled reflects societal expectations as much as any direct results of neurological impairment.

To acknowledge this is not to deny the reality of impairment which some people may suffer. It does involve looking at their experiences in a different light; looking at them as the experiences of fellow human beings. In doing this we begin to see how such experiences are frequently limiting and negative; we begin to recognise oppression.

The function of labelling is discussed at some length in the first article. Bogdan and Taylor are American sociologists committed to a style of research which gives a voice to people who would otherwise not be heard. In this way, their aim is not dissimilar from self-advocacy; though they themselves are not labelled 'retarded' they seek, in their book *Inside Out*, to allow two people whose autobiographies they have collected to speak for themselves. Our extract is taken from the introduction to the book. In it, the authors make both an impassioned and a carefully argued case against the label 'mental retardation'. Their argument is based to a large extent on the grounds of 'a shared humanity': that the similarities between those labelled mentally retarded and those not so labelled are greater than the differences. They do, however, go further than this and argue that the label is both subjective, depending for example on the person's life stage and the way they are assessed, and pernicious in its 'devastating effect on people . . . it is to be certified as "not one of us"'. Having been so labelled, people are then blamed for the results. We hope that this article will encourage you, the reader, to reflect on your own use of labels for others and yourself. If you do not agree fully with Bogdan and Taylor you will at least have had the opportunity to reconsider.

Bryan, Dadzie and Scafe do not write as experts in the mental handicap field. Their book *The Heart of the Race* is a personal account of black people's experiences in Britain. Their work, however, seemed very apt for us to use. The experiences described here, of the impact of the education system on black children, give us an insight into ways in which labels are applied, and how hard people must struggle to overcome the damaging effects. The common experiences of minority groups, black people and people with learning difficulties, are pursued in more detail in Section V of this book, but the special contribution of this extract 'Learning to resist', is that it illustrates not only how the experiences of the two groups have parallels, but also that to be labelled as having learning difficulties can actually increase the difficulties rather than improving the situation.

The parent's diary was sent to us by a sympathetic professional. We were keen to include it because it illustrates, at a different level, the dilemma of 'who knows best'. The professionals who came into contact with the mother who wrote this account may have been acting with what they thought were the best intentions. But from her point of view the experience was both distressing and confusing. She struggled not only with the problems of having a child whom she suspected was autistic, but also with the negative effect of being labelled as a mother who may be neglecting or, worse, abusing her daughter. The arrival of Fiona Martin illustrates the importance of a key worker who is prepared both to listen to the mother and to negotiate on her behalf the minefield of services available. The reader may be struck by the similarities of Fiona's role to that of the parent adviser described in the article by Davis and Ali Choudhury in Section I of this Reader. (All names in this account have been changed to avoid any possibility of identification.)

The next extract is taken from Michelle Stanworth's book *Reproductive Technologies*. It provides a clear and sober review of some of the implications of advances in scientific knowledge which open up a new vista: the eradication of undesirable characteristics by antenatal screening and genetic engineering. Stanworth's warning that 'the definition of "unfit" will become a mask for prejudice and intolerance' is a timely one. Genetic knowledge is a powerful tool; its implications for people with learning difficulties are potentially alarming.

The examination of the legal restrictions on the sexuality of people with learning difficulties by Gunn continues the eugenic discussion opened by Stanworth. He shows that many of the legal restrictions on sexual activity by people with learning difficulties are often contrary to human rights as defined by the United Nations and the European Convention of Human Rights.

Richard Jenkins' chapter, 'Barriers to adulthood' develops and extends the analysis of 'oppression' in considering what it means to be an adult. By drawing comparisons between young unemployed people and people with learning difficulties, Jenkins shows that adulthood is a slippery notion. To be an adult does not necessarily mean to be in paid employment, to be married, to live in one's own household. Young unemployed people do become adults, even if they do not fulfil those criteria. But in many respects people with learning difficulties are denied adult status, argues Jenkins, as a consequence of being denied their full humanity 'to really be an adult, it seems, one must first be fully human'.

John Swain has written for us a chapter on the theory of 'learned helplessness'. If people with learning difficulties are denied their adulthood by social and legal forces as Jenkins has argued, they are equally deprived of humanity at the level of individual learning. Swain's development of the original, and well-known, concept of learned helplessness suggests that it is not so much that the individual fails to learn to change and grasp control, but that circumstances and other people combine to teach helplessness. It is therefore the responsibility of other people to ensure that individuals are not deprived of opportunities to make effective choices.

This chapter ends the section on a more optimistic note, which suggests that steps can be taken to begin to undo the pervasive experience of oppression.

9 'What's in a name?'

Robert Bogdan and Steven J. Taylor

The meaning of mental retardation

'What's in a name?' 'Sticks and stones may break my bones, but names can never hurt me.' While these maxims are part of conventional wisdom, words – labels and names – structure how we think about and act toward others. Labels like 'retarded' have a dramatic effect on those who use them as well as on those to whom they are applied. They direct our attention to specific aspects of designated people. [. . .] Our research suggests, however, that the concept of mental retardation is not just less than useful, it is actually seriously misleading. The term's scientific aura is deceptive in that it conceals subjective moral and cultural value judgements. This would not matter particularly if mental retardation were not also a demeaning concept which implies a deficiency in the humanity of those tagged. People who are labelled retarded have, upon occasion, been denied due process, forced to undergo sterilisation, denied life-saving medical treatment, incarcerated without trial, and subjected to abuses that others without the tag are protected against. [. . .]

Is mental retardation real?

What is mental retardation? How do we know if someone is retarded? While professionals disagree on the answers to these questions, most answer them in terms of intelligence quotient (IQ) and so-called adaptive behaviour, waiting for the advancement of science to provide precise diagnostic techniques. They believe mental retardation is a condition people have. They do not question that; they only want to improve the ways we have of diagnosing 'it'.

This approach to mental retardation lies at the heart of the matter. As a concept, mental retardation exists in the minds of those who use it as a term to describe the cognitive states of other people. It is a reification – a socially created category which is assumed to have an existence independent of its creators' minds (Berger and Luckmann, 1967). To name something is, in a sense, to create it. Because the objective existence of the condition it is supposed to describe has never been questioned, the phrase 'mental retardation' has become an obstruction to understanding. Rather than pointing to a clear and discrete phenomenon, the concept creates the illusion that disparate and amorphous conditions and behaviours are similar. [. . .]

To suggest that mental retardation is not 'real' is not to deny differences among people in terms of intellectual ability. It is to say that the nature and significance of these differences depend on how we view and interpret them. We may distinguish between intellectual characteristics on the one hand, and social definitions and concepts on the other. Just as the existence of people who disturbed or upset others in the Middle Ages did not prove the existence of witchcraft (Szasz, 1970), the existence of people who appear intellectually deficient or incompetent to others does not now prove the existence of 'mental retardation'. [. . .]

Is mental retardation an absolute condition?

Mental retardation is thought of as an absolute condition – people are either mentally retarded or they are not. Indeed, the concept of 'pseudo-feeblemindedness' has been used in the mental-retardation field to retain belief in the absolute nature of retardation when professionals have been confronted with people who appeared retarded in some situations but not in others (Kanner, 1948).

Even the smallest reflection, however, suggests that mental retardation is a relative condition (in so far as it can be called a condition at all). The classification of people as mentally retarded depends on organisational and societal values, beliefs and processes. A person may be mentally retarded at some times or in some situations but not in others. Schools provide the clearest example of how organisations create mentally retarded persons. Through testing and sorting practices, schools classify a large number of children as retarded who function perfectly well at home, in their neigh-bourhoods and in other situations (Mercer, 1973). [. . .]

The proportion of persons identified as retarded in the general population has increased dramatically over the past century. Prior to the latter part of the 1800s, many who might be called retarded now either blended into the general population or were defined as part of the homeless poor (Rothman, 1971). They were not retarded! As North American society became increasingly industrialised and urbanised, and as new waves of immigrants arrived, social changes – the creation of surplus urban labour, mass social problems, crime, delinquency, vice – called forth new definitions, and 'mental retardation' (or 'feeblemindedness' as it was called then) became a salient concept (Sarason and Doris, 1969, p. 238; Platt, 1969, pp. 36–7).

In urban, industrialised society, the concept of mental retardation provided both a legitimation for the failure of some to succeed and a ready-made explanation for perceived social disorder. Around the turn of the century, early leaders 'discovered' a new class of 'feebleminded' persons and called attention to the presumed menace posed by this class. In 1915 Goddard, well known for his infamous hereditary study of 'feeblemindedness', *The Kallikak Family* (1912), wrote: 'For many generations we have recognized and pitied the idiot. Of late we have recognized a higher type of defective, the moron, and have discovered that he is a burden; that he is a menace to society and civilization; that he is responsible to a large degree for many, if not all, of our social problems' (Goddard, 1915, p. 307). [. . .]

Is mental retardation a non-arbitrary classification?

The associated concepts of intelligence and mental retardation are abstract and imprecise notions (Blumer, 1969). One cannot directly observe or otherwise experience either intelligence or mental retardation. Thus, while mental retardation is assumed to be a pathological condition, there is no specific, identified physiological or genetic impairment among the vast majority of persons classified as mentally retarded (Edgerton, 1967; Braginsky and Braginsky, 1971; Mercer, 1973).

Intelligence and mental retardation are concepts operationally defined by the IQ. IQ and adaptive-behaviour scales do not simply measure mental retardation, they define it. These concepts mean what testers say they mean. As Sarason and Doris (1969, p. 54) note, 'the assessment of intellectual functioning and the diagnosis of mental subnormality are based on conventional tests which tap a very restricted sample of intellectual functions or processes'. In addition, IQ tests are developed assuming that intelligence is normally distributed. Such an assumption assures that a certain proportion of persons will perform at the lower end of the scale, not because of their condition or competence but because of the design of the test. [. . .]

The determination of who is mentally retarded depends on where we draw the line or set the cut-off point on tests and scales. The cut-off point is arbitrary. Once the line is drawn, however, humanity is divided into two groups – the 'normal' and the 'retarded'. Which you are is based on performance on tests.

Burton Blatt (Blatt *et al.*, 1977) has discussed the arbitrary and changing nature of official definitions of mental retardation. Prior to 1959, professionals generally agreed that the incidence of mental retardation was 3 per cent of the general population, with a psychometric 'cut-off' point of 75 IQ or about 1.5 standard deviations from the mean on a normal curve. In 1959 a committee sponsored by the American Association on Mental Deficiency (AAMD) revised the definition of psychometric mental retardation to correspond to a score of one or more standard deviations away from the mean on general intelligence tests (Heber, 1959). According to this definition, 16 per cent of the population would be eligible to be designated mentally retarded. In 1973, a subsequent committee of AAMD once more redefined mental retardation to include only those who performed two or more standard deviations away from the mean on intelligence tests; according to this definition only about 2 per cent of the general population were retarded (Grossman, 1973). The irony is not lost on Blatt; with a stroke of the pen, he notes, a committee sitting around a conference table enormously reduced the incidence of mental retardation and 'cured' thousands of persons overnight. The classification of people as mentally retarded is arbitrary, resulting largely from an assumption underlying IQ tests and from the level at which the cut-off point is set. [. . .]

Perhaps the strongest indictment of the phrase 'mental retardation' lies not in its logical confusion and conceptual vagueness, but in its devastating effects on people. While mental retardation is assumed to be a neutral, value-free concept, it implies moral inferiority as well as intellectual deficiency. 'Retarded' is a demeaning and stigmatising label (Edgerton, 1967). To be called retarded is to have one's moral worth and human value called into question. It is to be certified as 'not one of us'.

The terms 'retarded', 'idiot', 'imbecile', and 'moron' are epithets in general use in our society. 'Moron' jokes pervade everday conversation. The mass media are filled with derogatory references to people with low intelligence (Bogdan and Biklen, 1977). Newspaper comic-strip characters use 'idiot' and 'stupid' as generic curse words. [. . .]

These negative stereotypes and prejudiced attitudes are by no means only the misguided views of an ignorant and backward public; such demeaning images of the retarded can be found in the works of scholars and professionals in the field of mental retardation. Public prejudice toward the retarded has its roots in professional myths. Professionals have actively promoted images of the retarded as dangerous, immoral and subhuman (Wolfensberger, 1975). Indeed, researchers and human-service providers have often been the strongest advocates of forced sterilisation, restrictive immigration policies, segregation and institutionalisation, and school exclusion (Sarason and Doris, 1969; Wolfensberger, 1975).

Labelling and testing provide a cloak of scientific legitimacy to social control and oppression. The so-called mentally retarded are a surplus population (Farber, 1968; Braginsky and Braginsky, 1971). That is to say, those who are called retarded often do not easily fit into society. They are perceived as deviant, different, and economically unproductive. They represent an embarrassment to others. People diagnosed as retarded on the basis of test scores can be treated in discriminatory ways. As Braginsky and Braginsky (1971, p. 176) put it: '"mental retardation" is, in fact, a sociopolitical, not a psychological, construct. The myth, perpetuated by a society which refuses to recognize the true nature of its needed social reforms, has successfully camouflaged the politics of diagnosis and incarceration'.

Studies of the effects of labelling and stigma have concentrated solely on the so-called mildly retarded (Edgerton, 1967; Braginsky and Braginsky, 1971; Mercer, 1973). However, the so-called severely and profoundly retarded are harmed as much as, if not more than, the 'mildly retarded' by labelling and related social processes. [. . .]

For even the 'severely and profoundly retarded', social definitions act as a self-fulfilling prophecy (Merton, 1957). Their life chances – how and where they shall live – are structured by people's understanding of mental retardation and the stereotyped reactions the concept brings forth. If we assume that they cannot learn, we will not teach them. If we regard them as subhuman, we will deprive them of their rights. If we regard them as a separate category of human being, we will segregate them and ignore their suffering. [. . .]

The mentally retarded have been abused, dehumanised, stigmatised and warehoused in impersonal and inhumane institutions (Blatt and Kaplan, 1966; Blatt *et al.*, 1980). Labelling confuses the issue of victims and villains. We blame the wounded for the failings and abuses of society and the service system (Ryan, 1971). When schools fail to teach children, the blame is placed on their retardation. When institutional neglect and deprivation result in 'maladaptive behaviour' – for example, rocking and head-banging – it is attribted to the condition of the inmates. Do labels help? Are labels useful? For the persons to whom they are applied – the judged – no. [. . .]

References

BERGER, P. L. and LUCKMANN, T. (1967) *The Social Construction of Reality*, New York, Doubleday.

BLATT, B. and KAPLAN, F. (1966) *Christmas in Purgatory*, Boston, Allyn & Bacon.

BLATT, B., BOGDAN, R., BIKLEN, D. and TAYLOR, S. (1977) 'From institution to community: a conversion model', in Sontag, E. (ed.) *Educational Programming for the Severely and Profoundly Handicapped*, Reston, Virginia, Council for Exceptional Children.

BLATT, B., McNALLY, J. and OZOLINS, A. (1980) *The Family Papers*, New York, Longman.

BLUMER, H. (1969) *Symbolic Interactionism: Perspective and Method*, Englewood Cliffs, New Jersey, Prentice-Hall.

BOGDAN, R. and BIKLEN, D. (1977) 'Handicapism', *Social Policy*, March/April, pp. 14–19.

BRAGINSKY, D. and BRAGINSKY, B. (1971) *Hansels and Gretels*, New York, Holt, Rinehart & Winston.

EDGERTON, R. (1967) *The Cloak of Competence*, Berkeley, University of California Press.

FARBER, B. (1968) *Mental Retardation: Its Social Context and Social Consequences*, Boston, Houghton Mifflin.

GODDARD, H. H. (1912) *The Kallikak Family*, New York, Macmillan.

GODDARD, H. H. (1915) 'The possibilities of research as applied to the prevention of feeble-mindedness', *Proceedings of the National Conference on Charities and Corrections*, pp. 307–12.

GROSSMAN, H. J. (ed.) (1973) *A Manual on Terminology and Classification in Mental Retardation*, Washington, DC, American Association on Mental Deficiency.

HEBER, R. (ed.) (1959) *A Manual on Terminology and Classification in Mental Retardation*, Washington, DC, American Association on Mental Deficiency.

KANNER, L. (1948) 'Feeblemindedness: absolute, relative and apparent', *The Nervous Child*, Vol. 7, pp. 365–97.

MERCER, J. (1973) *Labeling the Mentally Retarded*, Berkeley, University of California Press.

MERTON, R. K. (1957) *Social Theory and Social Structure*, Glencoe, Illinois, Free Press.

PLATT, A. M. (1969) *The Child Savers*, Chicago, University of Chicago Press.

ROTHMAN, D. J. (1971) *The Discovery of the Asylum*, Boston, Little, Brown.

RYAN, W. (1971) *Blaming the Victim*, New York, Pantheon.

SARASON, S. and DORIS, J. (1969) *Psychological Problems in Mental Deficiency*, New York, Harper & Row.

SZASZ, T. (1970) *The Manufacture of Madness*, New York, Dell.

WOLFENSBERGER, W. (1975) *The Origin and Nature of Our Institutional Models*, Syracuse, Human Policy Press.

10 Learning to resist

Beverley Bryan, Stella Dadzie and Suzanne Scafe

> When I sent my daughter to school, I can remember her coming home one day and asking me why God had made her black. That really hurt me. I asked her if she didn't like being black, and she said no, she didn't, because she was the only black child in her school. I told her God chose to make some of us black and some of us white, and there's no difference between us. But still she didn't want me to plait her hair, I had to put it in a pony-tail all the time, otherwise she would cry, because all the other kids had their hair flowing down . . . That made me aware that there was a lot of prejudice in the schools that was affecting the kids deeply.

The hurtful ignorance and implacable hostility of other children was probably the most common experience of the first generation of black children to enter British schools. It is no surprise that we were viewed as oddities, given the colonialist diet on which our peers were still being fed. Our hair, habits, language and customs were seen as the manifestations of savagery, confirmation of our uncivilised past. Even to young children and at a time when televisions were not a common feature of every working-class home, we represented the foreign hordes which had been tamed and disciplined under flag and empire. Indeed, it was the attitude of the teachers which did the most lasting damage. They were to interpret black children's disorientation and bewilderment as a sign of stupidity. Their concepts of us as simple-minded, happy folk, lacking in sophistication or sensitivity, became readily accepted definitions. Theories about us, put forward by Jensen in America and endorsed by Eysenck here in the late sixties, gave such views a spurious credibility by popularising the idea that race and intelligence are linked in some inherent way. The effect of this process was inevitable. Those of us who had lived in those 'foreign' places either built our own defences or learnt to reject the lessons and teachers that presented our lives in such a derogatory way:

> I didn't do geography after the third form, but when I realised that the countries the teacher was talking about in that far-off, abstract way were actually countries which black people came from, Africa, the Caribbean, etc., I realised that teachers didn't always speak the truth. It was so inaccurate, so biased, such a negative way of showing how we were meant to live, that I began to feel angry. But we didn't have a community, as such, in those days. There wasn't any way for our parents to get together to express their dissatisfaction. I just became more and more disheartened and frustrated with what was being presented to us at school.

Because of such reactions, we came to be labelled 'dull' and 'disruptive'. However, what appeared to teachers to be disinterest or unresponsiveness was often our only way of responding as children to the negative school environment we had to enter daily. Those of us who had come to England with a joy for learning and a deep-seated respect for the value of education often found our enthusiasm dampened by the arrogant, insidious assumptions of the school curriculum. In lessons and textbooks we were either ridiculed or ignored. Rarely, if ever, were we acknowledged in a positive way, on equal terms:

> I had always liked reading, and could have really enjoyed literature at school. I suppose I liked the strange and different world I found in books, especially the ones about life as it was supposed to have been like in Britain. This couldn't last though, because reading often became a nasty, personal experience. You would be getting deep into a story and suddenly it would hit you – a reference to black people as savages or something. It was so offensive. And so wounding. Sometimes you would sit in class and wait, all tensed up, for the next derogatory remark to come tripping off the teacher's tongue. Oh yes, it was a 'black' day today, or some kid had 'blackened' the school's reputation. It was there clearly, in black and white, the school's ideology. The curriculum and the culture relies on those racist views. [. . .]

Inevitably, the low expectations of teachers affected our performance in school. Our generally poor results in intelligence tests like the 11+ exam seemed to confirm their views. Throughout the sixties, this test was the greatest arbiter in our future, designed to select and grade the future workforce. Because of its class and cultural bias, we were bound to fail, as were the majority of working-class children. The consequence for us was relegation to the secondary moderns and later to the lowest streams of the comprehensives. The education authorities disregarded the fact that bad schools with poor resources and indifferent teachers had existed in the inner cities long before our arrival and our presence became associated with the lowest educational standards. For most of us coming through that system, we were well on the road to ESN (educationally subnormal) labels or dismal job prospects. [. . .]

The black women of this generation who were able to acquire the skills and qualifications they had set out to gain did so despite the discrimination and institutionalised racism we encountered in every area of our lives. Where we succeeded, we were projected as examples of the neutrality of the system, as token blacks who had proven the exception to the rule. Although a few did succumb later to the perks which relative success can bring, many black women, recognising how the system had been organised, went back into the schools as teachers, to wage an often solitary battle against the kind of racism which had made our own struggles necessary.

Many of the women teachers who did go back into the schools were to become involved in the black education struggles of the seventies, inspired by the Black Power movement with its call for social justice and militant resistance by black communities when under attack. This movement began in the States in the sixties, and its influence spread rapidly to black communities everywhere. Alongside parents and other black activists, we began to challenge some of the assumptions about black children and to take up the battles to defend their rights in school.

It was our community's growing readiness to mobilise in support of our children which ensured that our anger or bewilderment as parents could be channelled into a collective response. Probably the most important early initiative was the ESN campaign, which was spearheaded by black parents and teachers. Earlier bussing policies, designed to 'dilute' large concentrations of black low achievement, had been successfully opposed in some areas. The response of the authorities was quietly to transfer large numbers of black children into schools for the 'educationally subnormal', under the guise of providing 'special' education for them. The by now familiar arguments about 'low IQ', 'broken English' and 'hyperactive behaviour' were once again put forward to justify the disproportionate number of black children who were being classified ESN, some directly on arrival from the West Indies. The whole community, galvanised by Bernard Coard's exposé of *How the West Indian Child is Made Educationally Sub-Normal in the British Education System*, began to challenge these arguments. Foremost among those who opposed ESN schooling were black mothers:

> At first I didn't realise what was going on because I really thought they were sending her to a 'special' school. The school sent me a letter telling me they were going to transfer her and that she'd get more attention, they never really spelt out what kind of school it was. But when I went up and visited, the penny dropped. As soon as I saw that most of the other kinds there were black, I knew something was going on. There was a lot of kids there who had nothing wrong with them, and as far as I was concerned my daughter was one of them. I mean, how can you reach ten years of age and still be learning your alphabet? I didn't know what to do, I was so angry. The only thing I could think of at the time was to give her as much extra help with her writing and sums at home as I could. But I went along to this meeting one Sunday and there were a lot of people there with kids in ESN schools who felt the same way. That's how they came to set up the Saturday school, because everyone was saying if the schools wouldn't educate our children, we should do it ourselves. My daughter really got a lot out of those sessions, because it wasn't just about reading and writing. They taught the kids about black history and showed them that they had nothing to be ashamed of because black people are as good as anyone else. It took me three years to get her back into the ordinary school, and I really had to fight to get them to accept her back. In the end, she left school with two CSEs because they said she'd missed too much to do any other exams. But after that she went to college, and passed five O levels.

It was our recognition of the need to challenge racist assumptions about the intelligence of our children which gave rise to Saturday and Supplementary schools up and down the country:

> We were concerned about the education our children were getting. The teachers expected nothing from them. We formed a group because we wanted to see how we could get a better deal for our children in the school system, and how we could make sure that all of us parents knew our basic rights. Some of the parents hadn't been in the country for long, so we had to make sure they understood what was happening to the black children over here. We started running a school on Saturdays – it was too much to do it

evenings as well – and we all worked as volunteers, contributing whatever time we could. I worked in the school for over a year, and what it did for me was to make me more aware, more conscious. The children did well in the school, and this tended to encourage other parents to come along. A lot of black parents turned up to our meetings. We got all kinds of people to come along and talk to us – educational welfare officers, councillors, even the Social Security official. So we didn't just concentrate on the children's education, we organised meetings to educate black parents as well. But the school was the main thing.

Embracing the message of self-reliant community responses to the community's needs, enthusiastic black volunteers were recruited, many of whom were women, whose task was to teach black history alongside maths and English. There were many acknowledged successes, as black children, who had been classified ESN went on to take O and A levels. Such activities raised a high level of awareness and debate within our communities and were largely responsible for the militancy which characterised the behaviour of many black schoolchildren in the seventies.

By the mid-seventies increasing numbers of black mothers had begun to demonstrate a readiness to defend the rights of our children, both in the form of individual confrontations with the authorities and within organised campaigns. The response of the state was to round on us. Sociologists blamed our inadequate 'broken' homes and the fact that we went out to work, instead of providing the secure environment and stimulation necessary for proper intellectual development. They overlooked our history, and the fact that we *had* to work to support our children. They disregarded how seriously we had always regarded the education of our children. They undermined the deep sense of responsibility which we felt towards our children, who were battling daily to retain a sense of identity and purpose with the system:

> They (the schools) were pretending to do so much for people's children, and in the end they were doing nothing. They mucked up my kids and other people's children too, with their false pretences. They gave those children nothing to aim for for the future. But like many West Indians, I thought the teachers knew best, because that is how it was at home.

11   A parent's diary

Anonymous

We came across this contribution by sheer luck. A friend, working as a psychologist in a home-visiting support service, described how impressed she had been with one particular mother. She was the kind of mother whose views and experiences are seldom heard: a working-class mother of six facing the usual uphill struggle to get professionals to take her seriously. Yet she had, of her own accord, kept a written diary of the experiences she went through as she became more and more worried about her daughter's development. She has now made those diary notes available to us for this Reader. Through her eyes, we are able to experience with her the profession-als' blatant prejudices, first as they failed to take her concerns seriously, and then as they decided that she fitted their stereotype of a neglected or abusing mother. We do not often have the opportunity to know what that feels like.

Took Hazel to see the family GP because I am worried about her development and behaviour. Her development appears to have stopped and it is becoming more difficult to get her to do everyday ordinary things i.e. to come out of her bedroom, to get washed, or have contact with anyone except myself. Hazel is also behaving oddly i.e. since she started to walk last month she runs back and forward always in the same direction and very fast. She touches and rubs things i.e. table top, TV screen, mirror. She always runs on her toes can't get shoes or boots to stop on her feet. I told all this to Dr Black he could not examine her because she became so distressed but said he thought she was deaf and would make an appointment with Mr Stokes at the hospital. He also said her behaviour was not abnormal . . .

Hazel has had her adenoids removed. There is nothing wrong with her hearing. The staff nurse is surprised at Hazel's diet of rusks and milk which she takes out of a bottle. I told her I was concerned about Hazel's behaviour and at the distress she shows at the sight of a spoon. I later heard the staff nurse say that she thought Hazel was not being stimulated and that I needed some advice about child rearing. I later spoke to a doctor about my fears for Hazel and he said he only knew about ENT and could not help or advise me . . .

A new Health Visitor came to see Hazel. Hazel became very distressed. I told her my worries. She said Hazel appeared to be under stimulated. She asked if Hazel was our only child. When I said we have six children she asked if I was on the pill. I became angry. I told her about Hazel's fear of food. Health Visitor said I was not doing it right (I don't know what 'it' means) . . .

A letter came from a Dr Gordon at the child development centre I phoned Health Visitor and asked how the referral was made. The person I spoke to said I must have asked my GP to refer Hazel. I said I had not and cancelled the appointment. I rang my GP to ask about the referral he said the new Health Visitor was very concerned about Hazel and that I had asked her to contact him to make the appointment which I had not. The Health Visitor came and I rudely threw her out . . .

Old Health Visitor is back. I was very relieved until she said that because Hazel was the youngest of six children it is easy to neglect her and lock her away in a room and stick a bottle in her mouth every now and then. I am very upset. In fact I feel desperate and confused because I know everyone believes Hazel is being neglected but angry that no one believes she has a behaviour problem which I know can affect her development. I am confused that if people especially professional people believe that Hazel is being neglected why no one is trying to protect her. I am very scared she might be taken away from me because no one believes me. I took Hazel back to the GP but I was too scared to go in to see the Doctor . . .

Went to the doctors with Hazel again about her foot. She caught it on her cot weeks ago but even though I have bandaged it and put tights on her for bed she somehow rips the tights up to scratch at her foot. The doctor asks if I smoke and if I have burned her. I feel desperate. I tell him about her strange behaviour and eating. He gives medicine for her foot . . .

I think Hazel is autistic but I am scared to tell anyone. I told my mother and she said I was daft and that Hazel was just slow. But I have read a book about autism and I am sure. I also phoned a number from the Dr Diary that came through the door and everything the recorded voice said sounds like my Hazel. It even says that parents blame and doubt themselves, that it is a very rare condition. I keep phoning that message, more boys than girls are affected and I remember seeing an autistic boy years ago. Hazel does not seem like him except she has no eye contact and runs on her toes . . .

Health Visitor came and said if I tell the staff at St Mary's nursery I can't cope with Hazel they will find a place in their nursery for her. The staff told me Hazel would have to be examined by Social Workers every few weeks and any bruises would be investigated. I just cannot believe this, I can cope, I don't want Hazel to go to a nursery she is only 20 months . . .

I have had a blazing row with Patrick about Hazel. He is worried and wants her to go to the development centre. He does not know what is wrong with Hazel but says I am not to blame and should not be scared . . .

I phoned Dr Black and asked him to make another appointment with Dr Gordon. He asked why I had changed my mind I told him I thought Hazel was autistic he said don't be stupid. On the child development course the doctor there said a mother sometimes knows more about her own child than a doctor. I won't be put off. The hospital phoned and said take Hazel. I am terrified they will take Hazel away. When I think sensibly I know this won't happen but I feel useless. Patrick says we must tell Dr Gordon everything even about Hazel eating the contents of her nappy . . .

When we first went in to see Dr Gordon I was scared because I knew Hazel and I were being observed through a one way mirror. I did not know what exactly was being observed. A woman was physically forcing Hazel to play. Hazel was very distressed. I didn't know what was happening I was confused that the Dr did not examine Hazel but I was not scared anymore because I sensed Dr Gordon did not think Hazel was neglected. A teacher is going to visit Hazel at home she is probably another Health Visitor who will think Hazel is neglected . . .

Health Visitor came. She is suddenly very nice to me trying to convince me that these things happen and they are not the fault of parents. I am confused and angry at her changed attitude. She was pleasant to Patrick. She must not think Hazel's refusal to go to him is because he has neglected or been cruel to her now . . .

I think Fiona Martin is nice. I know she does not believe Hazel is neglected. Patrick says he feels silly because he poured all his feelings about Hazel to Fiona when I was out. I feel bad that we don't talk about Hazel and that Patrick can talk to a stranger about his feelings when he is normally shy. I will feel embarrassed when Fiona comes again . . .

Suddenly everyone is nice again, Health Visitor and Dr Black but I have told Health Visitor not to come back. There is no need if Hazel is seeing Fiona and Dr Gordon. Anyway I do not trust her anymore. I am happy that there is something wrong with Hazel though I wish she was alright but if there had been no medical reason for her then she may have been taken away. Patrick is unhappy that Hazel won't go near him but relaxed when Fiona said that it was not because she dislikes him. It is her behaviour problem . . .

Patrick's mam is trying to convince Patrick that Hazel's problems are my fault and that he should leave me and take Hazel to live with her. She says she has plenty of money to send Hazel to Hungary to be cured. If Hazel had been a boy she would not have bothered. We are happy with the way that Fiona works with Hazel because we know how to help her now . . .

Hazel is to have Brain Wave tests. Fiona says there is nothing to worry about . . .

Went for the results of the tests. I don't really understand what they mean. Hazel is to take some medicine for 4 weeks. Patrick is a bit worried and I am not too keen . . .

Fiona says the medicine won't harm Hazel at all and that it may help. We will try. She is going to come to the next appointment. The medicine is making Hazel sleep lots. I phoned Dr Gordon she said not to worry. Hazel is behaving aggressively towards herself she is biting her hand and punching herself in the face and crying lots . . .

Phoned Dr Gordon. She said stop the medicine. Hazel is learning to do little things she missed as a baby she looks for hidden things and drops objects into a bowl she seems to learn very quickly but loses interest soon.

12   The new eugenics

Michelle Stanworth

The first American physician who admitted openly that he had assisted in establishing a 'surrogate pregnancy' justified his action in the language of eugenics. 'I performed the insemination', Dr Simonds wrote, 'because there are enough unwanted children and children of poor genetic background in the world' (Keane and Breo, 1981, p. 36). He is not alone. For much of this century, reproductive technologies have been seen by some as tools for encouraging the propagation of the 'superior', or for reducing the numbers of the hereditarily unfit. The feminist campaigner Margaret Sanger, in 1919, saw the chief issue of birth control as 'More children from the fit, less from the unfit' (Gordon, 1977, p. 281). George Bernard Shaw was amongst those who, in the 1930s, were excited by the prospect of using artificial insemination as a means for multiplying the offspring of a gifted minority, not least himself:

> When I, who have no children, and couldn't have been bothered with them, think of all the ova I might have inseminated!!! And of all the women who could not have tolerated me in the house for a day, but would have liked some of my qualities for their children!!! (Kevles, 1986, pp. 191–2)

The naivety of these views became cruelly apparent with the sterilisation campaign launched by Hitler in June 1933. Aimed at mental deficients, schizophrenics, manic depressives, those with severe deformities and the hereditarily blind, deaf or alcoholic, it sterilised in the first phase, some 350,000 individuals and paved the way for Auschwitz (Lifton, 1986). By the 1940s, even the popular press in Britain was alert to the sinister eugenic potential of practices such as artificial insemination by donor.

Artificial insemination by donor has been in clinical use in Britain since the 1930s, with, as far as I know, little sign of the eugenic consequences that Shaw and his associates hoped for, or that others feared. What new ingredients have been added since the early post-war period to provoke the kind of anxiety about eugenics that surrounds discussion of reproductive technologies today?

First, the advance in genetic knowledge since the forties – accelerating rapidly with the development of recombinant DNA techniques – has been remarkable. Scientists have identified some 3,000 distinct conditions that are transmitted genetically from parent to offspring. These range from disorders that may threaten the life of a child, to others (such as male baldness or colour-blindness) which can be regarded, at worst, as minor afflictions. Clinical techniques for screening at the prenatal or postnatal stage (amniocentesis, chorionic villus sampling or the Guthrie test for phenylketonura (PKU)) make it possible to detect the likely presence of some of these conditions in foetuses or newborn infants. A number of techniques also exist for identifying, among adults, people who do not themselves suffer from a genetic disorder but who, as carriers, might pass it on to their children. Hence, genetic knowledge gives the potential to recognise the genetic basis of inherited conditions and susceptibilities in an individual long before there is any outward sign.

Secondly, this increase in genetic knowledge has taken place against a backdrop of revived interest in the biological basis of human behaviour, and of renewed attempts to target less privileged social groups as the source of society's ills. Rhodes Boyson, a member of the Conservative government in Britain, attributed the increase in single-parent families partly to artificial insemination, and blamed the procreative habits of single parents for 'violent crime, football hooliganism, mugging and inner city revolt' (*Guardian*, 10 October 1986). And on both sides of the Atlantic, the new right emphasis upon fiscal responsibility has allowed cuts in public expenditure for the unemployed, those on low incomes, the elderly, the chronically ill or the disabled to be cloaked in the mantle of 'economic realism'. The doctrine of survival of the fittest – which helped to inspire the growth of the eugenics movement in the late nineteenth century – has once again found fertile ground.

A short way behind the genuine interest in finding medical solutions to particular disabilities that bring suffering to some children and their families runs a concern merely to reduce public responsibility. In Britain, a spokesperson on behalf of embryo research exemplifies the tendency to argue for preventative research into genetic disorders in ways that further stigmatise the handicapped: 'We feel strongly that the lives of handicapped children are severely blighted and that the care of them is a considerable burden to their parents and the State.' (Peter Thurnham MP, quoted in Ferriman, 1985). More baldly, a former health-systems analyst in the office of the American Surgeon-General suggests that it is the existence of (genetically?) mentally deficient people that prevents the solution of other social problems: 'If we allow our genetic problems to get out of hand, we as a society run the risk of overcommitting ourselves to the care and maintenance of a large population of mentally deficient persons at the expense of other social problems' (cited in Kevles, 1986, p. 277). All these phenomena – the rolling back of welfare programmes; the return, in Britain, of some people with disabilities to 'community care' without the resources to protect their quality of life or that of their principal carers; the tendency to define handicap as a burden on the public purse – form the context in which attitudes to screening programmes develop. A large number of British Members of Parliament who are in favour of restricting women's rights to abortion strongly support at the same time proposals for a national prenatal screening programme that would encourage the termination of more pregnancies on genetic grounds (Farrant, 1985, p. 105).

Genetic knowledge, and voluntary programmes of screening and counselling, offer would-be parents the chance to prepare for the care of a child with special needs, or to terminate a pregnancy with which they feel unable to cope. But the technical capacity to monitor individual genetic make-up also raises, particularly in the current political climate, a number of major questions. Genetic knowledge enables the identification of inborn or inherited disorders or susceptibilities, major and minor, many of which can be neither treated nor cured. Will money that goes into developing screening techniques to identify such problems substitute for funds that might be used to develop treatments, or to provide better support systems, for those who suffer the effects of such disorders? If no practical medical help can be offered to people who carry potentially disabling genes, then what will be the impact of such information on the carriers? More importantly, to what purposes might this information be put by others? In the absence of strong legal protections, screening might, in other words, provide a burden of genetic knowledge which could be used to limit the autonomy of individuals and groups, rather than extend it.

These issues have already been aired to an extent in the United States, where in the early 1970s compulsory programmes of genetic screening were introduced, and where black people were particularly affected by employment restrictions placed, for example, by major commercial airlines and by the Air Force Academy on carriers of sickle-cell trait. In Britain, however, discussion of the implications of screening programmes has been confined to a greater extent to medical and scientific constituencies, although there is some sign that this is now changing.

In thinking about reproductive technologies and eugenics, it is not the bizarre fantasies of people like Robert K. Graham – the Californian entrepreneur who aims to encourage the 'mating' of superior women with the sperm of Nobel prize-winning men – that deserve detailed attention. Rather, it is the organisation of routine medical practice that needs scrutiny. A survey of consultant obstetricians in Britain found that 75 per cent of those questioned required women to agree to abortion of an affected foetus before they give amniocentesis; information that should be a resource for parents becomes, in these cases, an instrument of population control (Farrant, 1985, p. 113). It is not acceptable that the understandable desire of many women to have as healthy a baby as possible should become a duty, aimed at the welfare of the gene pool, rather than that of the parents or the child.

Screening of adults for genetic conditions, or prenatal screening of foetuses, works by influencing the reproductive decisions of would-be parents. The choices presented by these programmes – to give birth or not to a foetus with a potentially serious abnormality, to turn to artificial insemination or some other 'safer' means of having a child, to forgo procreation altogether – are often grim. Eugenists such as Sinsheimer see a more rosy prospect in genetic engineering: if developments in biomedicine eventually enable scientists to replace problematic genes with more meritorious ones (in the newborn infant, or the embryo), then the quality of the population could be improved not by the culling of the unfit, nor even by interfering with people's procreative freedom, but merely by 'the conversion of all the unfit to the highest genetic level' (Sinsheimer, in Kevles, 1986, p. 268). This, in essence, is the appeal of the 'new eugenics'.

Even if human genetic engineering is a science-fiction possibility at the current stage of development, the concern that it evokes is understandable. There is a worry that the definition of 'unfit' will became a mask for prejudice and intolerance; that information about biochemical differences will become translated into judgements about the differential value of persons. That, in short, we will not distinguish finely enough between scientific questions and political ones. More immediately, there is a danger that genetic knowledge will be seen not as a tool of human advancement but as *the* tool: that research which might reduce the number of genetic defects will replace research to improve the prospects of people with disease or disability; that attempts to reduce genetic variability will be substituted for efforts to create an environment in which the range of human variability can flourish.

But just as genetic engineering must be put in its place, by challenging the notion that medical technique can provide a sufficient response to issues of disability and physical difference, so too in our resistance to eugenic policies it won't do to overrate the importance of reproductive technologies. In Britain, despite the existence of a 'comprehensive' National Health Service, the maternal mortality rate and the infant mortality rate for women in the 'unskilled' working class is nearly double that for women in professional and managerial groups – and the gap has scarcely narrowed since the 1930s (Townsend and Davidson, 1982, pp. 70–1). This has little to do with eugenic policies or with new technologies, and everything to do with the routine effects of life in a society that is deeply stratified. To make resistance to reproductive technologies too central to a strategy for reproductive freedom plays into the hands of those who would equate 'family' welfare with the mere arrival of a child. The struggle for reproductive freedom must be embedded in a broader programme to create the forms of support that will enable people in varying circumstances to build secure and healthy futures for themselves and their children.

In a lecture given in 1986, the chair of the Warnock Committee mentioned a survey conducted by a popular women's magazine in which the overwhelming majority of respondents had said that they did not trust scientists to reveal the full truth about their research; Mary Warnock saw this as a reflection of appalling fear and ignorance about science. But it is not fear and ignorance that makes women wary of scientific or medical innovations; it is knowledge and experience of the ambivalent effects of medical technologies on women's lives. Because of the ambivalent effects, and because of the hidden agenda of many of those who promote and apply these techniques, assessment of risks and benefits cannot be surrendered to the 'experts'. We have no option but to ask: Does it work? Does it deliver what it promises? Does it involve risks to the health or well-being of the patient? – while insisting that there is no such thing as a purely technical answer to these questions. All assessments of the efficacy and safety of a technique contain a social dimension; what, after all, is 'an acceptable level of risk'? In trying to ensure that the criteria used for assessing technologies incorporate women's own priorities with regard to health, reproduction and well-being, we have no option but to engage with science. As Hilary Rose says [in Stanworth (1987)], science is far too important to be left to men.

At the same time, we must remain firm that technical knowledge does not dictate human choices, or even make such choices clear-cut. Knowledge of a likely abnormality in a foetus, provided by prenatal screening, may be useful background information for would-be parents. But none of the very different decisions they make in these circumstances can be 'read off' from the technical information provided by the geneticists. And, most importantly, none of these decisions is properly one for a medical practitioner, as opposed to a parent, to make. In circumstances where parents, and particularly mothers, assume the overwhelming burden of material and emotional responsibility for the children they bear, it must be parents – and particularly mothers – who decide under what circumstances they are prepared to parent. [. . .]

In the feminist critique of reproductive technologies, it is not technology as an *'artificial* invasion of the human body' that is at issue – but whether we can create the political and cultural conditions in which such technologies can be employed by women to shape the experience of reproduction according to their own definitions.

References

FARRANT, W. (1985) 'Who's for amniocentesis? The politics of prenatal screening', in Homans, H. (ed.) *The Sexual Politics of Reproduction*, Aldershot, Gower.

FERRIMAN, A. (1985) 'Embryo doctors hit back', *Observer*, 10 November, p. 3.

GORDON, L. (1977) *Woman's Body, Woman's Right*, Harmondsworth, Penguin.

KEANE, N. and BREO, D. (1981) *The Surrogate Mother*, New York, Everest House.

KEVLES, D. (1986) *In the Name of Eugenics*, Harmondsworth, Penguin.

LIFTON, R. J. (1986) *The Nazi Doctors: Medical Killings and the Psychology of Genocide*, Basingstoke, Macmillan.

STANWORTH, M. (ed.) (1987) *Reproductive Technologies: Gender, Motherhood and Medicine*, Oxford, Polity Press.

TOWNSEND, P. and DAVIDSON, N. (1982) *Inequalities in Health: The Black Report*, Harmondsworth, Penguin.

13   Sex and the mentally handicapped: a laywer's view

Mike Gunn

[. . .] This paper considers the extent to which English law restricts people with a mental handicap from developing sexually. It is to be considered in the light of the United Nations Declaration on the Rights of Mentally Retarded Persons[1] (hereafter UN) and the European Convention on Human Rights[2] (hereafter ECHR).[2a]

Neither declaration is specific on the sexual relationships of people with a mental handicap. Article 1 (UN) contains a generalised provision which could be interpreted to include such relationships. It states that '(t)he mentally retarded person has . . . the same rights as other human beings'. ECHR provides for the general right to private life, which includes a person's sexual life,[3] and to family life in Article 8 and the right to marry and found a family in Article 12. Only Article 12 (ECHR) has no restrictions expressed on its face. It does not grant an absolute right since its exercise is to be within the bounds of national law. The others do contain limitations. Article 1 (UN) indicates that equality is restricted by the feasibility of providing it. This reflects the problems of balancing the free exercise of rights by a person with a mental handicap with the need to protect such people from exploitation and abuse.[4] Indeed, Article 7 (UN) stresses the need to prevent such abuse. Article 8 (ECHR) is limited in so far as it is necessary 'for the protection of health or morals, or for the protection of the rights and freedom of others'. [. . .]

If sexual development and reproduction are to be possible, it must be legally acceptable for people with a mental handicap to enter into sexual relationships. Wholly unreasonable restrictions on such relationships would appear to fall foul of Article 8 (ECHR), where the right to private life, including sexual life, can only be restricted if the conditions in Article 8 (2) are fulfilled. It therefore needs to be considered whether the restrictions which are imposed by English criminal law are 'for the protection of health or morals, or for the protection of the rights and freedom of others'.

English criminal law may hinder and perhaps prevent the sexual relationships of people with a mental handicap through the offences created by the Sexual Offences Acts 1956–76.[5] Strictures are only imposed upon people who are severely mentally handicapped (in the legislation the phrase often used is 'defective'). This phrase is now defined by the amendment of the Sexual Offences Act 1956 introduced by the Mental Health (Amendment) Act 1982. It means 'a state of arrested or incomplete development of mind which includes severe impairment of intelligence and social functioning'. It would appear that this will cover a small number of people.[6] The borderline between it and mere mental handicap is unclear. Indeed, it leaves a considerable amount to clinical judgement of the professionals, whilst the terminology does not provide particularly clear guidelines.[7]

The offences are designed to protect the health and prevent the exploitation and abuse of this relatively small group of people. It is an offence for a man to have non-marital sexual intercourse[8] with a woman who is severely mentally handicapped. He will not be guilty if he did not know and had no reason to suspect that she was *severely* mentally handicapped. Sexual activity which falls short of intercourse could also amount to an offence, since a severely mentally handicapped woman cannot provide consent to prevent an act being an indecent assault. This is an irrebuttable legal presumption following on from her classification, and no account is taken of her individual capacity to consent. The same provision applies to severely mentally handicapped men. There are also a number of offences in relation to homosexual activities with severely mentally handicapped men.[9]

These offences have a very wide ambit. They can be committed by two people developing a true relationship as well as by the exploiters and abusers. The offence of indecent assault creates a problem for staff trying to teach a person, for example, how to masturbate appropriately and successfully. On its face, an offence is committed if the person (male or female) is severely mentally handicapped, since they cannot provide consent. It is possible that if the member of staff can establish that she/he has a decent motive then she/he cannot be guilty of an offence.[10] More of an obstacle is the offence committed by staff who permit a severely mentally handicapped woman to be on the premises managed by the staff for 'the purpose of having unlawful sexual intercourse'. It would appear that the only exception is when the couple are married; otherwise the offence is committed and the only protection for members of staff is that they will not be prosecuted if the relationship is a caring and meaningful one. It is also possible that in that instance the incident would not be reported to the police in the first place.[11]

These offences impose major restrictions, which it is arguable do not comply with the requirements of Article 8 (ECHR) since they do not give consideration to the capacity of the individual. The Criminal Law Revision Committee[12] (CLRC) in its recent report[13] has considered this issue and it is possible that it may have gone some way to redress the balance. It recommends that there should be no offence if two severely mentally handicapped people have sexual intercourse, whether they are married or not. However, if the woman were mentally handicapped only, an offence would be committed regardless of how caring the relationship and how devoid of exploitation it was. CLRC recommends the retention of the existing offence with that one exception. The man would not be guilty, though, if he did not know and had no reason to suspect that the woman was mentally handicapped. The recommendation does not refer to severe mental handicap, as does the present law, because of the borderline problem and because if a man knows that the woman is mentally handicapped, he is put on notice that she might be severely mentally handicapped. This could create particular difficulties in institutional relationships where there is no necessary segregation along these lines, but where it is quite possible that the man would know his partner is mentally handicapped and not realise she is severely mentally handicapped.[14] CLRC also recommends the abolition of the presumption that a severely mentally handicapped person cannot consent. This would mean that indecent assault could not be committed on a severely mentally handicapped person if she/he consented. But a new offence is recommended to fill what is perceived as a gap. The new offence would be one involving gross indecency with a mentally handicapped person. What gross indecency would cover is indicated, although not decided, in the following: 'The phrase "gross indecency" suggests a contrast with ordinary indecency. Perhaps it would be an act of ordinary but not gross indecency for a man to kiss another man with sexual intentions or in a way that had sexual overtones.'[15] Finally, CLRC recommends that no prosecution should take place without the consent of the Director of Public Prosecutions. If enlightened policy prevailed, this could overcome many of the problems. Indeed since the police at present have prosecutorial discretion, many of the apparent rigours of the laws just mentioned can be avoided, particularly if relationships with the police are fostered such as to provide them with the information to help in decision-making. A similar position will exist when the new independent Crown prosecution service is established.[16]

 ˙ The work of CLRC reflects one of the most difficult considerations in this area: achieving a proper balance between protection from exploitation and danger to mental and physical health, on the one hand, and the value of warm and caring human relationships on the other. Unsurprisingly, in the circumstances, the weight of CLRC's deliberations lies in favour of the former. That may well not reflect thinking in the caring professions. It is possible, though by no means clear, that CLRC recommendations impose boundaries which are unreasonable within ECHR. If it can be established that the restrictions are necessary for the protection of the health of severely mentally handicapped people as a group, then the recommendations can be justified within Article 8 (2) (ECHR).

The debate on reform of this area does not stop with the report. There is ample room and time for contributions to be made. One offence not mentioned so far and for which there is no recommendation, or probably even a move for change, is that which makes sexual relationships between staff and patients illegal. I refer to section 128, Mental Health Act 1959 which is still in force.

Sexual intercourse is then lawful for most mentally handicapped people. Many severely mentally handicapped people are likely not to be in trouble with the law because either the issue is not serious enough to be reported or a decision not to prosecute is taken. [. . .]

If the sexual relationships of mentally handicapped people are to be socially acceptable, marriage must be possible. Indeed Article 12 of ECHR states that 'men and women of marriageable age have the right to marry'. But this is subject to an open-ended qualification: 'according to the national laws governing the exercise of this right'. Clearly, however, no state could arbitrarily prevent mentally handicapped people from marrying and remain in compliance with the convention.[17] English law appears to fulfil this requirement since it does not arbitrarily prevent mentally handicapped people from marrying.

In order for a ceremony of marriage to take place,[18] the celebrant must be sure that the two parties are capable of consenting. It has been judicially stated that 'the contract of marriage is in its essence one of simplicity' which most people, therefore, can understand.[19] If a person cannot consent and this is obvious, no marriage can come into existence.

If, however, the person does apparently give consent, but is in fact incapable of so doing, the marriage is voidable.[20] This means that one of the parties may have the marriage declared non-existent if it can be established that one of the parties 'did not validly consent to it' because of 'unsoundness of mind'.[21] This could include mental handicap and so an appreciation of the particular individual's capacity is required. Since marriage is a simple contract, just claiming somebody is mentally handicapped would not be sufficient. The marriage is voidable on one other relevant ground: 'that at the time of the marriage either party, though capable of giving a valid consent, was suffering (whether continuously or intermittently) from mental disorder . . . of such a kind or to such an extent as to be unfitted for marriage'.[22] Mental handicap falls within 'mental disorder' but simply to claim that a partner is mentally handicapped is insufficient. It must be shown that as a result of the mental handicap the partner is incapable of 'carrying on a normal married life'.

In both these instances it is to be stressed that the marriage will be valid until one of the parties takes action to avoid it. If the full facts were known at the time of the marriage, this may make avoidance more difficult. In any case, proceedings must be instituted within three years of the marriage.

If the marriage is valid, it can be brought to an end by divorce. Mental handicap, in itself, is not a ground but it can help to establish that the marriage has irretrievably broken down because either the respondent has behaved in such a way that the petitioner cannot reasonably be expected to live with the respondent or the petitioner has been deserted by the respondent.[23]

A common theme does not run through these provisions. This is clear by the comparison with the provisions of ECHR and UN. What it suggests is that a more consistent attitude to the sexual relationships of people with a mental handicap would be fairer to mentally handicapped people and achieve the international demands, in particular, that 'the mentally retarded person has . . . the same rights as other human beings'.

Notes

1   Resolution of the UN General Assembly 2856 (XXVI) of 10 December 1971; see United Nations (1983) Action in the Field of Human Rights, 208.

2   The treaty was signed in Rome on 4 November 1950 and came into force on 3 September 1953.

2a   UN is not enforceable in any way in England and so is of persuasive value only. ECHR is enforceable since other states and individuals can complain to the Commission and, ultimately, the Court. The decisions of these bodies are obeyed by the English Government, often resulting in legislative change. The procedural details are not considered here, but can be found in, for example, van Dijk, P. and van Hoof, G. J. H. (1984) *Theory and Practice of the European Convention on Human Rights*, Deverikes, Kluwer.

3   See van Dijk and van Hoof, *supra*, n. 2a at p. 286.

4   Criminal Law Revision Committee, 15th Report on Sexual Offences (1984) Cmnd 9213, London, HMSO.

5   The Sexual Offences Act, 1956, the Sexual Offences Act 1967 and the Sexual Offences (Amendment) Act 1976. See Smith, J. C. and Hogan, B. (1983) *Criminal Law*, London, Butterworth, ch. 13. Gunn, M. J. with Rosser, J. (1987) *Sex and the Law: A Brief Guide to Staff Working in the Mental Handicap Field*, London, Family Planning Association.

6   See Craft, M. (ed.) *Tredgold's Mental Retardation*, (12th edn) (1979), London, Bailliere Tindall.

7   See Spencer, D. (1983) 'Classification of Severe Mental Impairment', *Mental Handicap*, Vol. 11, p. 174; Gunn, M. J. (1983) 'Reply' to Spencer, D., *Mental Handicap*, Vol. 11, p. 174; Gunn, M. J. (1984) 'Sexual Rights of the Mentally Handicapped' in Alves, E. (ed.) *The Mentally Handicapped and the Law*, London, British Psychological Society.

8   The phrase used in the legislation is 'unlawful sexual intercourse'.

9   These are to be found in the Sexual Offences Act 1967, which makes it an offence to bugger such a man who cannot consent and also to commit an act of gross indecency on him.

10   See *R. v Pratt* (1984) CLR, pp. 41–2.

11   This is considered more fully in Gunn (1984), *supra*, n. 7.

12   A body of lawyers and academics established by the Home Office to consider matters concerned with the reform of criminal law.

13   *Supra*, n. 4 and Gunn, M. J. (1984) 'Proposed reform of sexual offences legislation', *Mental Handicap*, Vol. 12, pp. 164–5.

14   See letter from Leyin, A. and comment by Gunn, M. J. (1985) *Mental Handicap*, Vol. 13, p. 37.

15   Honoré, T. (1978) *Sex Law*, London, Duckworth, p. 90.

16   See, on the present position, Royal Commission on Criminal Procedure, The Law and Procedure, Cmnd 8092–1, ch. 5 and Appendix 25 (1981) and Smith, P. F. and Bailey, S. H. (1984) *The Modern English Legal System*, pp. 477–86. For the future see two Government White Papers: 1. An Independent Prosecution Service for England and Wales, Cmnd 9074 (1983); 2. Proposed Crown Service, Cmnd 9411 (1984).

17   van Dijk and van Hoof, *supra*, n. 2a at pp. 330–40.

18   Which could take place in a hospital after the Marriage Act 1983.

19   *In re Park*, Law Reports: Probate 112–38 (1954) per Birkett, L. J. at p. 133.

20   See, in general, Cretney, S. M (1984) *Family Law*, 4th edn, at pp. 46–82, and Bromley, P. M. (1981) *Family Law*, 6th edn, at ch. 3.

21   Matrimonial Causes Act 1973, s 12 (c).

22   Matrimonial Causes Act 1973, s 12 (d).

23   See, in general, Creney, *supra*, n. 20 at ch. 4 and Bromley, *supra*, n. 2 at ch. 7.

14   Barriers to adulthood: long-term unemployment and mental handicap compared

Richard Jenkins

Like other life-course categories, 'adulthood' is socially constructed. In this discussion I shall examine two reasonably common contemporary social situations in which the assumption of adult status appears to be obstructed – long-term unemployment and mental handicap – in order to better understand the nature of adulthood as a social identity in modern Britain.

14.1   Long-term unemployment and the transition to adulthood

The rise of large-scale youth unemployment in the 1970s led research interest away from concern with the transition from school to work and towards the transition from youth to adulthood (Coffield *et al.*, 1986; Jenkins, 1982, 1983; Wallace, 1987). The process of becoming an adult is structured, among other factors, by gender. For example, the adult male wage seems to be central to 'becoming a man' (Leonard, 1980, pp. 71–5; Willis, 1977, p. 150). For young women, however, marriage and parenthood appear to be the most important criteria of adulthood (Griffin, 1985, p. 50; Lees, 1986, pp. 91–5; Leonard, 1980, pp. 259–60). The two situations are, of course, closely connected: for men the adult wage means the possibility of supporting a wife and children; for women marriage offers access to that wage during the period of responsibility for child care.

Bearing this in mind, it is likely that unemployment among the under-25s, particularly the long-term unemployment which is disproportionately their lot, will have implications for the move into adulthood of many young people. A number of researchers have suggested precisely this: that long-term unemployment consigns the young to a social limbo, suspended between being kids and being adults (Willis, 1984; see also Bostyn and Wight, 1987; Coffield, 1987). A study of unemployed young people on the Isle of Sheppey, Kent, provides us with more detail: the young men take refuge in the macho network of the street-corner peer group, while the young women spend more time than they otherwise might in domestic work at home, a form of 'extended adolescence' (Wallace, 1987).

One way out for the young women of Sheppey is a household of their own; since marriage seems to require at least one adult wage, this tends to result in consensual unions and/or single parenthood. Campbell (1984), describing single parenthood as an escape strategy from unemployment dependency in the family of origin, has attributed this trend to the effects of the recession. There may be a resultant move towards later marriage or the rejection of marriage altogether. However, research elsewhere suggests that the situation may be more complex than Campbell allows for (Youth Review Team, 1985, pp. 110–13).

Issues and topics such as these informed a research project into the family relationships of long-term unemployed young women and men, aged between eighteen and twenty-five years, carried out in South Wales between 1985 and 1987 (Hutson and Jenkins, 1989). Two of the project's central concerns are of particular relevance to this discussion: first, what are the implications of long-term unemployment for courtship and marriage; and second, does chronic unemployment prevent or obstruct the passage of young people into adulthood? I shall discuss each in turn.

With respect to courtship and marriage, a comparison can be made with Leonard's study of courtship and marriage in South Wales in the late 1960s (Leonard, 1980). *Then*, young people usually remained at home prior to marriage, which typically took place in a young woman's late teens and a young man's early twenties. Premarital sex was strongly disapproved of and cohabitation almost unheard of. Expenditure on socialising and courtship was the responsibility of men, although engaged couples typically co-ordinated their expenditure and saved together for a home of their own. The adult male wage was central to engagement and marriage strategies, and marriage was the final threshold or criterion of adulthood.

Now, in the late 1980s, premarital sex is a fact of life for young people in South Wales and is accepted as such by (most of) their parents. Many leave home at one time or another prior to marriage, sometimes for good. Cohabitation is common and some young men and young women put off marriage until well into their twenties. Marriage has also become less intimately bound up with adulthood; nor is marriage any longer seen as inevitable.

How much can these changes be interpreted as a consequence of the recession or unemployment? While there is likely to be some relationship between the two things, other factors present themselves more readily as contributing to the situation: changes in women's self-image and consciousness, an increase in female labour-market participation, readily available contraception, and 'new' attitudes to sexuality and its expression. There has been a clear and long-term rise in cohabitation, a trend which appears to be unrelated to the economic climate (Harris, 1983, pp. 209–11).

The relationship between these factors is likely to be complex and it is much too early to speculate about whether orientations towards marriage, or actual marriage patterns, will change in any marked or permanent fashion. It is, however, possible to be more certain about the question of adulthood: the South Wales study offers little, if any, support for the notion that long-term unemployment is preventing young people from becoming adults. Unemployed young men and young women continue, despite the many difficulties which they experience, to develop into adults. It is possible to say this with such confidence for at least four reasons.

First, many attributes of adulthood are unrelated to either employment or marital status. These are the various thresholds of adulthood which are defined legally or administratively by the state. Crossed at different ages, these include criminal responsibility, sexual consent, the conditional or unconditional right to marry, the right to vote and the right to donate blood or organs for transplantation. Adulthood is in this sense bound up, in a weaker or stronger fashion, with citizenship. It is not, however, marked by a sharply defined change of legal status: there is, instead, an incremental inclusion into jural adulthood, culminating in Britain at the age of eighteen with the right to vote.

Second, while social security benefits are much less substantial than a 'proper wage', they do allow young people a small measure of independence from their parents. It is a resource, the management of which permits them to display a degree of adult responsibility (or not). Claiming benefit is an adult transaction between the individual and the state. Within the family, benefit payments allow the giving in of 'lodge' money; this is another adult transaction. While recent changes in the social security rules discourage it, state benefits can still underwrite independent residence away from the family of origin.

Third, young women and men continue to become adults because most parents want them to. People have to grow up. It is the public proof that mothers and fathers have 'done a good job'. Mothers are particularly important, assisting in the process of growing up in all sorts of ways.

Finally, young people also want to grow up. Adulthood is a desirable goal. It is also seen as unavoidable; the possibility of its evasion does not bear thinking about. Within the boundaries of socially defined 'normality', there comes a point – imprecisely defined – when adulthood is simply taken for granted by most young people.

To summarise, while long-term unemployment does have detrimental effects on young people during the transition to adulthood, it does not seem actually to prevent them from becoming adults. Their potential *access* to particular situations and resources – marriage, for example – may be curtailed by economic constraints; their *rights* in those respects, however, remain intact. Adulthood in British society is a robust, if imprecise, identity, of which people can only be deprived by circumstances that undermine its central portfolio of rights and obligations. Unemployment, even in the long term, is not such a circumstance.

14.2 Mental handicap and the transition to adulthood

When is an adult not an adult? The answer to this somewhat contradictory question appears to be: when he or she is classified as mentally handicapped. The situation of people with learning difficulties or mental handicaps alerts us to the need to examine critically the notion that adulthood is somehow – as perhaps implied in the previous section – inevitable or natural. It is, in fact, neither.

What, in the first place, is meant by 'mental handicap'? There are three main conventional models (Anderson, 1982, pp. 25–8; Zigler and Hodapp, 1986, pp. 4–10): the *medical* model, which stresses physiological disorder or damage to the brain and the central nervous system; the *psychological* model, which emphasises impaired intellectual functioning, as determined by standardised tests; and the *behavioural* model, which relates to competence in routine, adaptive behaviours (this may also be measured using tests). These are the diagnostic models used by professionals such as clinical psychologists and physicians. Although the medical and psychological models are by no means superseded, the behavioural model is probably the more influential today, reflecting the shift from institutional, medically oriented care to community care, administered largely by Social Services.

What of popular or commonsense models of mental handicap? For centuries, medical science talked about 'idiots', 'imbeciles', or whatever. These notions became part of everyday discourse. Fear – of violence, of unbridled sexuality, of pollution or contagion – was also an important element of popular attitudes towards people with a mental handicap (Abbot and Sapsford, 1987, pp. 5–37). This is, in part, a model of mentally handicapped people as less than human, if not actually 'animals'. Such notions remain prominent in the modern British popular model of mental handicap; for example, it is for many people not a crime, or not a serious crime, to kill a mentally handicapped foetus or person through abortion or euthanasia (Shepperdson, 1983; Sinson, 1986, pp. 13–16). A fierce debate is going on in medical ethics about the legal killing of some mentally handicapped babies (Kuhse and Singer, 1985).

There is more to it, however, than the image of mentally handicapped people as subhuman. The other important component of the popular model of mental handicap is that of the 'eternal child' (Kurtz, 1977, p. 10): here one finds compassion, pity and a quasi-parental role for the non-handicapped. Religious beliefs about spiritual innocence may play their part (Hoffman, 1961). This is also an area where diagnostic and popular models meet in the allocation of 'mental ages' to people with mental handicaps. The influence of long-established popular imagery upon diagnostic models may be detected in the use of expressions such as 'subnormal' (less than human) and 'retarded' or 'developmentally delayed' (eternally children).

Policy models derive from both diagnostic and popular models; with respect to the latter, policy may also aim to change such models. In particular, community care policies and approaches deriving from the philosophy of 'normalisation', the idea that 'each person has the right to a style of life that is normal within his or her own culture' (Zigler and Hodapp, 1986, p. 214), aim to do just that. There is, however, little evidence so far that public attitudes have changed appreciably in Britain as a consequence of such ideas.

Policy is reflected in the organisation of Social Service and health provision for people with mental handicaps. There is, for example, a clear differentiation between 'adult services' and 'children's services', as symbolised by the transfer from special educational establishments into day care provision, such as adult training centres, which typically occurs in the late teens. This organisational divide does not necessarily reflect any marked change in the way in which the mentally handicapped young women and men concerned are treated, by either family or staff.

So far, then, we have seen that the diagnostic and popular models tend, whether explicitly or implicitly, to deny the adulthood of people with mental handicaps. Current policy models – particularly the normalisation approach, the community care model being agnostic in this respect – appear to accord adult status to the mentally handicapped. What, however, of the models which are perhaps more significant, those which have a force in law?

Statute law is generally of limited relevance. The 1983 Mental Health Act has something to say about 'abnormal aggression' or 'serious irresponsibility' with respect to people who are diagnosed as mentally handicapped, and regulates their compulsory institutionalisation. It has, however, little bearing upon the lives of most people with mental handicaps. There are also isolated references to mental 'subnormality' or 'impairment' in legislation such as the 1960 Road Traffic Act or the 1973 Matrimonial Causes Act. There is, however, no systematic, statutory legal model of mental handicap as a social status or identity.

Most of the legal model of mental handicap is, in fact, to be found in the common law, the law of case, precedent and judicial decision (Clarke, 1982, pp. 44–6). This covers such things as the status of a contract made by a mentally handicapped person and the incapability of 'idiots' to vote (despite the universal suffrage guaranteed by the Representation of the People Act 1949). It is in the common law that one can discern the coming together of diagnostic, popular and policy models within a framework of authorised and authoritative decision-making.

Although there is no space here to discuss them in detail, recent legal decisions have also highlighted important issues. One of the most fraught areas in the debate about normalisation concerns the sexuality of people with mental handicaps. It is a particularly difficult issue for parents and carers. In one prominent case during 1987, following hearings in the Appeal Court and the House of Lords, 'Jeanette', a seventeen-year-old with Down's syndrome, was sterilised without her consent. More recently, in the case of a 35-year-old woman with a mental handicap who enjoyed a relationship with another patient in the hospital where she lived, the High Court, while it could not legally *authorise* sterilisation in a person over eighteen, declared that sterilisation was not unlawful since the woman was incapable of consent and the operation was in her best interests. In February 1989 the Court of Appeal, while recognising the 'dilemma' in which this put carers and doctors, rejected this somewhat awkward compromise. Instead, each case will in future be subject to individual legal review prior to sterilisation in the absence of consent.

The arguments in defence of decisions permitting forced sterilisation are threefold, although they are related. The first has to do with the individual's welfare – protecting her from the physical and mental traumas of pregnancy and childbirth. Second, the woman is deemed to be incapable of recognising the connection between sexual intercourse and conception. Third, sterilisation is viewed as the acceptable form of contraception: it is permanent and does not require regular administration.

Two other kinds of situation crop up in recent case law. First, there is the authorisation of abortions for pregnant mentally handicapped women in the absence of their consent. Second, there is the case of a child born to parents who are mentally handicapped. In one such situation, in Wolverhampton in 1987, the child – the couple's first – was taken into care at birth by the local Social Services Department. The parents were subsequently described as 'very confused and upset'.

Three important themes are revealed by these cases. First, it is almost impossible, in a social democratic society, to imagine most of the above happening to people who were *not* mentally handicapped. Second, this is explicable by the clarity with which it emerges from the court reports that, although they are regarded as biologically mature or chronologically adult, the individuals concerned are, in fact, regarded as non-adult in any intellectual, psychological or social sense. Particularly important is the allocation of 'mental ages' by professionals and their acceptance by judges and other lay persons. Third, gender is also an issue here. While the sexuality of people with a mental handicap may be perceived as a general problem, the specific problem with respect to women is seen as their *fertility*. In the case of men, however, the concern is likely to be with the *threat* posed by their sexuality (as uncontrolled, or whatever).

In closing, there are two more general points to be made. The first relates to social change. One reason why the legal cases discussed above have arisen is the uncertainty which presently surrounds the status of adult people with mental handicaps. Community care and philosophies such as normalisation have resulted in a need to clarify and redefine the limits of the adulthood to which mentally handicapped people are to be admitted and the terms of their admission. Previously, people with a mental handicap who lived, for example, in mental subnormality hospitals were, in many senses, outside society. The effective legislators in their social universe were doctors, psychologists, nurses and care staff. If a woman was pregnant, then an abortion was simply done. Now, as deinstitutionalisation proceeds apace, things are different. Hence the need for legal guidance, definition and authorisation.

The principles of normalisation have also been influential, both through their impact upon public policy and as an ideology of change and advocacy. There is a public debate, involving parents, professionals and organised pressure groups (such as Mencap or CMH, the Campaign for People with Mental Handicaps), about the kind of 'ordinary' life which people with mental handicaps can expect and the nature of their entitlement to it. In the British absence of a constitutional bill of rights, the latter is particularly problematic: the common law is the guardian of citizenship. Increasingly, mentally handicapped people are also raising their expectations in response to the increased possibilities which are opening up before them. In consequence, the issue of their adulthood – and what it might mean at a level other than the rhetorical – has become contested.

The second point is that there is more than just *adulthood* at stake here; it is also the nature of the *humanity* of people with mental handicaps which is socially problematic. This is at the heart of questions of 'responsibility' and 'consent' and it is where popular models of mentally handicapped people as less than human meet up with images of innocence and eternal childhood. Social change – with respect to attitudes, policy and service provision – has blurred what was once a clearly marked boundary between the mentally handicapped and the rest of society. In Western culture, this has always been a boundary between full humanity and an ambiguous category of the half-human (or the half-animal).

At this point a comparative perspective may be helpful. One of the core notions of post-Renaissance Western culture has been the mind–body dualism: the human essence, the soul, is conceived of as 'lying behind the eyes'. Hence, perhaps, the ease with which society recognises the biological maturity of people with a mental handicap but has a problem in conceding their adulthood (and with it, of course, a degree of equality of status). And hence the importance attached to the issue. For all parties to the debate it is, one suspects, our *own* humanity and its nature which is the real point at issue.

14.3   Conclusions

This chapter has compared two apparently problematic examples of the transition to adulthood in Britain, in order to illuminate the contours of 'normal' adulthood. On the basis of this comparison, it is clear that adulthood is a complex and multifacetted social identity, a phase of the life-course marked by an imprecise threshold of transition. Adulthood also partakes of social, psychological and biological factors; to judge from the situation of people with a mental handicap, biology is the least important of these. Gender – another meeting point of the social and the biological – is, however, a major influence upon the transition to adulthood, for all people.

Social identities are, almost by definition, contextual and hierarchical. In some contexts gender, for example, is socially more relevant than adulthood, and vice versa. There is, however, one social identity – that of the full member, the 'human' – which has a claim to consistent pre-eminence and overarching relevance. This explains the contrast between the robustness of adulthood for long-term unemployed young women and men and its contested fragility for people with mental handicaps. To really be an adult, it seems, one must first be seen to be fully human.

References

ABBOTT, P. and SAPSFORD, R. (1987) *Community Care for Mentally Handicapped Children*, Milton Keynes, Open University Press.

ANDERSON, D. (1982) *Social Work and Mental Handicap*, London, Macmillan.

BOSTYN, A.-M. and WIGHT, D. (1987) 'Inside a community: values associated with money and time', in Fineman, S. (ed.) *Unemployment: Personal and Social Consequences*, London, Tavistock.

CAMPBELL, B. (1984) *The Road to Wigan Pier Revisited*, London, Virago.

COFFIELD, F. (1987) 'From the celebration to the marginalisation of youth', in Cohen, G. (ed.) *Social Change and the Life Course*, London, Tavistock.

COFFIELD, F., BORRILL, C. and MARSHALL, S. (1986) *Growing Up at the Margins*, Milton Keynes, Open University Press.

CLARKE, D. (1982) *Mentally Handicapped People*, London, Bailliere Tindall.

GRIFFIN, C. (1985) *Typical Girls? Young Women from School to the Job Market*, London, Routledge & Kegan Paul.

HARRIS, C. C. (1983) *The Family and Industrial Society*, London, George Allen & Unwin.

HOFFMAN, J. L. (1961) 'Catholicism, medicine and mental retardation', *Practical Anthropology*, Vol. 2, pp. 49–53.

HUTSON, S. and JENKINS, R. (1989) *Taking the Strain: Youth Unemployment, Families and the Transition to Adulthood*, Milton Keynes, Open University Press.

JENKINS, R. (1982) *Hightown Rules: Growing up in a Belfast Housing Estate*, Leicester, National Youth Bureau.

JENKINS, R. (1983) *Lads, Citizens and Ordinary Kids: Working-Class Youth Life-Styles in Belfast*, London, Routledge & Kegan Paul.

KUHSE, H. and SINGER, P. (1985) *Should the Baby Live? The Problem of Handicapped Infants*, Oxford, Oxford University Press.

KURTZ, R. A. (1977) *Social Aspects of Mental Retardation*, Lexington, Lexington Books.

LEES, S. (1986) *Losing Out: Sexuality and Adolescent Girls*, London, Hutchinson.

LEONARD, D. (1980) *Sex and Generation: A Study of Courtship and Weddings*, London, Tavistock.

SHEPPERDSON, B. (1983) 'Abortion and euthanasia of Down's syndrome children – the parents' view', *Journal of Medical Ethics*, Vol. 9, pp. 152–7.

SINSON, J. C. (1986) *Attitudes to Down's Syndrome*, London, Mental Health Foundation.

WALLACE, C. (1987) *For Richer, For Poorer: Growing Up In and Out of Work*, London, Tavistock.

WILLIS, P. (1977) *Learning to Labour*, Farnborough, Saxon House.

WILLIS, P. (1984) 'Youth unemployment: thinking the unthinkable', *Youth and Policy*, Vol. 2, No. 4, pp. 17–24, 33–6.

ZIGLER, E. and HODAPP, R. M. (1986) *Understanding Mental Retardation*, Cambridge, Cambridge University Press.

15 Learned helplessness theory and people with learning difficulties: the psychological price of powerlessness

John Swain

Helplessness is a psychological state that can result when events and outcomes are uncontrollable, that is independent of a person's responses and behaviour. The psychological consequences of powerlessness are an important dimension of the roles imposed on oppressed groups: 'always a feeling of powerlessness – the feeling that because one is black, female, working class, disabled or whatever, things are the way they are and one simply has to accept them because one doesn't have the power to change them' (Sutherland, 1981). This chapter begins with an examination of the framework that learned helplessness theory provides for understanding the experiences of people with learning difficulties, particularly as an alternative to the influential notion of 'a deficiency in spontaneous learning'. The chapter then critically re-examines the assumption that 'events and outcomes are uncontrollable' and outlines possibilities for overcoming helplessness which involve increased control for people with learning difficulties.

15.1 The original and reformulated hypotheses

The learned helplessness hypothesis states that if people are frequently in situations over which they have no control they can learn 'helplessness', that is the expectation and belief that they can do nothing to affect or change events. People can learn that events are independent of their actions and beyond their control. This is the cornerstone of a theory which has been elaborated, investigated and reformulated for over twenty years. The original research (Overmier and Seligman, 1967) showed that dogs who had learned helplessness would passively continue to receive high levels of electric shocks. This early research and development led to a full statement and review by Seligman in 1975, and *Helplessness: On Depression, Development and Death* is still the text most frequently referred to on this topic.

In the theory of learned helplessness there are three debilitating effects of experiences of uncontrollable events. The first is a lack of motivation to try to control events. If people have learnt that they have little effect on valued outcomes or undesired events, they will cease to try to solve problems or to overcome barriers. Second, the emotional effect typically involves resignation, depression and anxiety. Third, there is also a general disruption to learning which involves people having difficulty in learning that their behaviour does have consequences. Even when success is experienced, a person will have difficulty learning that what he or she did actually affected outcomes or events.

Learned helplessness is not the result of a particular situation. It is the impact of a series of learning experiences in which the person lacks control and choice, and it can begin in the first days of life. Seligman (1975) sought the roots of learned helplessness in early child development and particularly in the dimension of controllability of environments. He cites, for instance, Watson and Ramey's (1972) study in which they designed a very sensitive air pillow that closed a switch every time the infant moved his or her head and thereby moved a mobile hanging over the cot. They reported the results of exposing an eight-month-old girl with severe learning difficulties to this 'contingent mobile': her activity increased tenfold, and she smiled and cooed vigorously when the mobile was around. The importance of the responsiveness of parents in making a child's behaviour meaningful and significant is well documented in the literature. In interactions with infants, writes Newson (1979), caregivers 'make the assumption that the infant is attempting some form of meaningful dialogue, and out of this assumption the communication of shared meanings begins to take place'. The child's sense of mastery or of helplessness, argues Seligman (1975), develops in early interactions and from the information provided by the parents' responses to the child's actions.

The original theory was inadequate in explaining individual differences in learned helplessness. Some people in powerless situations seem far from 'helpless' in their struggle for change and for control over decisions which shape their lives. The reformulated version of the theory (see Abramson *et al.*, 1978; Garber and Seligman, 1980) explained such variations in response in terms of what the individual perceives to be the causes of failure and problems. It focuses on the person's reasons in explaining why he or she has no influence and control over events. These perceived reasons differ according to whether causes are seen as: personal or dependent on the environment (internal–external); long- or short-lived (stable–unstable); and unique to one or applying to various situations (specific–global). The reformulated theory predicts that learned helplessness is associated with internal, stable and global explanations for aversive events (for example, 'I am incompetent'), and external, unstable and global explanations for valued outcomes (for example, 'It was the luck of the draw').

There have been a number of studies based on learned helplessness theory which have involved people with learning difficulties. Floor and Rosen (1975) found that both institutionalised and non-institutionalised 'retarded subjects exhibited significantly more signs of helplessness than did the nonretarded control subjects'. Learned helplessness theory can also provide an alternative explanation for other research evidence. For instance, Clarke and Clarke (1974) drew together the main streams of experimental work and singled out 'a relative inability to profit from ordinary unstructured experience, a deficiency in spontaneous learning' as the most important overall finding about people with learning difficulties. This has been a highly influential notion, particularly in education where it is used to justify highly structured and didactic approaches, such as behaviour modification. Learned helplessness theory offers not only an alternative explanation of prolonged failure to learn, but also different implications for intervention. From this perspective it can be argued that didactic and structured approaches themselves deny learners choice and control of what and how they will learn. Guess *et al.* (1985) put it emphatically: 'The end result is more control for the caregivers and less control for the person being cared for. Ironically persons with handicaps are being treated with the very same "medicine" that made them "ill" in the first place – lack of control over their lives and circumstances.' We shall return to the implications for intervention after considering the limitations of learned helplessness theory.

15.2   'Learned helplessness' or 'taught helplessness'?

Learned helplessness theory has been criticised on a number of grounds. Some of the evidence from research has failed to support specific aspects of the theory (for example, Ford and Neale, 1985). The most far-reaching critical analysis, however, raises questions about the fundamental basis of the theory, that is the notion of 'uncontrollable and inescapable conditions' (McClure, 1985). This chapter concentrates on and extends this critical analysis.

Learned helplessness theory focuses on 'helplessness' as a condition of the individual, sometimes referred to by the medical term 'syndrome', rather than on the relationship between a person or group and the social environment. 'Helplessness' becomes a problem of the individual, albeit learned. The environment is generally characterised as an unalterable factor – 'uncontrollable conditions'. It can be argued that the seeds of this perspective are sown in the laboratory where learned helplessness has been the subject of much experimentation. In such situations the experimenter is always in control. As McClure (1985) points out, the so-called 'un-controllable conditions' are in fact being controlled by the experimenter. 'Helplessness,' writes McClure, 'is not only learnt; it is also taught.'

The emphasis on the attributes of the individual has implications for

intervention. Four categories of treatment were suggested in the reformulation of the theory (Abramson *et al.*, 1978) none of which is directly
concerned with giving people more control over their own lives. Three
types of treatment involve changing the person's perception of events,
controllability of events and causes of events. One of these is even directed
at helping the person accept their lot in life: 'Make the highly preferred
outcomes less preferred.' The fourth type of treatment does involve
changing the environment, but this is not a matter of increased control for
powerless people. Change remains in the hands of others (that is, social
agencies). As McClure says, 'Abramson *et al.* (1978) confound control with
philanthropic welfare arrangements.'

By concentrating on the attributes of the individual (including whether
they blame themselves), learned helplessness theory becomes part of the
ideology for blaming the victim. Ryan (1971) explains: 'the stigma, the
defect, the difference – though derived in the past from environmental
forces – is still located *within* the victim, inside his (or her) skin'.

15.3   'Uncontrollable conditions'

Learned helplessness can be understood in terms of social relationships,
characterised by the need to dominate and control via obedience, conformity and submission. McGee *et al.* (1987) have discussed such authoritarian and overprotective relationships in detail. They state, for instance:
'Punishment implies a need to dominate, rule over and control. It implies a
belief that the care giver's role is to bring about compliance. In effect, it
results in dependent persons who survive on the fringes of society.' When
learned helplessness is seen as a relationship between a person or group
and the social environment then it cannot be fully understood in terms of
the individual's responses to so-called 'uncontrollable conditions'. We
must look too at the conditions which deny people with learning difficulties
choice and control over their own lives. This involves a different approach
to research. Controlled laboratory experiments can tell us nothing of
people's opportunities for choice and control in their day-to-day lives.
Finding out about this requires studies of people at work, at leisure, at
home and in classrooms.

The available evidence confirms both the importance of opportunities
for choice for people with learning difficulties and the lack of such
opportunities. Edgerton's research, describing the lives of people released
from a large state hospital, began in 1960–1 (Edgerton, 1967) and the
fourth follow-up of people who are by now 'ageing in the community' has
recently been reported (Edgerton, 1988) (see this Reader, ch. 26). In
general, after thirty years of living in the community, the surviving
members of the original group have demonstrated and increased their

social competence, independence and 'zest for life'. Edgerton (1988) is unequivocal about the conditions for such successful living in the community: 'the right and obligation to make choices, large and small, for over thirty years. Their choices are often constrained in many ways, as they are for all of us, but they are choices nevertheless. They control their own lives.' He has also compared the conditions in the community with those of people living in restricted residential settings whose 'routine and crucial life decisions are typically made for them by others'.

Studies in the community, in residential care and in the classroom have begun to describe the powerlessness, restriction of choice and lack of control that people with learning difficulties can face. Houghton *et al.* (1987), for example, made an observational study to record opportunities that people with learning difficulties have to express their preferences and make their choices in a variety of classroom settings. They found that 'regardless of age level or setting, classroom staff responded at very low rates to student-initiated expressions of choice or preference'. A recent three-year study in Scotland involved repeated interviews with sixty-five people with learning difficulties living in hospital and at home. They also interviewed parents and staff. One of the features of people's lives that was described in detail is the powerlessness that characterises their position. 'The hospital residents', report Cattermole *et al.* (in press), 'lacked the opportunities to exercise the most basic choices such as when to have a cup of tea and whether or not to have milk and sugar in it.' Cattermole *et al.* (1988) also found that people living in their family home experience 'limited autonomy in very basic aspects of their lives, their parents exercising a large degree of control and protection'.

15.4   Power for the powerless

A view of learned helplessness as a social relationship focuses intervention on enabling people to take power over events and outcomes in their own lives. As argued earlier, this is not usually emphasised in the theory of learned helplessness. In statements of the original theory the main recommendations for so-called 'cure' are not concerned with any changes towards equality in relationships or transfer of control. Seligman's (1975) main suggestion was based on experiments in which dogs were repeatedly dragged to safety so they could avoid electric shocks. Significantly he called this approach 'directive' therapy. Nevertheless, he does make quite different recommendations specifically in relation to people living in institutions. Helpless people, he argues, should be given maximum control over all aspects of their daily life including 'choice of omelettes or scrambled eggs for breakfast, blue or red curtains, going to the movies on Wednesdays or Thursdays, whether to wake up early or sleep late'. It is this emphasis which is elaborated in this present chapter.

Guess *et al.* (1985) describe a model for categorising levels of choice which provides a framework for considering giving people power. Figure 15.1 shows the three categories and suggests related possibilities for empowerment.

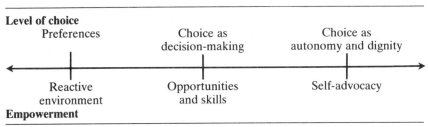

Figure 15.1   Choice and empowerment

Preferences: a reactive environment

The simplest form of choice-making is an expression of preference: a display of liking or disliking towards something. It is only conceptually 'simple' and in practice demands great sensitivity and empathy in communication and relationships. This level of choice-making is one of expression rather than action on decisions and is therefore directly dependent on the responsiveness of others. Expression of preferences is often through non-verbal signals and for some people, including people with profound and multiple handicaps, non-verbal can be the only possible form of communication.

The expression of preferences and responsiveness of others has been most extensively studied in early child–parent interaction. As stated previously, these early interactions are a foundation of helplessness or of mastery. The developmentally earliest forms of control for the infant are in initiating, maintaining, terminating and avoiding interactions (Trevarthen, 1977). The infant's eye movements, facial expressions, vocalisations and body movements are the basis for expression of preferences. At first the parent has to interpret the infant's non-verbal signals as communicative (such as expressions of discomfort or enjoyment). For example, activity level, muscle tone, facial expression and vocalisations can express preference for one type of position over another. Such early interactions are the roots of autonomy and self-direction and the basis of the child's growing ability to change and control the environment.

At this level of choice-making, intervention takes the form of increased responsiveness to expression of preferences. Guess *et al.* (1985) state: 'By providing consistent responses to the child's non-verbal behaviours and opportunities for utilising these behaviours in many interactions and environments, a systematic mode for communication of preferences may become meaningful for the child.' This general orientation has been developed by people working with deaf-blind children and also taken up in work with profoundly and multiply handicapped young people with learning difficulties. Goode and Gaddy (1976), for instance, developed a schedule of five categories of preference (from highly dislike to highly like) for observing expressions of choice and availability of options on a hospital ward. McInnes and Treffry (1982) have developed an approach for working with deaf-blind young people which is founded upon the creation of a reactive rather than directive environment. This is an environment which is characterised by social responsiveness founded on emotional bonding, the development of close personal relationships and two-way communication.

Choice as decision-making: opportunities and skills

Choice as a decision-making process incorporates the expression of preferences but also involves active selection amongst alternatives. Choosing at this level, then, is an act based on decisions which may take into account not only preferences but also the perceived needs of others, perceived constraints and future goals.

The first requirement for making choices is the opportunity to do so. In a small-scale study of students with learning difficulties being given choice over initiating and sustaining leisure activities, Nietupski and Hamre-Nietupski (1986) found students were able to initiate and select activities. Pictures were used as an aid to selection. They concluded: 'The implications of such findings are that practitioners should provide frequent choice opportunities in a structured fashion rather than assuming that students lack self-initiation skills.' Cattermole *et al.* (1988), mentioned earlier, also found that people with learning difficulties 'can participate in a real sense in major decisions about their lives *if given the opportunity*' (my emphasis). Another small study of leisure (Dattilo and Rusch, 1985) underlined the importance of opportunities for choice. They found that people with learning difficulties participated more in activities in which they were given control over participation than when they had no choice. A number of approaches have been more systematic in facilitating choice- and decision-making skills. Shevin and Klein (1984), for example, present a rationale and a framework for the inclusion of choice-making in curricula for students with learning difficulties. Cooper and Hersov (1986) have also described some of the ways that staff can help people with learning difficulties to make choices when they have had little or no previous opportunities for controlling their own lives.

Choice as autonomy and dignity: self-advocacy

Choice at this level incorporates the previous two levels into a more active empowerment of people in powerless conditions, particularly through group organisation and identity. Seligman (1975) himself wrote: 'When oppressed and impoverished people see all around them the possibility of power and affluence, their belief in uncontrollability shatters, and revolution becomes a possibility.' Nevertheless, self-advocacy in particular and self-help groups in general have received little consideration in either the original or reformulated theories.

One exception is the study by Baucom (1983) of women's achievements in legal and social changes that have to some extent lessened the 'uncontrollability of conditions' and increased the choices and control that they can exercise. Also McClure (1985) argues for relinquishing the assumption that the environment in helplessness-inducing experiments is uncontrollable and inescapable. Therapy for helplessness, he suggests, could include the option of giving people more actual control and also of encouraging people to exercise the control when it is not 'given'. Self-advocacy is a process of people with learning difficulties taking control over their lives and circumstances. Gary Bourlet, chairperson of the Participation Forum states: 'We are human beings not robots. We don't need people to control our lives. Self-advocacy enables us to make choices and make our decisions' (Shearer, 1986).

15.5 Conclusion

Learned helplessness theory offers a model of the psychological price of powerlessness in which oppression becomes internalised. What may seem to be enduring, debilitating characteristics of the people – such as apathy, fatalism, depression and pessimism – are actually 'the straightforward manifestation of the dynamics arising from lack of power. Man powerless is not fully man' (Ryan, 1971). Nevertheless it is still a 'personal tragedy theory' (Oliver, 1986). This chapter has argued that helplessness is an aspect of social relationships between people who are powerless and those who control so-called 'uncontrollable events'. Possibilities for overcoming helplessness essentially involve changes in social relationships with a transfer of control to disempowered people.

References

ABRAMSON, L. Y., SELIGMAN, M. E. P. and TEASDALE, J. D. (1978) 'Learned helplessness in humans: critique and reformulation', *Journal of Abnormal Psychology*, Vol. 87, No. 1, pp. 49–74.

BAUCOM, D. H. (1983) 'Sex role identity and the decision to regain control among women: a learned helplessness investigation', *Journal of Personality and Social Psychology*, Vol. 44, pp. 334–43.

CATTERMOLE, M., JAHODA, A. and MARKOVA, I. (1988) 'Leaving home: the experience of people with a mental handicap', *Journal of Mental Deficiency Research*, Vol. 32, pp. 47–57.

CATTERMOLE, M., JAHODA, A. and MARKOVA, I. (in press) 'Living in a mental handicap hospital – the view from the inside', *Mental Handicap*.

CLARKE, A. M. and CLARKE, A. D. B. (1974) 'Severe subnormality: capacity and performance', in Clarke, A. M. and Clarke, A. D. B. (eds) *Mental Deficiency: The Changing Outlook*, London, Methuen.

COOPER, D. and HERSOV, J. (1986) *We Can Change the Future*, London, National Bureau for Handicapped Students.

DATTILO, J. and RUSCH, F. (1985) 'Effects of choice on leisure participation for persons with severe handicaps', *Journal of the Association for Persons with Severe Handicaps*, Vol. 10, No. 4, pp. 194–9.

EDGERTON, R. B. (1967) *The Cloak of Competence*, Berkeley, University of California Press.

EDGERTON, R. B. (1988) 'Ageing in the community: a matter of choice', *American Journal on Mental Retardation*, Vol. 22, No. 4, pp. 331–5. (See the Reader, ch. 26.)

FLOOR, L. and ROSEN, M. (1975) 'Investigating the phenomenon of helplessness in mentally retarded adults', *American Journal of Mental Deficiency*, Vol. 79, No. 5, pp. 565–72.

FORD, C. E. and NEALE, J. M. (1985) 'Learned helpessness and judgements of control', *Journal of Personality and Social Psychology*, Vol. 49, No. 5, pp. 1330–6.

GARBER, J. and SELIGMAN, M. E. P. (1980) *Human Helplessness: Theory and Applications*, New York, Academic Press.

GOODE, D. and GADDY, M. (1976) 'Ascertaining choice with alingual, deaf, blind and retarded clients', *Mental Retardation*, Vol. 14.

GUESS, D. *et al.* (1985) 'Concepts and issues related to choice-making and autonomy among persons with severe disabilities', *Journal of the Association for Persons with Severe Handicaps*, Vol. 10, No. 2, pp. 79–86.

McCLURE, J. (1985) 'The social parameters of "learned" helplessness: its recognition and implications', *Journal of Personality and Social Psychology*, Vol. 6, pp. 1534–9.

McGEE, J. J., MENOLASCINO, F. J., HOBBS, D. C. and MENOUSEK, P. E. (1987) *Gentle Teaching: A Non-Aversive Approach to Helping Persons with Mental Retardation*, New York, Human Sciences Press.

McINNES, J. M. and TREFFRY, J. A. (1982) *Deaf-Blind Infants and Children: A Developmental Guide*, Milton Keynes, Open University Press.

NEWSON, J. (1979) 'The growth of shared understanding between infant and caregiver', in Bullowa, M. (ed.) *Before Speech: The Beginning of Interpersonal Communication*, London, Cambridge University Press.

NIETUPSKI, J. and HAMRE-NIETUPSKI, J. (1986) 'Self initiated and sustained leisure activity participation by students with severe/moderate handicaps', *Education and Training of the Mentally Retarded*, Vol. 21.

OLIVER, M. (1986) 'Social policy and disability: some theoretical issues', *Disability, Handicap and Society*, Vol. 1, No. 1, pp. 5–17.

OVERMIER, J. B. and SELIGMAN, M. E. P. (1967) 'Effects of inescapable shock upon subsequent escape and avoidance learning', *Journal of Comparative and Physiological Psychology*, Vol. 63, pp. 23–33.

RYAN, W. (1971) *Blaming The Victim*, London, Orbach & Chambers.

SELIGMAN, M. E. P. (1975) *Helplessness: On Depression, Development and Death*, San Francisco, W. H. Freeman.

SHEARER, A. (1986) *Building Community: With People with Mental Handicaps, Their Families and Friends*, London, Campaign for People with Mental Handicaps with King Edward's Hospital Fund for London.

SHEVIN, M. and KLEIN, K. (1984) 'The importance of choice-making skills for students with severe disabilities', *Journal of the Association for Persons with Severe Handicaps*, Vol. 9, No. 3, pp. 159–66.

SUTHERLAND, A. (1981) *Disabled We Stand*, London, Souvenir Press.

TREVARTHEN, C. (1977) 'Descriptive analysis of infant communicative behaviour', in Schaffer, H. R. (ed.) *Studies in Mother–Infant Interaction*, London, Academic Press.

WATSON, J. S. and RAMEY, C. G. (1972) 'Reactions to response-contingent stimulation in early infancy', *Merrill-Palmer Quarterly*, Vol. 18, pp. 219–28.

Section III Discovering a voice

Introduction

The articles in this section must convince us, if we ever doubted it, that people with learning difficulties are not passive. Despite oppression and despite denial of their humanity, people retain an individual dignity and spirit which is hard to destroy. This section allows the voices of some of those people to be heard. The voices are not new. They have always been there. But perhaps we are now more willing to listen.

These articles are essentially based on the experiences of individuals. Some are personal accounts written by the individual involved; others are descriptive, written by an observer, but still focusing on the experiences of individual people.

Detailed inside stories, like the first two in this section, have a fundamental importance which is easy to underestimate. It is against these experiential accounts that more formal approaches can be evaluated, for, when all is said and done, it is the impact of services and policies on the individual which is the hallmark of success or failure.

David Barron's account opens this section. As this is a Reader about people with learning difficulties it seemed appropriate, wherever possible, to allow them to speak through these pages. Inevitably, the label 'learning difficulty' means that it is unlikely that their strengths lie in the written word. David was, as the introduction describes, 'functionally illiterate'. Clearly this is not a barrier to empathetic and vivid description. Although this account is set in the past, David conveys vividly the experiences of someone who was apparently at the mercy of an inhumane system. Despite it all, he emerges able to speak about his experiences.

We searched long and hard for an account of self-advocacy, by self-advocates, which raised key issues, as opposed to providing a description of how to go about it, or summarising people's views. Diane Amans is a lecturer at Stockport College of Further Education. She attended the People First Conference held in London in September 1988. The information she and Christine Darbyshire provide about the conference, including the positive contribution of the local press, gives us a sense of the potential importance of such an experience. At the same time, Diane's diary goes some way towards illustrating the dilemmas of a person who wishes to facilitate people 'speaking for themselves'. The doubts she describes here may be familiar to many people. How far should you control or guide people 'for their own good', or because they have responsibilities to others, and how far do you allow them to make their own mistakes, even if it means losing what appear to be unique and valuable opportunities?

Following this is a short extract from a People First Conference Report. People First is an umbrella organisation which both encourages and co-ordinates the work of self-advocacy groups for people with learning difficulties, nationally and internationally. As the published extract shows, People First and similar organisations provide a platform for users to make an input into the planning of services, but this document goes further and the major statements give an indication of the breadth of topics covered, from the purpose of day services to the role of staff, from integration to labelling. It seemed appropriate for a Reader about making connections between the lives of people with learning difficulties and the lives of others to include a statement by people so labelled of where *they* would like to see changes.

The second trio of articles in this section deals with discovering a voice at one remove. The authors are – unlike Barron, Amans and Darbyshire, and the People First group – not speaking as the individual(s) involved, but about others. However, the accounts shade into one another: all the authors have been personally involved with the 'subjects' of their accounts; they have merely stepped back and reflected further before putting pen to paper.

Recognising that the severity of disability for some individuals prevents them from giving their own account, David Goode charts his attempt to enter the world of a young girl who has profound handicaps. In the process he discovers as much about his own limitations as about Chris's 'problems'. The article challenges us to begin to question our own assumptions about other people's apparently meaningless behaviour.

Valerie Sinason is a psychotherapist. The case study we have chosen illustrates her way of working with a young boy, Barry, who is apparently 'unknowable'. Her painstaking and long-term work with him, described in some detail here, allows us to begin to acquire an insight into his perception of the world. As in the case of Chris in the previous article, a child who at first sight appears both mysterious and inaccessible gradually begins to make sense, and a foundation is laid for further communication.

The final article in this section, 'Stigma and the self-concept of people with a mild mental handicap' deals with not one but several individuals. The researchers have set out to discover how twelve people with learning difficulties view themselves, and whether that coincides with how others view them. The conclusion, that although other people's perceptions are significant the individual can still resist negative labelling and develop a strong and positive self-concept, encourages belief in the strength of the human spirit. It brings us back to our starting point in this section where David Barron described his own resistance to the system which sought to dehumanise him.

16 Locked away: life in an institution

David Barron

In March 1939, I was taken, at the age of fourteen, from my foster mother to the mid-Yorkshire Institution at Whixley, near York. I was collected by two men and we were all met by the superintendent and the matron. I was instructed to wait until they finished talking. As the men left, they said, 'Goodbye, lad. We hope you'll soon settle in.'

I was marched from the room and into a large dining hall. It was massive. I had never ever seen so many people sat at tables. A patient told me that the hall held 485 people. I asked him lots of questions. Suddenly, he frightened me almost to death. He sent a pot of tea flying, fell from the chair and lay foaming at the mouth. Someone yelled 'Tom's having a fit', and an attendant came over.

I left the table to chat to other patients and was immediately told to sit down until the necessary permission was granted after the saying of grace. I was taken down a long corridor to the ward. The attendant pulled out a big bunch of keys fastened to his pocket on a long chain. Eventually he found the right one, we entered and he locked the door behind us. The ward seemed like a prison. [. . .] I was shown my bedroom and given a nightshirt to wear. The attendant locked me into the bedroom. I crawled into bed and cried my eyes out.

I learned later, I was in the punishment ward. It was an institutional ruling that you spent the first few months there. You weren't allowed to speak to other patients; all possessions were taken away; we were on half rations; a discipline of hard physical labour like scrubbing concrete with a brick and half a bucket of cold water.

After a few months, I was transferred to Ward Two. One night, I was woken up with a start. A hand had grabbed my bed clothes at the bottom. All the bedclothes were pulled expertly away from me. It was the superintendent.

'Come on now, son,' he said. 'Get them off.'

Playing dumb I just lay there.

'You know what I mean – those socks.'

I took them off.

'Right, son. Don't let me catch you with your socks on in bed again or you'll know what to expect.' He meant shunting back to the punishment ward.

On Friday, when I went up for my meagre pay, I had another shock.

'I have stopped your money for a fortnight,' he informed me. All for wearing a pair of socks in bed! [. . .]

Taste of freedom

Some months further on I got my first taste of freedom. One Sunday morning, I went to see outside the grounds for the first time since admission. At 9.30 a.m. prompt we left our wards to go round to the main drive where we lined up in twos for inspection. There were nearly 450 patients and some had their shoes on the wrong feet. Some had no ties on or had tied them incorrectly. Others, like myself, had failed to comb their hair or clean their shoes.

After an age, we marched off. I called it the 'Whixley Crawl' or the chain gang. It was an ordeal we should never have had to undergo. The superintendent deliberately made us a spectacle for all the surrounding villages to see. I suppose it was OK for the lower-graded patients who had no way of knowing they were the laughing stock. But we could sense the public's ridicule. It was a two-hour walk. I made it for eighteen years until I could have walked it blindfold.

16.1   Opening the door

[. . .] Besides having non-qualified attendants, there were also tradesmen in four different trades – tailors, the mat shop, the occupational therapy room and the cobbler's shop. [. . .]

For four years, I worked in the cobbler's shop. I felt no longer a patient working among the boots and shoes. I felt as if I was working outside. The cobbler, Mr Webster, was a good man. However well we were treated here, we had to remember we were patients when we returned to the ward in the evenings. He taught me all about repairing shoes. With his passionate temper and ripe language, he was full of respect and kindness. When Mr Webster died suddenly, the cobbler's shop was taken over by a private firm.

Pre-discharge ward

After this I was transferred to Ward Four. This was the pre-discharge ward. I was allocated to work with Mr Tynegate in OT who had forty patients under him, mostly epileptics. My task was to put out the various jobs for patients – painting, drawing, sewing and basket work. Eventually I became an assistant instructor, learning a lot on the medical side, coming to know and understand the patients in the same way that a parent understands his children.

When certain patients were about to have a fit, they seemed to gain the strength of a horse and took off their boots to throw at the staff. It was all Mr Tynegate and I could do to see they came to no harm. We inserted a special medical implement in their mouths to stop them biting their tongues.

We had to guard against patients who had fits without warning. They often became violent. Some people got injured as they fell. It used to break my heart but Mr Tynegate gave me a piece of sound advice.

'You mustn't let your emotions get the better of you, David. They need a bit of understanding.'

16.2   Getting out

Rumours were going around about lots of patients being sent out to hostels in Tadcaster, Bubwith and further afield. It spread like wildfire when tons of suitcases were delivered and every other day, patients were sent for by the tailor and measured for new suits.

A good twelve months rolled by and I had just returned from a walk. Mr Tynegate called out, 'The tailor wants you, David.' I was to be fitted for a discharge suit.

Hostel

A few days later, my suitcases were put in the back of the superintendent's car and I was taken to Bubwith Hostel near York. After a few months there, I went under licence to Leeds to live with Mrs Shaw. I found her harsh but got most of my company through the Salvation Army.

One day, when I came in from work, Mrs Shaw was waiting for me. 'Don't go to work in the morning, David, someone is coming to see you.'

At 10.30 a.m. the following day, I sat in her front room when in came Messrs Perry and Hoyle, the same two men who had taken me to Whixley Institution nearly twenty years before.

'Hello,' said Mr Hoyle with forced cheerfulness, and turning to Mrs Shaw, 'you are sure you won't change your mind?'

'No,' she cried out harshly, 'he's a bloody menace. Get him out of my house.'

Too much

The fear of going back to the institution was too much for me. I bolted for it. I ran quickly down the back alleys to my friends in the Salvation Army – Mr and Mrs Sharpe.

Mrs Sharpe gasped, 'Why, David – you look as if you've seen a ghost.' Breathlessly, I explained.

'I will arrange for you to go and stay with my sister who lives in Tingley – just near Wakefield.'

I was on the run. The Yorkshire police would be out looking for me. After a cup of tea and a bite to eat, I caught the various buses to Tingley. I had to change buses bang opposite Dewsbury Road police station.

I had to explain to Mrs Furniss, Mrs Sharpe's sister, who was most welcoming. I knew that it was only a matter of time until the police caught up with me. At 6.30 p.m. on the Friday, the policeman's knock came.

'Come on David,' he said, 'I don't like having to do this but it's my job and you have to come with me.'

Escort

I was kept overnight in Morley police station. I cried myself to sleep. In the morning, the superintendent called with an escort to take me back to Whixley Institution. I was taken out of the car and with sickening inevitability placed in Ward One.

Next Monday, I was completely taken by surprise when they came for me.

There, outside the board room, to my joy, was the Sharpe family. As I greeted them, the superintendent called me into the board room. I stood at one end of the long room so the committee could see me. The superintendent spoke.

'Well David, what have you done wrong to make Mrs Shaw have you brought back here?'

'Nothing sir.'

'Nothing, eh?'

'I couldn't put a razor blade down but what it took legs and walked.'

The committee laughed and a few words were exchanged. The superintendent turned to me. 'All right. You can go and wait outside.'

Mrs Sharpe and Mrs Furniss asked me how I had got on.

'I don't know.'

Then they were called into the board room. They were a long time. Afterwards they told me about the questions. The committee wanted to know why they were offering me a home. Was it because of the money? 'I told them,' said Mrs Sharpe, 'the money never entered my head. I had come to know you as one of the family. You spent most of the time with us when you weren't at work.'

The superintendent came out. 'David. You can go back with Mrs Furniss on licence and I will send her the necessary forms to fill in in due course,' he said.

I left with the two ladies, in great joy, never to return.

17 A voice of our own

Diane Amans and Christine Darbyshire

Christine Darbyshire and another delegate from Stockport College of Technology attended the People First International Conference in September 1988 in London. They were accompanied by Diane Amans, a lecturer at the college. The following extracts are provided as a way of illustrating what this experience involved for them and what some of the outcomes were.

This is not an exhaustive account, nor is it simply a summary of the conference, but it reflects experiences and documents a process which others may share. It also raises some issues and dilemmas which may well be an integral part of the process of emerging self-advocacy.

It starts with a brief written explanation from Christine Darbyshire.

People First is about speaking up for yourself. We went to a conference at St Mary's College, Strawberry Hill, London. People came from Canada, London, America, Australia, Switzerland and all over Britain. Some of them talked about their own meetings and some talked about where they live. Some of them were talking about being sterilised, which means stopped from having babies. We do not like being called mental and disabled, when we are just as normal as anyone else. We are just a bit slow at learning but we will soon catch up. I enjoyed having the meeting and I enjoyed the social life, meeting other people. I want to start People First in Stockport to help people speak up for themselves.

The next People First conference will be in Canada in 1992. I want to go to Canada and say what I think about having a paid job and living on my own. If you are interested in People First ring Christine Darbyshire.

Diane Amans also wrote a summary of the conference.

3–10 September 1988
St Mary's College, Twickenham, Middlesex
Last week I accompanied two delegates to the above self-advocacy conference. For the past four years a group of thirty people with learning difficulties has been meeting regularly to plan this conference. It was the first international conference in the United Kingdom to be organised entirely by people with learning difficulties and the first event of its kind this side of the Atlantic. There were eighty delegates from overseas (USA, Canada, Australia) and 200 British delegates.

The following is a brief summary of the notes I took during some of the workshops and plenary sessions. (NB I was there in the role of 'supporter' and we were asked to 'take a back seat' – only speaking when invited to.)

Monday am   Plenary session

Nancy Ward (Nebraska People First)   What is self-advocacy?

> Self-advocacy teaches people with a disability to speak out for themselves . . . Self-advocacy is really important in people's lives – until I learned self-advocacy skills I didn't really see myself as a person . . . With all the labels people put on you – you don't have the confidence. Self-advocacy is seeing yourself as a person – start by just saying your name out loud.

Washington People First

Self-advocacy is about:

- standing up for yourself and speaking up for yourself;
- standing up for your personal rights and getting a better job;
- working together to make things better for people with handicaps.

London and Thames People First

> Four years ago I went to an international conference. I feel proud of myself – very strong and willing to speak up . . . We got the label changed from 'mental handicap' to 'people with learning difficulties' (referring to a local Social Services committee) . . . We changed the bus passes – now it doesn't say mental handicap . . . we've written to magazines about labelling (referring to correspondence in *Community Care*).

Notes from small-group discussions   Monday and Tuesday

On labelling

> I much prefer 'people with learning difficulties'.
>
> Throw it all out – get that 'retarded' out of there (referring to the ARC – (American Association for Retarded Citizens).
>
> How about 'American Association for Community Living' like they have in Canada? (Canada now has a 'Canadian Association for Community Living').

People First in Nebraska have worked with the senators and succeeded in removing the labels 'moron', 'idiot' and 'imbecile' from all their documentation (!). A Bill has been passed so that the term 'people who have mental retardation' will be used in future. Self-advocates saw this as a step in the right direction – 'At least they put the people first!'

> We don't like the name mentally handicapped – because we're not – are we?
>
> We might be a little bit slow, but we're just as good.
>
> I hate labels, I don't like being called 'spastic'.
>
> It makes me angry when people give me a label.
>
> The label 'retarded' follows you wherever you go.

Would you like labels on your back? We don't like it.

I'm just a slow learner but I catch on to things.

I am mentally retarded and I have to live with that for the rest of my life.

On living in the community

'Course we're going to have problems living in the community. Everybody has problems living in the community.

We learn from our mistakes.

We need to talk about what choices are open to us.

Biggest disability of all is people's attitudes – it's not us.

When I go shopping people keep knocking me with their handbags. They talk to my mum instead. Children usually say 'Mum, why is she in the chair?'

I'm working at McDonalds. I love it there.

On institutions

K: I got friends in an institution because their parents want them to have care and to be looked after.

P: But they can get that in the community. I was in an institution for eighteen years to control my epilepsy. My epilepsy wasn't controlled till I came to live in the community.

J: My mum didn't want me.

R: I live in a hospital with a thousand other people . . . lots of them don't know who their mum and dad are. I'm lucky, I know what my mum and dad look like. Some of them were left on the doorstep, or in a black bag.

M: It's like cruelty to animals. They don't want the animals so they throw them out.

R: A cat and a dog can get chucked out of home and go feed itself – a little new born baby can't.

On work

Licking envelopes, packing diapers – what I call them is real silly jobs. I was promised I would get a job from there sometime but I never did.

Workshop jobs aren't real jobs. They're just segregated programmes that'll put you there and keep you there.

Let them work for our job and get peanuts. All those that go out for these fancy lunches.

I came out of school in 1974 and had nowhere to go. I went to the workshop for five long years.

I hope these notes give you the 'flavour' of the conference.

Diane Amans also made notes in a personal diary, reflecting on some of the behind-the-scenes dilemmas she experienced. 'C' and 'S' are Christine Darbyshire and Steven Smith, the delegates she accompanied.

Sunday 4 Sept. – Monday 5 Sept.

C and S went for a walk. I heard them come back. I went to sleep. They stayed up all night. I didn't hear them but some people heard them talking.

I feel a real dilemma here. It's a self-advocacy conference – I shouldn't be wielding the power. But if they stop up all night are they going to participate during the day? Student's Union have funded them to be delegates – it's not just a free week in London. (They woke me at 6.15 am to see if I was all right!)

Monday – plenary session 9.30 am

C and S arrived five minutes late. I was relieved they'd turned up. They sat apart from me (understandably). After twenty minutes C came over to complain about S swearing. S came over – he was swearing about the overhead projector because he couldn't see it.

I pointed out that swearing upsets people.

Shortly afterwards they both left. I had a quick look but couldn't see them. Again the dilemma – how directive/bossy to be? I *feel* I should leave them to it but they are conference delegates and have a responsibility to participate. Think I'll have another chat and emphasise the responsibility. Don't want to be too heavy handed but I feel like taking them back home!

Despite the uncertainties reflected in the diary notes, there was a very positive follow-up to the conference. A press release was drawn up resulting in three local newspapers printing the story of Christine's ambition to found a People First group in the area.

Date   6 October 1988
Ref   L/263/88/CLG
Subject STARTING OUT

Christine Darbyshire, a student at Stockport College of Technology, is hoping to establish a 'People First' group for the borough.

'People First' is a world-wide organisation which encourages people with learning difficulties to be confident and independent individuals.

Christine's ambition to establish a local branch was fuelled by a recent visit to the 'People First: Voice of Our Own' conference in London.

This was organised by and for people with learning difficulties. It gave delegates the chance to discuss and share their problems.

Steven Smith, who studies with Christine, also attended. They were accompanied by Diane Amans, a college lecturer who runs courses for people with learning difficulties. Both students are in their mid-twenties.

Anyone interested in finding out more about 'People First' should contact Christine.

Put people first, pleads Christine

CHRISTINE Darbyshire, a student at Stockport College of Technology, is hoping to establish a People First group for the borough.

People First is a world-wide organisation which is designed to encourage people with learning difficul-ties. Christine's ambition to establish a local branch was fuelled by a recent visit to People First's 'Voice of Our Own' conference in London.

More information about People First can be obtained from Christine on 061-442 8772.

Manchester Evening News 26/10/88

Christine's crusade

STUDENT Christine Darbyshire is hoping to form a 'People First' group. The Stockport College of Technology student's ambition for a local branch was fuelled at a conference in London. 'People First' is a world-wide organisation which encourages people with learning difficulties to become confident and independent. Anyone interested should phone Christine on 442 8772.

The North Cheshire Herald 14/10/88

People first

A STOCKPORT student, Christine Darbyshire, is hoping to set up a 'People First' group in this area.

'People First' was estab-lished by and for people with learning difficulties. Christine's ambition to establish a local group of the world-wide organisation stemmed from a recent visit to the 'People First: Voice of Our Own' conference in London.

The Stockport Messenger 14/10/88

18   Day services: a users' account

People First

It seemed important to include in this Reader the views of people with learning difficulty on services provided for them. People First is an umbrella organisation for self-advocacy groups within the UK and internationally. Self-advocacy groups are a means of enabling people with learning difficulties to speak up for themselves, to share experiences and to begin to shape what happens to their lives. We have included this extract from the Report of a conference where people met to consider day services as it is an important contribution to some of the issues discussed in the Reader as a whole. The demands are hard-hitting and radical, and overall imply a change of control of services from service providers to service users.

18.1   Introduction

1   At the South West Core Group Workshop for People with Learning Disabilities held in June 1986, it was decided that the views of attenders at day service resources should be sought, to hear what they had to say about the way care is provided and organised.

2   This document is the users' account from a two-day conference, 'Day Service Users', held at the Exeter Moat House on 10 and 11 November 1986 to begin this process of consultation. It was arranged and supported by the members of the South Western Regional Core Group Day Services Working Party.

3   People who attended came from a variety of backgrounds throughout South, West and East Devon and Cornwall. There were thirty users of services of existing day services and nine paid personnel from Health and Social Services acted as notetakers, listeners and enablers.

4   As a result of the conference, this document has been produced as a verbatim report of that consultation process. It is very important to stress that the document represents an unaltered account of the views of consumers of our services. Some of these views are very challenging to paid employees of these services but this document shows that consultation is not only possible, but virtually necessary in the planning of services.

5   On the first day the users of services had a general discussion followed

by more specific discussions in small groups and on the evening of that day they decided for themselves the topics they wanted to discuss in detail on the second day. The statements made by the groups were recorded on flip charts and are produced in this document as a true and unaltered account.

6 It is planned that another conference will be held towards the end of April 1987, when the same participants will be invited back to decide how they would like the consultation process to proceed. One of the objectives of this conference will be to produce a formal consultation document setting out the views of users as to how future services could be developed in ways they consider to be relevant to their needs.

7 The participants themselves have already decided that local groups of consumers should be established. They also decided that they wanted their document to be sent to you. Your response to this document would be welcomed and will be fed back into the next conference.

18.2 The main aims of the two days

1 To provide an opportunity for people who use existing day services to present *their* comments on how these could be improved upon or altered.

2 To give people who use existing day services an opportunity to discuss how *they* want future day services to be planned and organised.

3 To record and publish these comments and ideas for presentation to whoever the people attending the two days feel to be relevant.

Hopefully this document and the follow-up will draw the attention of service planners to the vital importance of genuine and meaningful 'user' consultation, approval and support when planning, implementing and running future day services.

18.3 Major statements

The following major statements were highlighted by the participants as being those that were the most important to them arising from the discussions held over the two days. They arose from the final session of the conference.

- A fair day's wage for a fair day's work.
- The chance to train in a valued choice of experiences, with a range of

work that will enable us to achieve job satisfaction, and take our place as people.

- Big homes should be closed.
- ATCs should help us to get work but they are not places of work.
- We should have a total right to decide what we are called.
- Everybody should be able to attend their own review, all of it.
- Every ATC and residential setting should have a committee.
- We should change the name 'mentally handicapped' altogether.
- Attenders should be involved in interviewing for staff.
- There should be a trial period for appointment and attenders should be involved in assessment of performance.
- Training is needed for staff to change their attitudes and the way they 'work'.
- There should be opportunity for exchange of information and ideas between centres locally and nationally.
- If staff don't like more independent views of attenders . . . they can get on their bikes.
- Attenders and staff should not be segregated.
- Training should be a set period of time.
- Staff must answer to people and they must listen to what people say.
- People should choose their key workers and change them if they are no good.
- Key workers should help *you* to control all your money and help you to have more choices.

19 The world of the congenitally deaf-blind: towards the grounds for achieving human understanding

David A. Goode

David Goode spent eighteen months as a researcher on a ward for children who were congenitally deaf-blind. Here he describes in detail his approach to trying to discover and understand the world of one girl, Chris, who was deaf, blind and mentally handicapped as a result of rubella damage.

19.1 Meeting Chris on her 'own grounds'

The staff's institutional rationale and its concomitant 'purposes at hand' (maintenance and teaching) were directly related to the particular features they formulated about the residents. I came to understand that I could take advantage of my institutional position (my not being charged with maintenance and teaching) to pursue a particularly interesting line of research. I could examine the staff's construction of certain of the residents' behaviours as retarded (that is, as faulted) to discover the logical underpinnings behind their system of practical reasoning – a system which produced behaviour-displays-as-faulted. By doing this I hoped that I might also be able to unmask some of the skills the children exhibited – skills which the remedial stance of the staff was 'hiding'. This enterprise would entail establishing intersubjectivity with the residents on a somewhat different basis from that of the staff.

I saw my task as an attempt to establish intersubjectivity with Chris on more or less her 'own terms'. The problem was how to recognise what her 'own terms' were. First I attempted to approximate her perceptual environment by the simultaneous use of ear stops and blindfolds. I discovered that I was quick to make the necessary adaptations to the features of the visual/auditory world I already took for granted. This is not to say that the blindfolds and ear plugs did not cause me a lot of trouble, that they did not render me essentially helpless without the aid of a sighted and/or hearing person. Rather, the cognitive categories I already possessed allowed me to be deaf and blind in a fashion which bore little resemblance to the *congenital* deaf-blindness of the residents. There was no simple technology by which I could accomplish my purpose – any procedures would have to be accompanied by a 'willing suspension of belief'. It

seemed impossible to bridge this gap between our worlds and the consciousness interior to each. [. . .]

Obviously Chris did not share the staff's evaluation of her behaviours.
The construal of these behaviours as deficient was clearly an interpretation
of our seeing-hearing world view. I thought I could begin my task of willing
suspension of belief by attempting to separate the evaluative from the
descriptive components in my accounts of Chris's actions. This pursuit was
manifested in the following fieldnotes:

> Watching Chris walk it was clear that her arm movements were spastic, her
> gait wide, and her movements and balance awkward. She also did not seem
> to walk purposively – that is, she would walk a few steps, stop, bend over or
> stare into the sun, run, twist around, laugh, sit down, get up, walk, etc. *She
> seemed to enjoy the physical sensations involved in her admittedly 'abnormal'
> techniques for ambulation.* While it is clear that she does not walk correctly, it
> is equally clear that it is only incorrect with respect to the dominant
> seer-hearer culture's version of walking – a version, by virtue of her impaired
> sensors, almost inaccessible to her. Most importantly, while watching her we
> were occasioned to ask ourselves, 'Who is getting more from the activity of
> walking, Chris or us?' [. . .] The question is, how *should* we evaluate what we
> see? Is it 'wrong' to act abnormally, and does one's detection of 'abnormal'
> or 'faulted' behaviour require that remedial work be done upon the child to
> correct the observed flaws? These questions seem particularly important
> when asked with regard to persons who, in very obvious ways, do not share
> the perceptual cognitive world that occasions 'normal' walking.

[. . .] I felt I could use certain interactional procedures (changes in my
purposes at hand) in order to provide myself with an experiential basis for
the kind of understanding I sought. Achieving this understanding was to be
my new purpose at hand. I stopped trying to remedy the obvious faults I
perceived in Chris and tried instead to intuit, while interacting with her,
what purposiveness or rationality her activities might have from her
perspective. My first major change in interactional strategy was to allow
Chris to organise activities for both of us by *'remaining obediently passive'*.
On the first occasion I did this, she organised the following activity for us:

> *Activity No. 1, or 'MMmmm . . . mmm . . . K . . . h'*
> Chris manoeuvred me in such a way that she was lying on my lap face up and
> had me place my hand over her face. By holding my hand she eventually
> manoeuvred it in such a way that my palm was on her mouth and my index
> finger was on her right ('good') eye. She then indicated to me that she wanted
> me to tap on her eyelid, by picking my finger up and letting it fall on her eye
> repeatedly, smiling and laughing when I voluntarily took over this work as
> my own. (She has also 'shown me', by moving my body, that she wanted me
> to speak in her ear and flick my fingers across her good eye.) While I tapped
> Chris's eye, she licked and sniffed my palm occasionally and softly hummed
> seemingly melodic sounds. *We did this* for about ten or fifteen minutes.

I named this activity by the sound Chris produced while doing it, in order
to remind myself, even in the reading of my own material, that my purpose
was to burst the 'bubble' [of my own perceptual world]. To do this
consistently I could not *properly* code my sensory experience of the activity

into a natural language (as Chris apparently cannot do) because the 'bubble' and the 'language' were so intimately related that to sort one from the other would have been a practical impossibility. Thus, in my first encounter with Chris's desired form of interactional activity, I became aware that in my writing about the activity I necessarily transformed what it was she could possibly intend in organising it as she did. The description I sought to suspend belief in was itself imbedded in the very language I used to formulate my attempt. I realised that *my enterprise was a standing contradiction*, but I was willing to let this be, since to do otherwise would have meant to abandon all attempts to communicate to others what I was discovering. I was in much the same position as the anthropologist trying to code the native's language into his (the anthropologist's) own tongue. [. . .]

An interesting example of the use of natural language categories in 'making sense' of the residents was the staff's use of the category 'play'. Resident-initiated activities were considered by staff 'play' activities and not particularly relevant to their purposes at hand. Usually these activities merited a smile from the staff or an utterance such as 'Cute'. [. . .]

I introduced Chris to a small toy electric organ and observed the following:

> Chris would place her left hand on the keys of the organ which produced the lower frequency sounds. She would then engage in two related sets of body movements. One was to move her head and body in a rhythmic rocking motion which brought her right (good) ear closer and farther from the organ sound source. The other set of movements involved her leaning her head back so as to face the overhead light, and swivelling it back and forth, from side to side, accompanying these actions with vibrating her lips (something like the way little children imitate motorcycle sounds but without the vocal component). In both sets of body movements there was an obvious rhythmic quality – such as to suggest the kind of thing seer-hearers do when they are engrossed in the activity of keeping beat to music. In Chris's case, however, there was no clearly available beat to the droning sounds she was producing by holding the organ keys down.

As with Chris's brand of walking, my initial encounter with these behaviours was characterised by my engaging in the 'vulgarly available'. I 'naturally' saw that these behaviours were obstacles which I would have to overcome in my pedagogical enterprise (my initial purpose at hand) – a pedagogy designed to make Chris attend to sound in the 'right' way. Once I gave up this remedial stance towards Chris, her alternative treatment of light, sound and tactile stimulation took on a rational and even intelligent quality.

> I decided to *mimic her actions* in order to gain more direct access to what such activities were providing her. I utilised wax ear stops (placed more securely in the left ear, i.e. Chris has 'better' right ear than left ear) and gauzed my left eye with a single layer of lightweight gauze to simulate the scar tissue which covers Chris's left eye. I proceeded to imitate Chris's behaviours at the organ. While the procedure had its obvious inadequacies, with respect to my gaining access to Chris's experience of these activities, I did learn a number of interesting things in this way.

In both sets of body movements *the motion of the head itself gave the experienced sound a beatlike quality, and this was uniquely present by virtue of performing those movements.* In adapting to deficient eyes and ears and their resultant degraded perceptual fields, Chris had developed a way of 'doing' hearing, so as to make any long-term and reliable sound source available as a source of music. [. . .]

I discovered that Chris's head rolling provided not only for a beat to the music (which in its performance it does), but also for what one observer called a 'light show'. By 'light show' I mean that the head rolling, which Chris performed with her head leaned back and her eyes facing the overhead fluorescent light, provided an overall effect something like the following: alternative musical beats, occurring when the head was accelerating from one extreme position to the other, were culminated, when the head came to rest, in either light stimulation (when the head rested on the left shoulder, thus directing her good eye toward the light) or a lack of light stimulation (*when the head rested on the right shoulder, thus interposing her nose between the light source and her good right eye*). [. . .]

Another excerpt from my fieldnotes is relevant to the present discussion. This was written after a particularly interesting teaching session with Chris (Goode, 1974). I was trying to demonstrate the use of various music-making toys *vis-à-vis* the 'familiarising' procedures described by Robbins (1963)

[. . .] Initially, our play sessions consisted in precisely my attempting to provide for her the 'proper' cultural formula – that object X is a rattle and is to be used (in satisfaction of the criteria of a rational course of action) in such and such ways. I would hand her the rattle after demonstrating its use to her by placing the rattle in her hand and placing her hand within my own, then engaging in the appropriate shaking motion. While such demonstrations were successful in that Chris would hold and shake the rattle appropriately and unassisted (for ten seconds or so), she invariably brought the rattle to her right (good) eye or mouthed it. She would bring it within two inches of her eye with the apparent purpose of determining what it could visually supply for her (parts of the rattle were metal and reflected the fluorescent light in the room). This visual examination would be of short duration (less than fifteen seconds). Of the longest duration, often lasting till I would interrupt her somewhat intense involvement, was her use of the rattle as an object with which she could obtain various forms of stimulation in and about the mouth. Parts of the rattle were employed as tongue thumper or lip thumper, licked inside and outside the mouth, rubbed against the front teeth, banged against the front teeth, pushed against her cheek, and so on. Characteristically, when Chris was through with or had exhausted the immediately present and interesting possibilities of the rattle, she would drop it with no concern as to where it fell, its breakability, or its future uses. While such actions were easily accessible as 'problems' with regard to teaching Chris to use objects appropriately (similar behaviour was observed with regard to many objects), I was occasioned to ask myself: Who is getting maximum mileage out of the rattle? Is it we, who use it singularly and for specific purposes, or Chris, who uses it in a variety of ways? Let's put it another way. What Chris's not knowing how to use a rattle might mean is problematic. Her not knowing disqualifies her from membership in the category of persons who know how to use a rattle. However, it also *qualifies* her as a member of a category of persons who, by virtue of their not knowing how to use a rattle, do things with it which are inaccessible to persons who 'know' its proper use. *The superordinate ranking of our use of the rattle, on the basis that we realise its intended purpose by our actions, constitutes the 'ground' for the pejorative figure 'Chris does not use the rattle appropriately'.*

[. . .] My initial reading of these observations provided me with two general categories of finding. One concerned the reasoning embedded in my (and the staff's) 'fault-finding procedures' with the residents, and one concerned the rationality of purposiveness (from Chris's point of view) behind these same behaviours. [. . .]

With regard to Chris's purposiveness, she was basically self-seeking, hedonistic and amoral in her interactions. She would often rub her genitals against me or pantomime her (our?) recognised 'behaviour display' to denote a rocking or swinging activity. She did not seem to care whether I was getting pleasure from the activity. Instead she focused on structuring the interaction so that she could get as much of what she inwardly recognised as 'good feelings', though I really don't 'know' what those words index in terms of her experience. This seemed quite understandable to me since, in terms of her life on the ward, Chris did not live a life particularly filled with gratification – especially when she was interacting with others. However, left to herself, she was quick to provide herself, through varieties of autostimulatory behaviours, with experiences which she apparently enjoyed. Generally she occupied a powerless and frustrating position in many of her interactions and did not have the cognitive equipment (concepts, language, logic) through which she could rationalise (understand). She could only accept or reject, and on rare occasions 'puzzle'. She did not have the physical capability to aggress or, for that matter, to even defend herself against 'attack'. Compliance with sometimes not understood pulls and pushes from staff was characteristic. When staff could not force compliance (for example, when her language teacher could not get her to make the sound 'Mmmm'), she seemed to sit in a sort of dull passivity. Other times she seemed to be puzzling – that is, trying to 'code' what it was I was trying to do into some understanding or feeling she could deal with – what a programme administrator called her interior 'language' system. Generally when she initiated interaction it was to seek as much pleasure as she could, however she could. We often index such a behaviour pattern by the term 'infantile', but Chris was no infant. She was nine years old and had lived long enough to have gained some sophistication in achieving her pleasure-seeking activities.

Within the limits of hospital routine, I co-operated with her in achieving her goals. I became a sort of 'superplaymate' – perhaps (with the possible exception of her father) the only one in her life she had ever had. While there were a number of sympathetic and loving custodians and teachers in her life, the institutional definition of their relationships to Chris prevented them from simply co-operating with her. From time to time I did observe activities in which the staff's role was precisely to be Chris's playmate (for example when it was hot out and they would sprinkle the residents with a hose, or when they took the residents to the pool to 'swim'), and on these occasions the staff and residents seemed to enjoy themselves immensely. By the end of my stay on the ward I had become a little sad about the way in which the institutional and medical 'contexting' of the children seemed to victimise the staff as well as the children. An even sadder thought was the impossibility of ever changing this situation under the present approach in the fields of human servicing. [. . .]

> For Chris, *objects can only be sources of perceptual stimulation of the sorts outlined above.* When I watched her 'do her thing', it was with both joy and sorrow that I appreciated what I was seeing. *Her blindness and her deafness constituted her strongest asset as well as her greatest deficiency.* They sometimes provided her with incredibly intense enjoyment of the simplest things. At other times they were a source of 'troubles' as equally intense.

My abilities to see and hear allowed me to engage in the practices by which the culturally defined objects and activities of my world were realised. These abilities allowed me to experience certain pleasures as well as pains. Obviously, Chris did not comply with culturally prescribed courses of rational activity. Yet in a more generic sense, she seemed to conduct herself quite rationally. Perhaps she could not give her hedonistic pursuits names like 'self-realisation', 'the pursuit of personal power' or 'transcendence', but that she was a pleasure-seeking creature made her quite understandable to me. In this most basic enterprise, we were in basic agreement. We just used different technologies to accomplish our goal.

19.2   Concluding remarks

All creatures, that is, all subjectivities, seek, in their own terms, to fulfil needs and to gratify themselves. They do not do this in any haphazard fashion. Certain needs must be met before others, and in Chris's case survival-related needs were almost exclusively taken care of for her by others. Next in her 'motivational' hierarchy were emotional and perceptual gratification, and in this regard she was not dissimilar to other humans. She differed primarily in the forms in which these needs would be met. Many of the rational activities of our culture are built upon these very motivational projects. But the specification of these enterprises into culturally acceptable forms is not what defines our humanity to ourselves or to others. If we learn to believe this, then we have stopped one of our basic self-deceptions and have moved away from a view of man which raises us above other creatures – which affirms our presence here as an 'emergent' phenomenon. We are not 'better' than other creatures. We are 'different'. I was not 'better' than Chris; I was, in many ways, 'different'.

Acknowledgments

This research was supported by PSH Grant No. HD 04612 NICHD, The Mental Retardation Research Center, UCLA, and No. HD 05540–02, Patterns of Care and the Development of the Retarded. My special thanks for their assistance in guiding my enterprise to Robert B. Edgerton, Harold Garfinkel, Melvin Pollner, and Michael Gaddy. My thanks to Harold Levine for his editorial assistance.

References

GOODE, D. (1974) 'Some aspects of interaction among congenitally deaf-blind and normal persons', unpublished Working Paper No. 1, Mental Retardation Center, UCLA Medical Center.

ROBBINS, N. (1963) *Auditory Training in the Perkins Deaf-Blind Department*, Perkin School Publication No. 23.

20 Barry: a case study

Valerie Sinason

20.1 Personal history

[. . .] Barry (not his real name) was the second child born to working-class parents whose marriage was already in difficulties after the birth of the oldest daughter who suffered from spina bifida and died six months ago. Depression over the precarious existence of the daughter (who had additional severe medical problems) meant that, apart from a painful forceps delivery, Barry was perceived as a perfect quiet baby. It was only a routine clinic visit that determined he was cerebral palsied and slow to develop. However, mother was only concerned by Barry when he began attending a special day care nursery at two years and displayed aggressive disturbed behaviour. At the age of three his attacks on himself were so dangerous that he was admitted to hospital. It was at this time his father left home, after a violent deterioration in the marital relationship. Father behaved violently to mother in the last months of their marriage and there was some worry that Barry might have been hurt too whilst father was in an alcoholic state. Shortly after, Barry was admitted to a special assessment unit for the mentally handicapped and an intensive behavioural pro-gramme began with some intitial improvement. However, two weeks after the termination of the programme he was damaging himself again. In April 1980 he was admitted to a residential home for severely mentally and physically handicapped children and attended the linked special school.

Further help was sought from the assessment unit but the effect on Barry was to make him attack different parts of his body, instead of his head. The children's home were worried that if he continued being so violent they would not be able to contain him much longer and they did not want to see him transferred to a subnormality hospital. His mother cares for him and visits him each weekend but cannot be left on her own with him as he is so violent.

The staff of the children's home, together with his mother, referred him three years ago as 'he has been treated in the well-tried and trusted method of behaviour modification which is usual for mentally handicapped children displaying behaviour problems but it has not been successful'. At the age of seven he caused concern not just over his own safety from head-banging, but also for his violence to staff. The referral letter made the point that the staff felt he would respond to something psychoanalytical but no child guidance clinic nearby wanted to take on such a patient. They made clear they would provide an escort, driver and his mother to accompany him if we would take him on.

It was agreed that I would make an initial visit to the children's home. The referral letter had mentioned difficult staff systems in the short-staffed home and we wondered whether some of Barry's fury was linked to that. However, a visit to the home emphasised the fact that, although the shift system was disturbing, the home was an extremely caring one that gave the children ample warning of all changes. Barry, it was emphasised, found all changes unbearable, even down to standing up from having been in a sitting position. We agreed I would meet with Barry for some exploratory sessions.

20.2   Clinical material

In the waiting room a slumped, twisted, ferocious-looking boy was jammed between his mother and a key worker. I could not see his face. When I introduced myself his legs went into an amazing forceful action as if they had a life of their own. Before the moment of seeing him I had disbelieved the social report which stated his mother could not be on her own with him. I could not believe that a seven-year-old could be so violent. Now I did. This primitive infantile biting and kicking had tremendous power. I realised I would not be safe on my own with him and asked the mother and worker to bring him to my room and stay. I was very impressed by the kind and calm way they helped him, heaving and spitting, along the corridor, clearly helped by the behavioural advice they had received from the special unit.

Inside the room they placed Barry on an armchair and sat at the side on ordinary chairs. Barry grunted and screamed all the way to the room, but the moment he was sitting he moved into a foetal position and then said clearly and distinctly the word 'Shy'.

Tears filled his mother's eyes. The social worker looked sad and I felt immensely moved. His mother said he had never said the word 'shy' before. She did not even know he knew it. Barry started head-banging ferociously. The sound really hurt. But I restrained his mother from moving to him to hold his hands.

I started talking, saying how he had said he was 'shy' and that wasn't surprising since I was a stranger to him. He didn't know me. His fist stopped in mid-air. I carried on speaking, saying he was telling all of us that he knew his mum and key worker and all the people at the children's home. He was used to seeing lots of people, but he didn't know me. His fist flopped on to his lap and I was at peace, knowing that meaning was there and I was at work.

I then explained why he was coming – how people were worrying about him hurting his head and how they felt he was sad. I explained he would come to this room a few times and there were toys on the table. The moment I mentioned toys, he ferociously banged his head. When I said he was worried about being in this new room, looking inside a bag at new toys he stopped banging. Other features of the first session were that he banged his head whenever there was a sound from outside the room. Alternatively, he would curl up and close his eyes like a baby. When I said there were five minutes left he moved the vestigial fingers of his deformed hand and then hid it under his head. I wondered aloud whether he was showing me his struggling hand now it was time to go and maybe there was a struggle between the Barry who had powerful legs and could run and a handicapped Barry. When it was time he kicked the table with great force at me.

On the second meeting, again with his mother and worker, he screamed and banged all the way to the room but was quiet on sitting down. Not a single word came from him, just a piercing cry at odd moments. He banged his head whenever the wind blew or there were footsteps. At one time when there were particularly loud footsteps outside he went into a newborn falling reflex. I wondered here whether the tiredness was because of all the energy that went into maintaining an unborn state where no other life existed.

It took me until the third meeting to dare to say aloud to Barry that I did not feel ready to see him on my own yet until I felt I could protect myself and him from his violence. I thought we must be connecting more for him to allow me to have that thought and utter it and for him to not bang his head when I said it. Fifteen minutes before the end of the session he fell asleep.

During the fourth session, a major change happened. For the first time, with his head still twisted away from me, Barry held up both his hands to show me very clearly the differences between them: not just the organic difference between the ordinary and the handicapped hand, but the secondary handicap he had inflicted on himself by his own banging. He then held up the hand he banged with in such a way as to conceal it from his mother and key worker. I was very struck with the injuries he had made. There was a huge swelling on two knuckles with a red bruise at the tip of each. I was aware of the thought that he had made two breasts – that maybe he was attacking his mother in fury at the handicapped body he had been endowed with but also adding to his body at the same time. I did not feel I could make such a comment in front of his mother and worker. I said instead that he was showing me how angry he was about being handicapped and that when he banged he showed that anger as well as making his knuckles larger. I then said, feeling terrified and daring, that I would see him on his own next week but that his mother and worker would bring and collect him. As usual he fell asleep fifteen minutes before the end of the session.

The fifth session was the first on his own. It was also crucial as it would determine if therapy was possible. After the usual banging and kicking on the way he was put on the chair by mother and key worker who then left quickly, looking relieved and apprehensive at the same time. Barry was in his usual foetal position. It was only in this session that I became aware that he always curled up with the normal side of his face showing and the handicapped side hidden. Gritting my teeth, I wondered this aloud. For a moment I sat in terror. To my amazement he suddenly sat bolt upright and faced me. He looked proud and furious. I felt overwhelmed.

The feelings he evoked in me at that moment made me realise with terrible clarity that the twisted postures he took up were a terrible self-made caricature of his original handicap, so that he could not be seen as he truly was. I was filled with images of subnormality hospitals and all the twisted movements and guttural speaking which I had previously taken as inevitable consequences of brain damage or retardation. I found myself wondering about that. Barry fell asleep at his usual fifteen minutes before the end of the session and this time I was able to comment to him that he knew the time was coming to an end and wanted to be asleep. He would spit quietly and wake up when I spoke. I was also struck by the unborn stance he seemed to remain in, where living tired him so enormously. The home said he slept long hours as well as catnapping. Right at the end I asked him if he wanted to continue coming to see me. There was no reply. I asked him to raise a finger if he wanted to carry on seeing me. He raised a finger and has continued coming for three years to date, with only two absences for colds, both on the last session before a holiday!

There was a big visual change in Barry over the next few weeks. In the waiting room he could be seen sitting upright or standing hugging his mother. Several therapists told me their patients were mentioning this boy in the waiting room who used to look terrible but was really nice-looking. The home commented that he was calm for the rest of the day after coming to see me and for the next day and we were agreed that the next important stage would be for me to dare to take him from the waiting room to the therapy room myself and back.

The last session before Christmas, he got a cold and the staff were very aware of the clear meaning in that and reported that his sense of time had become very accurate as well as his memory. Although he was visibly alert, he was still not using speech with me apart from a chant, 'Your chair my chair' and 'Piss off'.

After Christmas I started taking him to the therapy room on my own and returning with him to the waiting room afterwards. I felt extremely frightened but he managed and has managed ever since, apart from a regression following the death of his sister, when he would not come to the room without his mother and worker escorting him. The triumph Barry and I both felt at managing the fear of his violence was visible in the proud way he hugged his mother and worker on his arrival back for the first few months of going alone with me. His mother even said 'Well done, you brave boy'.

The changes that came in the next three months (after which we decided to continue therapy indefinitely) are at one level slow and yet they were immensely exciting and moving. My affective responses have been a mixture of hope and terror.

The changes almost make a visual graph of gradual movements towards closeness. Here are examples.

21 January (1984). He says, 'Hello.'

28 January. He asks, 'Time yet?' just before the end of the session. He also looks briefly at the toys. I realise that our chairs are not opposite as Barry's has been placed in the corner to give him the security of two walls. I mention this and tell him next week I will move his chair.

4 February. He says his longest sentence as we walk back to the waiting room: 'Hello, did you see my mum?'

11 February. He stares at the toys all the time.

18 February. His nose runs and he looks desperately at the box of tissues on the table. I offer him one. He cannot bear to be helped and says, 'No thank you.'

25 February. He kicks the toy bag over in order to see the toys. I realise the drawing paper is creased from having been brought in weekly for months without being used. I mention this and say I will bring new paper next week. I also mention the desk is too far for him to be able to reach it. (I had moved it after our first session as a protection against his violence.)

4 March. I bring new paper and move the desk near him. He kicks the toy bag accurately so all the toys spill over and looks at them carefully.

The most important change was one year after therapy. I was suddenly aware that when Barry banged his head he was making enormous spitting noises and sound effects but in fact he was miming banging his head. When I said he was not hurting his thoughts so much, he was thinking more about what I said, he lifted his hands to show me the bumps had subsided. I told the home my observation and they then realised it was true too.

After 1½ years Barry stopped falling asleep and I realised how sleeping must have been a protection for all the exhaustion he felt at being in the world trying to control all the noises and actions around him. When I gave a comment he did not like he would mime a head-bang and then mime sleeping and then open his eyes and say 'Shut up.' He was losing his secondary handicaps, his defences against meaning, and he felt very mixed and exposed about it. It was at this point that he suddenly burst into a terrible caricature of handicapped singing, 'Old MacDonald Had a Farm'. He was singing in the guttural voice I had often felt was intrinsically linked with handicap, just as I had felt previously the twisted postures were. But there was something in the meaning he was conveying that made me say, with great terror, that maybe he felt there was room here for the animal noises and feelings in him; but maybe too he wanted to see if I was an idiot who thought that was his real singing voice. He looked at me in a startled but proud way and then started to cry terribly and deeply.

This pitiful crying was a strong feature for the next six months and is difficult to put into words. It is not crying that is asking for a word or a hug. It is a weeping that is to do with a terrible sense of aloneness and the reality of that. Neville Symington has commented that weeping comes when there is a breakthrough with this kind of patient and it represents a real awareness of all the meaning that has been lost in the years up to that moment as well as the aloneness of handicap.

His mother and worker were very distressed to see the weeping state Barry was in when I brought him back. They were worried therapy might be too cruel for him. I felt worried at the pain he was in and when he desperately wept 'Go now. See Mummy' I had to struggle not to give in. We both managed to keep him in the room for this phase.

Then a change happened. It was heralded by a session in which, when I said it was time, Barry reached in his pocket and threw a toy watch at me. There was a lot of anger in his throw and a lot of accuracy. It was also a toy he had brought from the home, not one of the therapy toys. Nevertheless, it was at this point that the terrible crying stopped and several changes were noted at the home. Barry was more affectionate and responsive. He had stopped injuring himself. However, he was not only still violent to staff; he was more dangerous because he could aim accurately. Previously, he just had to be sat in a chair and he would go to sleep and stop being violent. Now, he would stand up immediately and attack as he did not mind physical changes so much!

In the last year other changes have happened. Barry tried masturbating for a while, at the home and in his sessions, to provide himself with another piece of self-comforting since banging and sleeping were no longer available to him. However, this stopped very quickly. He understood it too well.

He is no longer startled by external noises and does not need as much sleep as he did. After two years of therapy there was a session in which, in the silence, my stomach gurgled loudly. His face lit up. 'Your tummy?' he asked. I said yes, it was my tummy. He giggled. I said he knew the sound was inside my tummy. He agreed. It started raining. 'Rain outside,' said Barry with a happy smile. There was a startled pause. A telephone could be heard next door. Barry put a hand to his ear. 'Outside the room,' he pronounced. From that moment there was an extra degree of hope and aliveness in the sessions. Barry had differentiated between inside and outside and had achieved a 'psychological birth' within the room. In the same session he called the toys I provided 'Horrible toys' and giggled.

A few months ago I bought a soft toy, a puppy, for the therapy room as Barry always gives me a Christmas card with a dog on it, and when he sang 'Old MacDonald' it was the dog he sang of first. On the first occasion he saw it, having been warned for several weeks, he held it to him and hugged it with his back to me the whole session, not uttering a word.

He has not touched it since but looks at it wistfully. When I comment on his fear of getting close to me, the dog and the toys, his fear that he will be violent because he won't be able to bear it, he says 'Stupid.' He knows the meaning of the word 'stupid' because he knows that is not what he really is.

In the last few months Barry has begun to talk softly, so softly I can hardly hear, to the blanket on his armchair or to parts of the chair or the dog. It feels as if there is a transitional talking space he has made, linked to the transitional object of the toy puppy. At his home they say he spends a lot of time that he used to spend being asleep talking to objects in his room, his bed, his shoes, his pillow. He has been able to spend the first tentative moments with his mother without being violent. At the same time his violence to staff is still very worrying and includes kicks to the eye, stitches in the thigh for bites, impetigo on the face from his spitting attacks.

When his sister died his mother did not want it mentioned and staff were very worried about what to do. Barry solved it for them by taking advantage of a cot death in a soap opera to say 'Baby dead. Mary dead.' Again, nobody knew he was aware of the word.

Now Barry has been in therapy for three years. His home sent me a report last week saying:

> Since his visits to the Tavistock, staff have noticed progress in his development. He is sometimes able to warn of his aggression and is now guilty for some of the hurt he causes. He has started to say who he will miss and asks questions about staff who leave. He has been able to get closer to his mother. However, although he shows he can develop through understanding his violence can be so great it is difficult to restrain him.

When his sister died, Barry was terrified his mother would not visit him. In the sessions he would return to his old painful crying of 'Mum, now, please' and then be absolutely silent and still. In these moments I was aware that my mind wandered from him to other events. I was shocked and then realised he was wanting to be good and dead, the 'perfect' baby, so I could be preoccupied with other things. I commented that he was not just calling for Mum in the waiting room, but had a painful feeling of a longed-for Mum-in-the-room who might be so upset about an ill Mary (and now a dead Mary) and a furious husband leaving home that she just wanted a good, quiet, dead baby Barry. It had taken three years to move through the issues to do with his handicap to the events in his physical family life. Last week, when we were looking at these issues, Barry held his hand for me to hold at the end of the session. As I reached for it he looked at the untouched toy dog and cried and then said 'Arm hurts' and kicked the toy mother and father dolls lying on the floor from his earlier throws. It brought back a query in the minds of staff as well as myself as to whether in addition to witnessing marital violence he had been beaten himself. There was also the question of the injury he felt had been done to him by his handicap and the possible relationship in his mind between the violent sexual couple and his hurt arm. In these three years Barry could easily have wrecked his therapy time by being too violent for me to manage or by being too difficult to take on a two-hour journey. He was violent once in the car coming and was told, after the staff and I discussed it, that if he did that again a different larger car would be needed to provide room for another escort. This would mean a different therapy time too and possibly another room. Barry firmly stated 'Not another room' and has not been violent since on the journey, two hours each way! [. . .]

21 Stigma and the self-concept of people with a mild mental handicap

Andrew Jahoda, Ivana Markova and Martin Cattermole

21.1 Introduction

Most of the past research concerned with the study of the self-concept of people with a mild mental handicap used self-concept tests standardised for the general population (for reviews see Schurr *et al.*, 1970; Gowans and Hulbert, 1983). The results of this psychometric approach are commonly expressed as quantitative statements about the location of the self-concept of people with a mild mental handicap on a continuum from 'positive' to 'negative'. Since such scores are purely external to the person whose self-concept is so measured, they are uninformative. They do not help one to understand the internal mental processes of the individuals sharing the common experience of having difficulties in mastering certain skills considered important by society. Neither do such scores enable one to understand the stigma imposed by the society on individuals with a mental handicap.

The classic work of Edgerton (1967) employed participant observation for studying the lives of people with a mental handicap who had moved out of an institution into the community. In a subsequent paper, Koegel and Edgerton (1982) investigated a group of black Americans who had recently left a school for people with a mild mental handicap. The main concern in these studies was to identify the reactions to stigma, using investigation strategies based on the concepts of Goffman (1963). In the former study, Edgerton argued that people with a mental handicap 'denied' their handicap, while in the latter study the authors divided the respondents into those who 'denied' or avoided the topic, and those who declared themselves as 'handicapped'. Zetlin and Turner (1984) produced a more extensive typology of how the participants coped with stigma, and related the 'type' of response to features of the participants' backgrounds and circumstances. The crucial element identified by these authors in determining how the participants dealt with stigma were the attitudes and socialisation practices of their parents. Although these studies made a valuable contribution to the understanding of the meaning of stigma for people with a mental handicap, they did not attempt primarily to gain insight into the relationship between the experience of stigma and the self-concept. [. . .]

At present, the most commonly adopted approach to the study of the self is based on social construction theory. According to this theory, one's self-concept is largely determined by the ways in which one is treated by significant others. [. . .] On the basis of this theory, one might expect that those people who are stigmatised by their significant others are likely to internalise a stigmatised view of themselves. Thus, according to this theory, it would be expected that people with a mental handicap and, in particular, those who have been segregated from their childhood in special schools, who attend clubs for people with a mental handicap and who work in segregated centres, must have developed a view of themselves as essentially different from those who live in ordinary, that is unsegregated, social environments. The purpose of this study was to explore this expectation. In order to do so, an attempt was made to combine two rather different approaches: the phenomenological and the quantitative. The primary aim of the study was to gain as much understanding as possible into the experience of people with a mental handicap and into the nature of their self-concept. [. . .]

The time-consuming intensive interviews meant that the samples had to be small, though they were not unrepresentative. While this is a disadvantage, one can have considerable confidence in those statistically significant relationships that emerged from this approach.

21.2   Method

Sample

Thirty-six people participated in this study. They consisted of the following groups: five men and seven women with a mild mental handicap, aged 21–40 years, living at home and attending adult training centres (ATCs); their mothers (in one instance an aunt); and the member of staff at the ATC who worked most closely with the person with a mental handicap in each of the twelve cases. While all thirty-six participated in the study, the term 'participants' will be reserved for the people with a mental handicap, and mothers and staff will be described as such. [. . .]

Procedure and interviews

Semi-structured interviews were carried out with the participants, their mothers and staff. Prior to the interviews, about twelve hours were spent gaining the confidence of the participants and an undertaking was given to maintain strict confidentiality. The interview was not solely concerned with their feelings about attending the ATC, it was about their lives outside the ATC as well. Therefore, the interviewer attempted to spend time with the participants at clubs and other leisure activities outside the ATC. [. . .] The interviewer had a list of areas to cover while attempting to promote a dialogue and allowing the participants to raise issues which they saw as important. The areas covered in the interview were the following: social life, autonomy, handicap and stigma. Information about social life and autonomy was obtained first by a direct line of questioning, and was entered on structured information sheets. The subjects of stigma and handicap were approached indirectly. The interviewer did not use the word 'handicap' or assume that participants felt stigmatised in any way. Instead, he explored their experience and raised issues which were thought to be pertinent to the participants' views of themselves. The same line of questioning was adapted for obtaining mothers' and staff's attitudes toward the participants as persons, and the issues covered in these interviews remained essentially the same as for people with a mental handicap. Those issues relating to stigma and handicap were: (1) the participants' attendance at specialist services and how they thought that these services were regarded by people outside the ATC, (2) the extent to which they had experienced abuse or discriminatory treatment (for example, the relation between their own and their siblings' social life), (3) how they felt they were treated by significant others at home, at the ATC and at leisure activities, and (4) how the participants regarded themselves relative to others (for example, peers at the ATC, non-handicapped peers and people more handicapped than themselves). The data on social activities and autonomy provided by each participant, his or her mother and staff member were then collapsed into one set of data to produce the most complete account.

Most of the participants and mothers involved appeared glad of the opportunity to discuss these issues, and their emotional response indicated its importance for them.

Analysis of the data concerning stigma and handicap

The scrutiny of the participants' interview transcripts has revealed a common thread in these transcripts: the participants' perception of themselves in relation to non-handicapped people. This perception was directly based on the participants' acceptance or rejection of a stigmatised view of themselves. Since this perception stood out from the remainder of the interviews as a central feature, the authors have decided to use it as a framework within which to analyse the participants' concepts of the self. This does not mean that the participants' self-concepts are static over different contexts and over time. Individual and environment are relational phenomena, and the individual's concept of the self and his or her social world are mutually interdependent. It is to be expected that when the individual's personal and social circumstances change so does his or her self-concept.

The purpose of the categorisation as described below, therefore, is not to produce a discrete dichotomy of people's self-concepts. Rather, the categories provide a framework for the understanding of the individual's perceptions based on his or her own diagnosis of the self. The following categories were adopted for the analysis of the participant's responses.

Essentially different from non-handicapped people   Participants who fell into this category felt globally handicapped. They did not just regard themselves as having a disability but accepted the imposed stereotype of a handicapped person. Thus, on the whole, these participants did not expect to receive the same opportunities (that is, for work, leisure, or having a relationship and taking everyday risks) as non-handicapped people. Their belief that they needed 'special' treatment was justified by them by their 'handicapped identity', as opposed to their actual disability.

Essentially the same as non-handicapped people   Participants who fell into the second category felt that they were only different in so far as they had a disability or a learning difficulty. They did not feel that their handicap affected their personhood or that they deserved to be seen or treated as less worthy individuals than non-handicapped people.

These categories also proved a valid framework within which to place the mothers' and staff members' views of the participants. Thus, the material from mother and staff interviews was also examined to determine the category which the participant best filled. The process of categorising the views of the participants, and the attitudes of the parents and staff, brought out the different ways in which the participants saw themselves and were seen by the parents and staff.

The interviews were rated by a second judge for one-third of the sample (four participants, parents and staff), making a total of twelve judgments. There was agreement between the two judges on ten out of the twelve ratings.

21.3   Results

All twelve participants had an insight into their situation as 'stigmatised individuals'. They knew that to be regarded as a 'handicapped' person often resulted in being treated as someone who did not deserve parity with non-handicapped people. [. . .]

Participants

Essentially different   Three participants accepted a primarily handicapped status. They felt that they could not engage in the same kinds of activity as non-handicapped people. Two of them resented this. A woman aged twenty-seven years said:

> Well the people who are outside working, like shops and the bank and everything . . . I says to myself they're all right, they're no handicapped, they can do anything outside the centre they like. They can go away to pubs or

discos or anything like that which I cannae do, you know. Not that it really bugs me, but I like to do these sort of things and I just cannae do it. It's just one of these things that happens.

Essentially the same Two distinct perspectives characterised the nine participants who rejected an essentially different status (one participant expressed both views at different points of the interview). The first group of two participants set themselves apart from the other people with a mental handicap, arguing that they did not have a *general* cognitive deficit but had *particular* difficulties with activities such as reading and writing. They felt that they only attended a day centre for people with a mental handicap because they could not obtain jobs. However, they felt they were different from other people with more severe disabilities who really were 'handicapped'. They were aware, though, that 'non-handicapped' people treated them in a stigmatised manner, or in a way they regarded as unjustified by their actual disability. For instance, they all reported being treated in a child-like way in the ATC or at home. These participants did not simply want to assert that they were not globally 'handicapped', but they also wanted to distance themselves from the stigma associated with handicap. For example, a woman, L, aged twenty-six, repeated what the organiser of a club for people with a mental handicap had said about her to other club members: 'L is not mentally handicapped because she's a leader. She can camp out, use public transport. If L was mentally handicapped she would not be able to go on holiday. L is not mentally handicapped. She's only at the ATC because she cannot get a job.'

The second position adopted by six participants was a 'minority group' approach. Although they recognised that their disability was very mild relative to that of many of their peers in the ATC, the participants showed solidarity with these people. They did not just reject the stigma attached to themselves but the stigma attached to all people with a mental handicap. These participants thought that to set themselves apart from other people in the centre would make them guilty of stigmatising others. A man aged forty years with Down's syndrome expressed this position as follows: 'Nobody is different on this earth, nobody is different, you are in this world what you are and how God made you. You've got your nature, everybody has, you've got your feelings.'

Mothers

Essentially different There were two distinct levels of 'global handicap' presented by mothers. The more extreme group of four mothers perceived the participants' very personality, emotions and interpersonal relationships as essentially different from those of ordinary people. These mothers considered that the very fact that the participants had a handicap meant that they were cut off from the wider social realities, and that they were 'happy in their own wee world', to quote one of them. It was inconceivable that their sons or daughters should have ordinary aspirations for interpersonal relationships or obtaining jobs. The notion that people with a mental handicap remain in a child-like state was put forward as an explanation by three of these mothers. As the mother of a woman aged twenty-nine said: 'She can be quite sensible and quite astute at times, but when it comes down to the bottom line she's still a child . . . if you look at them they do not age'.

The other set of four mothers saw their sons or daughters as equal to anyone on a person to person level, but 'handicapped' in a wider social context. Thus, they respected the individual, but doing things in the wider community like ordinary leisure activities or work was forbidden not because of the individual's disability as such, but just because he or she was 'handicapped'. One mother had told her daughter that she had to go to a special school: 'Because you're handicapped, you're special, you're different from other people. (On a personal level the mother had a different outlook) . . . Well, we just treat her as normal – well in the house we do.'

Essentially the same   There were two different attitudes adopted by the mothers who saw their sons or daughters as essentially the same as non-handicapped people. Two mothers recognised the person's disability and sometimes they referred to the individual as 'handicapped'. However, they resented the discrimination which resulted in their son or daughter's exclusion from mainstream social activities or employment, and rejected negative stereotypes of people with a mental handicap. As the mother of one woman aged twenty-four explained: 'I'll tell you why she works better than anybody: because they've got to prove to themselves and everybody else that they're as good as anybody.'

Two mothers in this group denied that their son or daughter had a handicap or disability and did not regard stigma as a problem.

Staff

Essentially different   There were five members of staff, like the mothers, who viewed the participant as a different kind of person with different needs and an outlook on life defined by being 'handicapped'. As a staff member said about a man aged forty-six years: 'I think, for his mentality, it (his social life) was quite satisfactory.'

Essentially the same   The attitudes expressed by two of the staff members would fit well with those of the first two mothers who regarded the participants as essentially the same. The feature of five staff members that differentiated them from the mothers was their preoccupation with ability. The staff members did not necessarily think that people with a mental handicap deserved equal status to ordinary people. Rather, the participant was simply considered too able to be labelled as 'handicapped'.

Social life

The participants' social lives revolved round activities organised for people with a mental handicap and/or activities with parents, siblings and relatives. The participants' ordinary activities normally took place in the company of relatives, friends from the ATC or people they met at the above-mentioned clubs. [. . .] Their degree of isolation from mainstream society was highlighted by the fact that none of them had any non-handicapped friends or even knew anyone they could go out with for an occasional evening.

No significant relationship was found between the participants' involvement in ordinary activities and their mothers' attitudes toward them as persons. All the participants who were seen by their mothers as essentially the same as non-handicapped people did regularly participate in ordinary activities. In comparison, only three out of the eight participants who were seen by their mothers as globally handicapped took part in ordinary social activities.

Level of autonomy

Information was obtained about the amount of autonomy afforded to the participants in the following nine items: having key to door, choosing clothes to buy, choosing time to go to bed, allowed to stay in house on own, allowed to go out on own, allowed out at night on own, choosing where to go out to, choosing time to return home and control over money. [. . .]

It was found that the mothers whose attitude towards the participant was that he or she was essentially different gave the participant less autonomy than those mothers who considered him or her as essentially the same. Thus, the level of autonomy did not necessarily determine the participant's acceptance of a stigmatised identity. Several people who were not even allowed to make the most basic decisions, such as the time at which they went to bed, still rejected a primarily handicapped view of self. In contrast, the mothers' attitudes towards the handicap of their sons or daughters were related to the level of autonomy given to them.

21.4   Discussion

All participants were aware of the stigma associated with being identified as a 'mentally handicapped' person. Stigma was not for them an abstract notion but something with which they had to cope in their everyday lives. However, only three participants accepted a view of themselves as essentially different from non-handicapped people. The rest rejected a globally handicapped view of themselves. In contrast with Edgerton's (1967) study, the participants' rejection was not a denial that they had particular learning difficulties or a mental handicap; rather, they did not accept that this meant that they were less worthy as persons.

The participants' self-concepts were not related to the way they were perceived by mothers and staff, to their involvement in ordinary social activities, or to the level of autonomy which they were afforded. In fact, a significant difference was found between the mothers' attitudes toward the participant as a person and the participant's own self-concept. Thus, four participants rejected a globally handicapped identity although their social life and contacts revolved around a 'handicapped' world, and their mothers and staff regarded them as globally handicapped people. This finding could not be explained by the mothers having an insignificant relationship with the participants. The maternal attitudes were related to the amount of autonomy given to the participants and it is possible that they are also related to the participants' opportunity to take part in ordinary activities.

Although the sample is small this finding has important theoretical implications because it cannot readily be interpreted in terms of the social constructionist theory (Gergen, 1977). On the basis of the social construc-tionist theory, and given the conditions of the lives of the people with a mental handicap described above, one might have predicted that all participants would have internalised a 'handicapped' view of themselves. However, this study has shown that the participants actively made sense of the situation in which they found themselves; they were aware that a globally handicapped status was distinct from their disability and was imposed on them as a result of social prejudice. Perhaps this awareness is best expressed by a thirty-six-year-old man with Down's syndrome talking about how he was treated by people that he met:

> Generally they're good towards me, anyway, but not because of what I am, because they know me. Not because of what I am, but because they know me personally. Because you don't judge a book by the cover. When we walk on a street or a bus or a train it's wrong to confront a person on a picture of a different source. Because people should realise that we are people like them and want to be treated like them, so that you are in the same standards. But not saying, Well, I want to be your friend because you're handicapped. To me that's wrong, totally, generally. It would be much nicer to know people coming up to say, I'm your friend and I want to know more about you as a person, not just that big word that doesn't mean anything.

This quotation clearly demonstrates this person's awareness of himself as a human being, that is, as a human agent equal to other human agents, and his wish to be treated as such. It is both human agency and the ability to internalise others' views about oneself that contribute to the development and maintenance of one's self-concept (Markova, 1987a, 1987b). The social construction theory focuses only on the individual's internalisation of others' views of him- or herself, without acknowledging that individual as an agent who is aware of his or her capacities to do things and actively to evaluate his or her actions. [. . .]

It is apparent in the present study that the participants were expressing feelings rooted in knowledge and experience of what it means to be treated as an inferior person. Even if, through their actions, they could not achieve a position where they were treated by others on a more equitable basis, they sought to maintain as far as possible their own self-respect and dignity.

The above discussion does not account for the fact that three people in the study were found to accept a globally handicapped view of themselves. In the case of one individual, the reason might be that the rewards associated with being treated as a 'special' person at home outweighed the negative aspects of the stigma; consequently, she wanted this protected existence to continue. However, there are no obvious reasons which can be identified in the case of the other two participants and salient aspects of their personal histories may have been overlooked in the interviews.

The findings also have implications for the services for and treatment of people with a mental handicap. The fact that the parents who viewed the participants as primarily handicapped gave them less autonomy and less opportunity to take part in ordinary activities demonstrates that attitudes do count. Perhaps an effective method of countering these negative views of parents and staff would be to try and make them aware of the sensitivity and feelings of the people with a mental handicap who are hurt by such attitudes. Similarly, those in the services for people with a mental handicap should take account of the sensitivity of those they are there to help, and seek to create and enhance the individual's sense of personal worth. People with a mental handicap require support to achieve more of the rights and opportunities in the social and other spheres of life that are ordinarily taken for granted.

Acknowledgments

The authors are grateful to Mrs Anne Goldie for typing the manuscript and Dr Ranald Macdonald for statistical advice. This research was supported by the Scottish Home and Health Department.

References

EDGERTON, R. B. (1967) *The Cloak of Competence*, Berkeley, University of California Press.

GERGEN, K. J. (1977) 'The social construction of self-knowledge', in Mischel, T. (ed.), *The Self: Psychological and Philosophical Issues*, Oxford, Blackwell.

GOFFMAN, E. (1963) *Stigma*, Englewood Cliffs, New Jersey, Prentice-Hall.

GOWANS, F. and HULBERT, H. (1983) 'Self-concept assessment of mentally handicapped adults: a review', *British Institute of Mental Handicap*, Vol. 11, pp. 121–3.

KOEGEL, P. and EDGERTON, R. B. (1982) 'Labelling and the perception of handicap among black mildly mentally retarded adults', *American Journal of Mental Deficiency*, Vol. 87, pp. 226–76.

SCHURR, K. T., JOINER, L. M. and TOWNE, R. C. (1970) 'Self concept research on the mentally retarded: a review of empirical studies', *Mental Retardation*, Vol. 8, pp. 39–43.

ZETLIN, G. and TURNER, L. T. (1984) 'Self-perspectives on being handicapped: stigma and adjustment', in Edgerton, R. B. (ed.) *Lives in Process: Mildly Retarded Adults in a Large City*, Monograph No. 6, American Association on Mental Deficiency.

Section IV   Support in the community

Introduction

Community living is currently the favoured policy option for people with learning difficulties. But what, in practice, does it entail? And how is it best supported? This section explores support in the community from a variety of angles.

We begin this section with the view of a carer. Pat Henton is the mother of a twelve-year-old girl who is 'profoundly handicapped'. This account seemed to us to illustrate both the negative and the positive sides of being a carer. Pat has suffered a nervous breakdown and a near marriage breakdown since having Vicky: yet she also loves Vicky dearly and cannot contemplate her life without her. The emphasis is very much on Vicky as part of Pat's life; services could make life easier, but the reality for Pat seems to be just her and Vicky.

Larraine Eastwood, on the other hand, is a paid carer. As a 'landlady/ supervisor' she describes her 'job', which seems to be not so much part-time employment as a way of life. Larraine's account vividly echoes the dilemma felt by Diane Amans (Section III). 'Letting go' and allowing people to live their own lives is not easy; they may not want or be ready for the independence on offer. And facilitating independence and choice-making is time-consuming. More time-consuming, you might conclude, than had been foreseen when Larraine's job was planned and costed.

As editors we chose to include 'Mary M' . . . for different reasons. One of us chose it as an excellent example of a structured approach to teaching someone the skills necessary for community living. The other saw it as an illustration of a moral dilemma central to the principle of normalisation: to what extent service providers are justified in imposing their own values on a person who is not in a position to articulate choices. It is a tribute to this account that it serves both purposes admirably.

By contrast, Roger Blunden's account of Robert Griffiths' life shows that, despite the efforts of all involved, community living is not a straightforward option: 'I looked at her and she looked at me – a psychologist standing in the corridor in the middle of the night with two night staff, screaming and crying – and I thought, this is not my idea of community care'. Although Robert's experience of community living was not a happy one for anyone concerned, people have not given up, nor have they blamed Robert. As the postscript suggests, there remains the possibility that an environment and appropriate support will be found which will enable Robert to make a go of community living in the future.

Robert Edgerton is well known for his longitudinal study of people who left a long stay hospital in the 1950s. This article describes people who, unlike Larraine Eastwood's 'ladies', have been 'in the community' for many years. It is encouraging to realise that, for these people, some of the pitfalls of community living were transitional; that many years of making choices, both small and large, have equipped the people in Edgerton's study well for a full and satisfying life, in many respects barely distinguishable from their 'non-retarded' compatriots. Edgerton's article ends on an enigmatic note, 'Would all of this make them happier?'

Linda Ward's honest review of the Wells Road Service five years on widens the focus. Despite its fame, despite its successes, 'its only real failure, however, was fundamental – its failure to survive'. But failures, too, can teach valuable lessons and the article offers several positive suggestions which might better safeguard future projects of this kind.

The final article in this section, 'Community care: the ideal and the reality', written for us by Gillian Dalley, draws together the various themes of community care and shows that as a concept it means different things to different people. Some of the conflicts over community care become easier to understand in the light of Gillian's analysis; whether such clarity of vision also makes them possible to resolve is a challenge to all of us.

22 Caring

Pat Henton

Vicky is 12½ and profoundly handicapped, with a mental age of about five months. She is doubly incontinent, bottle-fed and can eat only minced food. She is unable to play with toys or sit up without back support, but thankfully she is small for her age, weighing only three stone. Vicky is my husband Ken's only child; I have three from a previous marriage, they are twenty-four, twenty-two and eighteen. They live in Norfolk. We are very close and they are really good with Vicky; I stay with them in the summer and they help with bathing, feeding and changing her.

That all paints a rather bleak picture but it's not as bad as it sounds. She is very pretty and very responsive; although she can't speak, her eyes and smiles say it all. She is able to laugh, watches mobiles, likes musical toys and loves watching television. She also smiles when she hears a piece of her favourite music. I enjoy looking after her most of the time. When she is ill, and she often is, I tend to get very low, always expecting the worst – the prognosis is rather bleak. The day-to-day caring, when she is well, isn't too bad. I have osteoarthritis of the spine and lifting can be painful and difficult, but I try to avoid doing things I know are painful. My husband gives Vicky a bath and washes her hair on Sundays, and she has her hair washed at school midweek. I asked if it could be done as Ken works away from home quite often. We are lucky, he is in a well-paid job as a computer consultant.

We don't have a social life really, I choose to stay in with Vicky most of the time. Occasionally when she's in hospital we go out for a meal, and if something special is on Vicky goes into hospital overnight. We are very lucky with our paediatrician – if I ever feel I need a break she can go into hospital almost at a moment's notice. I find that, knowing I can have a break whenever I want, I don't seem to need one too often.

Ken and I don't mind the change in our lives; we are in our early forties and are happy staying in most of the time. At the moment he's doing an external mathematics degree, so he is busy in the evenings when he's at home. We try to have a holiday without Vicky every two years, but we have lots of weekends and holidays in Norfolk with her. My family all live there, we live in the north-east of England and Ken's family live near, but as his mother is disabled and a widow and we rarely see his other relatives we are very much on our own with Vicky. Our marriage has been under a strain several times in the past twelve years. When we were first told about Vicky's handicap she was fifteen months old (I knew something was wrong but I didn't want to be told). I couldn't accept it, she was five before I came to terms with it and up until then I was taking valium, librium, etc. and took four or five overdoses. It was a very trying time for Ken. My older children lived with us until ten years ago when I had a nervous breakdown and Ken and I separated for a year. He had Vicky, I was unable to look after her. I feel really guilty about that and it still hurts just remembering. I sometimes feel we don't need each other now – he is very involved in his work and degree, and I centre my life around Vicky. I don't know what I will do with my life when she dies, I haven't worked for over twenty-five years, my home and children have been the centre of my life for so long. Vicky will leave a void I will never be able to fill. Life will go on, it has to; I'll find something to do. I'd like to go back to Norfolk near my children but it will depend on Ken's job. We've lived here for eight years because the school and hospital are so good.

We try hard not to be a handicapped family. So often a whole family thinks it can't do things other families do. I went through that when Vicky was much younger – I wouldn't take her out, all the nappy changing and feeding were awkward. I manage much better now yet she's so much bigger. I used to find myself apologising because she was handicapped, then I stopped feeling sorry for myself and got on with living.

Vicky goes in the car a lot and enjoys travelling. She likes going to school, her face lights up when I put her in the taxi and she recognises people she sees regularly. The school is a very good one; the atmosphere is always welcoming and friendly. Parents are encouraged to visit whenever they want. I often pop in when I'm out shopping. I have to do the heavy shopping when Ken is able to take me in the car. Vicky has to come but she seems to enjoy the noise and bustle and all the people around her. I am unable to drive because I am epileptic through an injury twenty years ago, but I am controlled with drugs. Vicky is epileptic too; her fits are more difficult to control but she hasn't had a grand mal for eighteen months. We're really pleased about that, it's much easier to take her out in her wheelchair. We had great difficulty with wheelchairs until the Variety Club of Britain bought one for her. It's really nice, it has a thermal cover which is ideal in the winter, and a large shopping bag on the back. Its very stable even with heavy things in the bag. I have difficulty taking it out when the pavements have frozen melted snow on them; I tend to stay in more and live on food from the freezer.

I will always look after Vicky at home. She is regressing, but I will always manage somehow. I love her dearly and couldn't consider residential care. I have a reasonably happy life, I enjoy cooking, cleaning, knitting and sewing. I don't really have any close friends, I don't make friends easily, but I'm happy doing what I do. I don't always like being alone when Ken is away but it's part of his job and has to be done. We have happy holidays with and without Vicky – for a week or two I can be Pat, not Vicky's mum. It's nice for a week or so but I'm always so pleased to come back to her. I cry when I leave her but I'm all right when I get away. The nurses at the hospital are our friends. We've known some of them for eight years, so Vicky is never with strangers, and she's in hospital, ill, often enough to be used to it. When she's there, I sit with her from 10 am until 7 or 8 pm and I do it because I want to. I love Vicky the way she is and wouldn't want her any different. If I need help I usually get it. I am able to go to the hospital and say I need a rest and Vicky goes in for a few days. I still sit with her all day but she's not my responsibility and I think that's the really tiring part in caring for someone you love, you feel so responsible for everything that happens to them. I feel very guilty when I am unable to cope or if I have to ask for help because so many people are in a much worse position than we are. I rarely contact my social worker, it's only when I need a piece of equipment. At the moment we are waiting for Social Services to install a shower. We've been waiting for nine months but these things always take time. I could manage Vicky in a shower but not lifting her in and out of the bath. It's lifting and carrying her that I find most painful. When my husband is away I sometimes have to ask a neighbour to carry her up to bed, he's always happy to do it. Having her has made me much more tolerant and I try to understand other people's problems more. We all have problems, they are just different in each family.

The three of us usually go somewhere for lunch on a Saturday, it's my day off! When we're in Norfolk Ken always gets Vicky washed and dressed in the mornings so I have a break, and he enjoys doing it. When he's at home he feeds her at teatime and puts her to bed, he always plays with her then. On the rare occasions when I'm ill and have to stay in bed he is quite able to look after us both, he can cook and is as helpful as anyone in his situation can be. I am able to get out as often as I want when Vicky is at school, so I'm only confined to the house when Vicky is off school ill or the weather is too wet or cold to take her out.

Over the years things have improved a lot, there is more back-up help for carers. Ten years ago I felt so alone, but maybe I cope better now. If I could turn the clock back thirteen years, knowing all the worry, heartache, tears and fears we've had and the sorrow still to come, I would still have had Vicky. The joy outweighs the anguish and she's been such a pleasure and delight to all of us who know and love her.

23 A group home/landlady scheme

Larraine Eastwood

In 1979 the local Social Services Department embarked upon an experimental project, embracing the philosophy of community care for
mentally handicapped people. The basic concept was that the more able
handicapped person should be cared for in a 'normal' environment, with
minimal supervision provided on a landlady/supervisor scheme.

For this scheme the Social Services acquired two semi-detached houses
from the Local Authority Housing Department. The houses were situated
next door to each other on a local housing estate. The majority of the
occupants of the estate were of the mining fraternity. In close proximity to
the houses were an assortment of shops, a launderette and a post office.
The town centre was approximately one mile from the estate and offered
the usual amenities. Both houses had three bedrooms, bathroom, through-
lounge, kitchen and gas central heating, with large gardens to front and
rear.

The landlady/supervisor lived in one of the houses with her family, and
by way of remuneration the Social Services Department paid the rent. The
landlady was responsible for all the usual household bills incurred, and
furnishing of her own accommodation. The department also paid the
landlady's telephone rental, and £1 each quarter for calls.

In return for the services of the landlady, each resident paid £10 per
week from the weekly DHSS benefits. The residents were also responsible
for their rent, gas, electric, food, replacement items for their home, and
any other bills incurred.

It was envisaged by the department that the landlady would work on a
part-time basis (no more than twenty hours per week), and that her
services would be of a supervisory nature only, helping no more than four
residents to budget, plan menus, shop, etc. and cope generally with a more
independent life-style. [. . .]

The agreed 'back-up' service from the hostel proved to be totally
ineffective. The first occasion on which I sought assistance was when one of
the ladies reacted violently to her new environment, which happened only
days after the arrival of the residents. It was explained by the hostel that
they could not offer the help required as their beds were fully occupied. It
took a further four weeks to resolve this crisis and necessitated me living
and sleeping in the house to ensure the safety of the other residents.

On a later occasion, the response was so slow that the situation could not
be contained any longer in the home environment; consequently an
emergency admission to the mental handicap hospital resulted.

Realising the impracticalities of this system I approached the department, suggesting that a more efficient service be sought. The department,

however, did not agree, and argued that with the agencies involved every eventuality was catered for.

Experiencing the inadequacies, I accepted isolation as part of my position and learned to deal with other problems with little or no support from these areas. [. . .]

Later the department suggested that because I felt so isolated I could benefit from a regular visit from someone from their office. Consequently, every few weeks a lady would arrive to offer a sympathetic shoulder to cry on. Although this lady offered no practical assistance, she was extremely useful to me as a sounding board. [. . .]

In the following I have opened my diary at a time three months after the arrival of the residents. It shows very clearly how difficult those early months were, and the impracticalities of the department's expected role of the landlady.

Monday
Crawled from my bed feeling numb and tired at 6.00 am. Enjoyed a coffee in the quiet of my own home before running next door. The path was frozen this morning, and so my feet stayed dry!

Wished the ladies a cheery 'Good morning' before observing them wash. Lucy requires a lot of supervision in this area, but this must be done gently as she appears to resent my intrusion and growls at me – cannot blame her really, I would not like it either!

Emma refused to rise and needed coaxing from her bed; however, once up copes well, although she does tend to put dirty clothes back on, including her knickers.

Doris copes well and offers no problems – she is a love.

May was reluctant to rise, only because she dresses before going to bed, a habit I am trying to break.

Lucy set the table this morning; on it she placed a milk bottle, cups (no saucers), plates, a packet of sugar, a spoon, and a packet of butter, complete with a knife in upright position.

Emma helped her to reset the table.

Doris made a pot of tea, but forgot to boil the kettle.

May requested a cup of tea whilst sitting on the toilet – constipated again!

Ran back home to call my children for school at 7.30 am.

7.45 am Returned to the ladies with the drug box, and taking each lady in turn allowed them to open their own bottles, and take their medications. I never realised taking a couple of pills could be so time-consuming!

8.15 am Doris washed the dishes, Emma and Lucy dried, and May disappeared to the toilet.

8.30 am Walked the ladies half way to the Training Centre to escort them across the busy road.

Emma and Lucy cope well with the crossing of roads; Doris, however, relies on them. Perhaps she is deaf!

9.00 am May still in the toilet but complains of the housework and shopping.

9.15 am Found a note from my husband asking me to collect the children from school.

9.30 am   Organised May and the housework. I did not think that dusting and using a hoover could be such hard work! Escorted May to the shop and helped her prepare some lunch.

12.00 pm   Returned to make some lunch for myself.

1.00 pm   Washed the ladies' clothes, had to do this in my own home as there is no washing machine next door.

3.00 pm   Returned to May – she complains of toothache, her teeth are in an appalling state.

3.15 pm   Rang the dentist to make May an appointment (Wednesday 10.30 am).

3.30 pm   Picked the children up from school and made them some tea.

4.00 pm   Met the ladies from the centre to see them across the road – they seemed pleased to see me.

4.45 pm   Helped them to prepare the dinner. More truthfully – they helped me!

6.00 pm   Observed medications.

6.15 pm   Observed Lucy wash the dinner pots, what a mess – water everywhere! Lucy resented being asked to clean up afterwards but I stood firm.

7.00 pm   Returned to be with my own kith and kin.

9.00 pm   Raised voices from next door. Lucy and Emma do not appear to get on too well. Lucy stormed from the house. Emma refuses to talk with me.

9.15 pm   I put my shoes on to go and find Lucy. It's cold outside and she left without her coat.

9.30 pm   Returned with Lucy. Emma had gone to bed, probably without washing. I went to Emma's bedroom to say 'Goodnight' but she did not reply. Because she is epileptic I switched on the light to make sure she was all right. My actions were met with verbal abuse and we had firm words.

10.00 pm   Bathed May (her frame is so fragile) and tucked her in bed.

10.30 pm   With the ladies safely in their beds I returned home, kissed my children as they slept, and retired at midnight.

Tuesday
Slept in this morning, rising at 7.30 am. Called my husband and children before running next door. There is snow on the path today but it is pleasant.

8.00 am   Everyone was still in their beds. Emma was still very annoyed about last night and we had words again! May must have dressed after I left last night – she rose fully clothed. I made her remove her clothes, wash and redress in clean. Hurried the ladies through breakfast. Doris set the table and did very well. I feel that she is really bright but lacks confidence.

8.30 am   Observed medications.

8.45 am   Walked the ladies across the busy road before returning to May and the breakfast dishes.

9.15 am   May had made no attempt to clear the pots or the table. I asked her again before returning to collect my diary.

9.30 am Had a coffee with May and listened to her endless list of complaints, headache, constipation, etc. While she talked I noticed that her body continually moved. After consulting my diary I realised that the district nurse was due to administer a medication injection. Left May to finish the washing up whilst I ran to the shop. It would have been so easy to collect May's pension, but felt that May would come to expect it of me on a permanent basis.

11.30 am May had just finished the dishes. As I gave her the pension book she asked if Lucy could collect it for her later. Reluctantly May put her coat and shoes on and left.

12.00 pm Received a telephone call from the local shopkeeper. May had called for her cigarettes and left her pension book and purse on the counter.

12.15 pm May returned to collect her belongings from the shop. However, on this occasion left her gloves.

1.00 pm Rang the DHSS regarding Emma's pension book – now two weeks overdue. They do not seem to understand that she needs that money to meet her commitments.

1.30 pm The daycare officer called to check that all was well. I pointed out once more that this was no part-time occupation, but just as the discussion got going he had to leave.

2.00 pm Checked that May was all right and had washed her lunch pots before enjoying a quiet afternoon.

3.30 pm Walked down the road to meet the ladies from the training centre. Emma was a little more sociable.

4.15 pm Spent a little time with my children. My daughters informed me that some other children had been calling them names, and asked if they liked living in the looney bin. When I asked what they had said my eldest replied, 'Nothing, we hit them'.

5.00 pm As the children left to play with their friends I returned to the ladies. Lucy was peeling potatoes – what a mess, but she was showing initiative.

5.45 pm Left the ladies to enjoy their dinner.

6.15 pm Observed medications. Doris washed the dishes. Emma began knitting. May settled in front of the television. Lucy, however, was thumbing through a book obviously wanting some help. I spent some time with Lucy listening to her read – she does very well. I promised her that I would try and find someone from adult literacy to help her.
  Doris made everyone a cup of tea and it was warm!

7.00 pm Returned to my own home.

10.00 pm Observed bedtime routines. Told May firmly that if she dressed after I left, and got into bed, she would have to strip and wash again in the morning.

10.30 pm Wished everyone 'Goodnight'. [. . .]

A home of this type certainly has a great deal to offer. It caters for individuals' needs at their level, and offers an opportunity for personal development in areas often excluded in hostels or larger institutions.

However, I do feel that the landlady and residents are both open to exploitation if great care is not taken in the planning of such a scheme.

Although the time spent with the ladies was unremitting hard work for myself and my family, the satisfaction derived from observing four individuals exercise their rights as people was such that I would not hesitate to do it all again.

24 Mary M . . .

David Felce and Steven Toogood

24.1 Mary: before moving

[. . .] Mary moved into the house in the second week of November. She moved from an environment which had aspects of prison security – for example, being confined to a locked dormitory from early evening until morning. Her contact with the outside world was non-existent. She did have disruptive behaviour, the reason for her initial transfer there. She displayed temper tantrums at least two or three times per week, which were sometimes so intense that she fell to the floor and forcibly removed her clothing. She also damaged property, pummelling surfaces with her fists and breaking windows. She had attacked staff over a long period, although these outbursts, as well as the more extreme forms of self-injury, had declined of late. Therefore her disruptiveness should perhaps not be overstated; she was living on a pre-discharge ward and her move was considered appropriate by the professionals involved in her care.

Mary was severely mentally handicapped with few self-help skills. She ate using a spoon and her fingers, could drink unassisted but with considerable spilling, and dressed (given that she wore loose tops and elasticated trousers) with help. She was fully ambulant but with a lopsided gait. She was basically continent but did not wash even her hands herself. Mary had been assessed on the Fairview Self-help Scale in 1976 as having a score of 31.4 months. Reassessed in 1978, she seemed to have regressed (19.9 months), but whether she had in fact done so or whether these scales are prone to such variability is open to debate. The ward staff gave no indication of anything other than Mary being in a fairly stable state. After her move, she was reassessed as having a mental age of 28 months. [. . .]

In the first six months after moving in, Mary received a greater than proportionate share of the clothing budget in order to obtain a suitable range to her wardrobe, a new top coat, dresses and shoes. As well as looking right, it was found that more fashionable adult women's shoes with a slight heel in fact helped her to walk with a more normal gait. She had appointments at the hairdresser's and chiropodist's and began a course of dental treatment which was to lead to the provision of dentures. She was proud of her appearance, liked having her hair done and enjoyed brushing it herself. Apart from a slight awkwardness in movement, in time Mary's appearance became such as to give little indication of handicap.

It is important to emphasise that, in distinguishing the issues of ability and appearance and in highlighting the separate importance of appearance, one is not denying the presence of real functional handicap. It is of course also true that an individual's behavioural deficiencies or problems make the task of attending to appearance more difficult. For example, when Mary received her dentures she had difficulty in wearing them without gagging. The problem might have been due to the dentures not fitting properly, which in turn might have been due to the difficulties found in getting Mary to help the dentist obtain an adequate impression. There was also the question of teaching her to wear them – getting her used to having teeth after many years of being without them. Thus in order to attend to this aspect of her appearance, staff had to set about a long-term programme of structuring occasions when Mary would wear her dentures for increasingly longer durations. Meanwhile, if they were successful in getting even short but significant usage, the dentist was willing to put further effort into obtaining a more precise moulding that would fit more closely.

This example serves to illustrate the complexity of co-ordination and effort that may be required to obtain personal services for handicapped people which accord with the broad range of standards for ordinary individuals. There is an interaction between seeking high-quality involvement from the various branches of our helping professions and the development of client behaviour appropriate to the activities involved in maintaining such standards, achieving personal care or using materials to good effect. However, in relation to severely and profoundly mentally handicapped people, learning cannot be achieved both quickly and on a broad front simultaneously. One therefore needs to be wise in one's decisions as to what to teach. Targets need to be things that are important to the client's life. However, one also needs an alternative strategy for more general behavioural development. A teaching strategy for wearing dentures was unavoidable given that nobody could help Mary wear her dentures for her. But an alternative strategy is possible in many other circumstances. That alternative strategy is the notion of staff helping to bridge the gap between personal accomplishment and what is required. In many ways staff act as a prosthetic device – just as spectacles bridge the gap between the current ability of an individual's eyes and the visual acuity needed, so staff act as a social prosthesis helping the handicapped person to behave as others do in similar environmental circumstances. The analogy with spectacles also helps to give an image of the extent of help to be given. In just the same way as an overly strong prescription for glasses will lead to a deterioration in the muscles of the eye and an increasing dependence and worsening of sight, so excessive staff help leads to overdependence and often overprotection. Staff have to give the minimal help required, in order for the handicapped person to contribute as much as they can for themselves. [. . .]

24.2 Behavioural development

Early priorities for teaching were concerned with Mary's mode of feeding, her table manners, her ability to wash and to dress, her joining in the activities of the house and her getting more appropriate social interaction. The temper tantrums and screaming described in hospital probably functioned to avoid demands, to avoid becoming involved and to keep herself to herself. For example, it was found that Mary particularly disliked washing her hands, and the cracks in the plaster above the hand basin in the kitchen still bear testimony to her displeasure at being requested to do so for herself. [. . .]

As Mary became familiar with joining in more and learning simple domestic tasks such as emptying the dishwasher or pegging out the washing, her agreement to follow requests became easier to obtain. Once occupied, she participated with good grace, enjoying the social situation. [. . .] Mary liked to celebrate her achievement by saying, 'I done it' and returning to the living room to sit down. Care had to be given to allow her the opportunity to be pleased with doing what she had been asked to do; the breaks between activities did not have to be prolonged. [. . .]

During the year following her transfer, Mary had a thorough, progressive review of her medication. On arrival, she was being prescribed 200 mg Epilim twice a day, 5 mg Valium morning and night, 10 ml chloral hydrate at night and was written up for 100 mg Largactil by intra-muscular injection when needed. The latter two were immediately stopped. It was not anticipated that behavioural disturbance would be treated by sedation. Moreover, with a longer day and progress toward a new sleeping pattern, it was predicted correctly that Mary would sleep without need of medication. The Valium was reduced soon after moving in. Meanwhile the psychiatrist wrote to find out whether the Epilim was prescribed as a result of a history of epilepsy or as a response to behavioural disturbance. As epilepsy had never been apparent, this drug too was reduced successively once the administration of Valium had been phased out entirely. By the end of 1982 Mary was receiving no medication at all and the psychiatrist's notes record improving behaviour alongside drug reduction. [. . .]

The new opportunities for Mary on moving to the house within the general context of staff support led to fairly rapid development. She quickly learnt to use a knife and fork at meal times. She was so thrilled at this new accomplishment that for a period of a few weeks she chose to eat even her toast and marmalade at breakfast by that means. In hospital, she had been described as taking food from others' plates and as being terribly messy, but now she learnt to follow the normal conventions of waiting for others to finish before taking more, offering serving dishes (when prompted) to others and using language to express preferences and wants. Proficiency at feeding herself improved enormously. She participated in the routine domestic tasks of the house: clearing the dining table, putting the things on the kitchen hatch, wiping surfaces and sweeping or hoovering the floors. She went shopping almost daily. Of course, the majority of these things would be done with staff instruction and direct guidance, but through regular practice and some specific teaching she increased considerably the part she played and the level of independence she showed. [. . .]

Specifically programmed teaching taught her many whole and component skills for her personal care and household life. She was taught to wash her hands using soap and subsequently to dry them. Having learnt this, tantrumming when asked to wash her hands died out. She also learnt to put clothes on a hanger and then in her wardrobe, to put folded items neatly in her drawers, and to look for and take out items without totally disturbing the remaining contents. Previously, she had undressed by pulling off all items of clothing worn above the waist together, and all clothes worn below the waist together. This damaged her clothing and meant that it needed to be unravelled before she could redress. So Mary was taught to take items off singly. By careful structuring of natural opportunities, Mary learnt to collect the dirty washing from people's rooms and bring it to the laundry room. [. . .]

Other changes important to Mary's development occurred in relation to her language and socialisation both in the house and outside. Mary had an extremely sociable personality which should be viewed as an asset. But her pattern of social interaction was so odd that her sociability had been cast as an inappropriate trait. The repetitiveness of her speech was extremely wearing and the way she approached and greeted people could be off-putting, particularly to the unaware. She physically grasped and held people, and was generally over-intimate. [. . .] Going to shops and having a meal in a restaurant or a drink in a pub represented a significant source of new opportunities. To use these to the best possible benefit and to avoid the kind of negative reaction which her mother had predicted, it was an urgent matter following her arrival to teach more appropriate social skills.

At first, Mary greeted all visitors to the home, people returning to the house and even people inside the home in an inappropriate manner. In order to teach her to keep an appropriate distance and to offer her hand to shake instead, every physical contact Mary initiated in an overly intimate way was met by an impassive correction. This comprised releasing her grasp, moving back slightly, taking her right hand to an offering position, taking her hand, shaking it and at that point smiling and saying the normal social pleasantries. This was rapidly successful in shaping Mary's interactions with people within or coming to the house. A similar effort was made when Mary reached for and held people when shopping, such as the cashier or sales assistants. [. . .]

Another aspect that was detrimental to Mary's image and her ability to participate effectively in the domestic round was a habit of carrying her possessions, particularly two large and worn teddy bears, around with her. [. . .] Therefore a positive approach was followed to supplant their role in Mary's life by acquiring other more age-appropriate accessories which she would prefer to keep about her. Mary purchased a handbag which, given the interest shown in it by the people around her and the opportunity to be similar in this respect to the other adult women in her immediate surroundings, she began to choose to have with her instead. The teddies were first kept in her bedroom and later discarded. The handbag also served as a repository for items Mary treasured – a number of handkerchiefs, combs and some small picture books. In time, she was further taught to put her handbag down when in the house and to collect it when going out or moving to sit in another room. Moreover, as her personal property increased, the tendency to hoard items reduced.

24.3   Community living, recreational pursuits and social life

Mary had considerable exposure to shopping and going to cafés or pubs. She was able to push the trolley in a supermarket and collect goods from shelves with instruction. She learnt to ask for a coke and had to wait for change when making purchases. Her sociability led to many genuine social exchanges as she became a familiar and regular customer. She had a tendency to show people new clothes or possessions, such as when getting new ear-rings. This could be repetitive and still marked her out as socially immature for her age, but was a far preferable and more appealing peculiarity than her earlier means of contacting people.

One story can illustrate how well Mary was accepted in and involved with the community. She had become a regular shopper at a local bakery. One day, when the shop was particularly crowded, she and a member of staff entered the baker's and waited at the back of the queue. Totally on the assistant's initiation, Mary was asked to help serve behind the counter. The assistant said something like 'Come on Mary, come and help – we are busy . . . This lady wants six bread rolls in this bag here.' Between the shop assistant and Mary, the lady was served. When Mary later became terminally ill, many people asked after her, and for someone who knew no one when she came to the locality some thirty people attended her funeral (the combined staff and resident group at that time was seventeen. [. . .]

When she first came to the house Mary gave every impression of being someone who had lived in an environment in which personal belongings were not respected. In hospital she had gathered all her possessions to her person in a number of carrier bags. When first in the house she had carried her teddy bears with her, and when getting the handbag to replace the teddy bears she had then carried that with her at all times, collecting small things to keep in it so that it was overflowing. As time went by she was taught to lessen the number of items she kept close to her person and to use the cupboards available in the living room and her own bedroom instead.

She gradually learnt that in this house other people did not interfere with her personal belongings. [. . .]

In the one summer she spent in the house, she had had a holiday with Shirley and two members of staff. They stayed in a caravan at a seaside resort. The caravan park had a restaurant, bar and entertainments complex which they used as adults. In her time in the house she went to the cinema a number of times, went to music concerts, attended church, visited a riding stables and attended a gymkhana, went on all-day shopping excursions to neighbouring cities, ate lunch and dinner out in restaurants, visited the homes of staff, used public transport and played pub skittles. Many recreational events such as eating or drinking out or doing the house shopping occurred in the evening. Mary kept the hours of an adult, a distinct difference to her life in hospital.

Mary had no family contact. What did grow was personal friendship with a few local citizens, something that staff kept an eye open for opportunities to encourage due to her particular circumstances. Other than the relatives of other house residents, about four people visited Mary. Two developed a particular friendship. The shop assistant who had invited Mary to serve bread rolls in the baker's became a regular visitor. Her fiancée (later her husband) also became involved. They visited Mary personally and did other things which friends may do, such as, when meeting her in town unexpectedly, deciding to go off together to a café for a coffee. Mary was able to entertain them in the house, offering them coffee (with staff help), or inviting them to stay for a meal. Staff fostered the friendship and began to talk to the couple about whether they would be prepared to act as an external advocate for Mary's welfare at her six-monthly individual programme planning review meetings. They had agreed to do so and would have attended the next meeting in such a capacity had not illness intervened. Mary was invited to and attended their wedding.

Mary appeared to be extremely happy in her new life in the house. Although staff did take a consistent approach to tantrums and behaviours damaging to property, their decline may equally be attributable to the generally more stimulating environment, her own increasing capability and the direct experience of the results of her contribution to household life. A structured approach to changing her initial tendency towards non-compliance into a likelihood of co-operation was important in maximising her development and use of the opportunities available. Care always had to be exercised in inviting Mary to engage in household activity: without such care she could easily refuse.

In a world of greater activity, greater material enrichment, personal possessions and range of clothing, more opportunity to go shopping for food, household requirements and personal belongings (toiletries, cosmetics, tissues and jewellery), and increased social contact, Mary's vocabulary exploded. It increased by leaps and bounds, aided by her echolalic capacity to copy speech. Learning what objects were called was not difficult for her, she had a well-established tendency to imitate other people. In order for her speech to develop some functional meaning, all that was required was the consistent creation of situations in which she needed to use language in order to obtain the outcome she wanted. Her sociability gave her a strong desire to gain other people's interest in and approval for what she was doing. It is very likely that her developing language helped her sustain her sociable world. [. . .]

24.4   Serious illness

About the time of Mary's second Christmas in the house, staff first began to observe worrying signs. Mary appeared slightly frail at times – a slight stumble, a lack of balance or a failure to stand up from the armchair at first attempt. She also started to become slightly less co-operative again. [. . .]

Over the next two months, the tendencies which had first alerted staff that something was wrong accelerated and Mary started to hit her head and pull out her hair. Even if staff could contemplate Mary going to such lengths to be left alone (which they found difficult to accept), the form of disruptive behaviour chosen struck them as incongruous. In the past, her opposition had taken a different form – tantrumming, screaming and hitting floor, table or wall with her fists – so why did she not return to these rather than adopting a different behaviour? Mary was also particularly proud of her appearance, especially of her hair. Staff therefore suspected that she was experiencing pain and again asked for a medical opinion. [. . .]

Mary was admitted to the neurological unit in the teaching hospital of the health authority region. There a rapidly-growing and inoperable brain tumour was diagnosed. Mary received medication to relieve pressure within her head, which in expert opinion must have caused her considerable pain. She remained an in-patient for about a week, the medication successfully controlling pain, as judged by the cessation of hair-pulling. There was no curative treatment and she was now ready to return home. [. . .]

Mary returned home after arrangements had been made to ensure her comfort and care. She moved to a bedroom on the ground floor. She had a hospital bed installed which would allow ease of lifting and turning (the easier it was for staff, the more comfortable it would be for Mary) and discussions were held with the community nursing service so that they could be called upon if necessary. The two senior staff were trained nurses but were certainly not specialists in caring for a dying person. However, their experience helped them to teach staff how to give Mary food and drink, how to care for her skin and how to lift her into and out of a bath. The community nursing service was employed for specialist advice, but not to supply direct labour. [. . .]

With these arrangements for her comfort and nursing care, Mary was still able to have what benefits she could appreciate from home life. Fellow residents returning from their day care setting often went into Mary's room to see how she was. Two people clearly showed their concern. Afternoon tea was taken together in Mary's room and she was visited regularly by friends. Her care was beyond reproach, a credit to the staff. She died in June 1983. [. . .]

25 Robert Griffiths

Roger Blunden

Robert is a young man who, despite his many problems, is described affectionately by most of the people who know him well. He also shows a great deal of affection to those around him and has created a strong sense of loyalty and concern in many of the people who have lived and worked with him. Robert's parents explain that he has always been a very loving boy, who enjoys a cuddle and gets a great deal of satisfaction when he successfully communicates with others:

> He can be very demanding, but he can also be very lovable. He can have you going up the wall all day long and then he'll do something he's never done before. Then you'll forget all about the horrible day you've had, when he's kicked you and scratched you and bit you and done everything else – because he's done something that he's never done before.

Robert is his parents' first child and was born prematurely in December 1964. His mother contracted German measles before becoming pregnant. Although she was told at the time that this would not affect her pregnancy, it soon became apparent that Robert had difficulties. A cataract was found on one of his eyes when he was about three weeks old and later his other eye was also found to be affected. By the time that Robert was two years of age, it was confirmed that he had little or no hearing. In spite of various operations for his cataracts, he has very limited sight.

When Robert was three, he went to a local school for children with hearing impairments. However, after about a year, the school decided that it was unable to help 'rubella-damaged' children because of their additional visual handicaps. He was also assessed by a special school catering for children who were deaf and blind, but it was concluded that Robert had additional mental handicaps and could not be helped by them:

> They told us that he was mentally handicapped. That was the first time that anyone had told us that he was mentally handicapped. We'd put it down to the fact that he couldn't hear and couldn't see very much, so how can you make yourself known and do things if you have these problems?

Robert was then transferred to a special school for children with mental handicap situated on the other side of the city.

When Robert was three a brother was born and the two played together, although needing a watchful eye kept on them. In spite of his considerable handicaps, Robert's parents received little advice or practical assistance. 'Nobody told you anything. The less you asked, the less you got.' When he was aged fourteen, his parents found out about the availability of short-term care at a local hostel and Robert started going there occasionally at weekends. Apart from this occasional break, they coped alone with Robert at home, with him attending the special school during the day.

Robert and his parents developed a set routine, from getting up in the morning to going to bed at night. His clothes and personal belongings were kept in particular places so that he could find them with his limited vision. In spite of his vision and hearing difficulties, Robert showed a great deal of 'common sense' while living with his parents. He enjoyed manipulating objects such as Lego and bricks and had a well-developed sense of balance. However, his inability to communicate caused him a great deal of frustration. He would sometimes take off his shoes and socks, or undress to avoid having to go out for a walk. He also developed violent temper tantrums, throwing objects, breaking windows, kicking and scratching his parents, and mutilating himself. This had become a major problem by the time Robert was sixteen years old. He was admitted for emergency short-term care to the local mental handicap hospital and, for the first time, drugs were used in an attempt to control his violent outbursts. Robert continued to attend the hospital for emergency short-term care from time to time. On occasions, the hospital staff were called out, sometimes in the middle of the night, to help deal with his problem behaviour. In spite of his increasing temper tantrums, Robert's parents stress the positive aspects of life at home, 'We've had some laughs, mind. They bring a different aspect of your life altogether.' They also wonder how much of his supposed 'mental handicap' is caused by his vision and hearing problems and his difficulty in communicating with others. 'The trouble with Robert is that he knows what he wants but he can't make us understand.' However, they admit that 'whatever you do, Robert will always get the upper hand'.

25.1   Living in a NIMROD staffed house

[. . .] During the period leading up to Robert's move to the house, NIMROD care staff had an opportunity to get to know him. A report, written later, stated that:

> We found a young man of 17 with the stature of a 13 year old who spent most of his time twirling or playing on a swing. We learnt from his carers and parents about Robert's strong sense of territory and time, and the nature of the problem behaviours which made his care in the home so difficult. In a temper sparked by deviations from an established routine, or demands that couldn't be interpreted or met, Robert would be capable of physical aggression towards people (scratching, butting, hitting and, in extremes, biting), and towards objects (windows, furniture, ornaments, etc). Outside of a close relationship with his parents, and getting on well with his teacher, Robert had developed into something of a 'loner'.

The staff discovered Robert's like of bright lights, plastic shapes, Lego and a swing and arranged for these to be available to him at the house. They found that the light from an overhead projector was a powerful reinforcer for him, and used this as a basis for developing a range of activities. Once moved into the house, Robert settled very well. Staff engaged him in play activities, for example Lego, 'rough and tumble' and playing on his swing in the garden. The staff reported a number of occasions when Robert collapsed with laughter after these activities. He became more co-operative, would wait patiently for a bus, carry his plate to the kitchen, and learned not to enter other residents' rooms.

However, a worrying trend was also developing:

> On Thursdays and some Fridays, particularly at night and for no reason that we could fathom, Robert became steadily more disruptive. The behaviour would begin as (often creative) mischief, e.g., tipping furniture over, upsetting sanitex bins, entering and disrupting other residents' rooms, blocking washbasins with towels then turning taps on and leaving them to overflow. Efforts to keep tabs on Robert and restrain or contain this behaviour would then often lead to more serious disruptions involving broken windows, cups, tearing of curtains and so on.

This behaviour had a serious effect on other residents, the staff and the neighbours. The problem was particularly acute at night. Indeed, a member of the night staff left after several traumatic nights with Robert. He developed a very erratic sleeping pattern and did not seem to require a great deal of sleep. The house was terraced and the neighbours on both sides were complaining about the noise at night. Considerable damage was also being done to the house and all windows had to be fitted with strengthened glass. On a number of occasions, Robert set off the fire alarms in the house, resulting in fire engines arriving in the street. He also managed to flood the washing machine, causing considerable disruption.

The house staff were extremely concerned about this situation, but also determined to persevere. They developed strategies for dealing systematically with the disruptions. On occasions, day staff worked 24-hour shifts so as to provide extra night-time support for Robert. Medication was also prescribed at this time, including 5 mg Mogadon, as necessary, to help him settle at night. There is some evidence that Robert had his first epileptic fit during this period while on a regular weekend visit to his parents.

From January until October 1983 the staff made considerable progress with Robert. They devised ways of communicating with him, using the Makaton sign language and various objects. His disruptive behaviour became less frequent and he began to learn a number of new skills, including signing, dressing and preparing breakfast. Robert developed a set routine and became much more compliant and co-operative. He laughed a great deal. [. . .]

In October 1983 Robert's behaviour again gave serious cause for concern. He became intolerant of new or relief staff, unco-operative in the mornings when setting off for school, and aggressive towards staff and other residents. On one occasion he threw one of the other residents across the room, and on another, hit a member of staff on the way to the bus pick-up point. He also began a pattern of frenzied jumping, tearing his clothes, head-banging and other forms of self-mutilation. These problems were again particularly acute at night.

The consultant psychiatrist was again involved, together with the NIMROD clinical psychologist. Staff kept careful records of Robert's behaviour and his sleeping patterns. Various drugs were prescribed in an attempt to sedate him, but seemed to have no effect after a 'honeymoon period' of about ten days. At various times, Robert was prescribed Largactil, sodium amytal, haloperidol and 'cocktails' of haloperidol and Valium. On occasions, he was receiving up to 1,000 mg Largactil in a day, and local GPs were called in, day and night, to administer drugs.

Staff persevered with a number of strategies for dealing with Robert's problem behaviour, including organising a consistent regime for him. [. . .] Staff report that Robert's parents were particularly supportive at this difficult time. However:

> despite all these strategies, Robert's behaviour continued to get worse. So far as the quality of life in the house was concerned, this not only had a direct effect on the other residents, but also an indirect effect. Staff energies became more and more absorbed in strategies for Robert and house repairs necessitated by his behaviour. Leaving the house became more and more difficult, it being highly undesirable (and dangerous) for one staff to be left alone with Robert for any length of time.

At the beginning of June 1984 staff began to notice a deterioration in Robert's sight and an appointment was made for this to be examined. Before this appointment, Robert apparently 'woke up blind' one morning and was extremely distressed:

> The most vivid and horrifying sight for staff working that morning was of Robert feeling his way along the hall and tumbling down three steps that lead to the dining room, laughing in confusion and desperation as he picked himself up . . .
> As might be expected, Robert found the loss of his partial sight an extremely traumatic experience, and the behaviour that resulted from it amounted to the worst we had encountered – especially the self-mutilating aspects of it: continuous falling to the floor, banging his head, scraping fingernails and teeth on concrete of the backyard, scratching himself very badly.

At this time, the staff felt that it was important that thorough investigations be made of any possible medical causes of Robert's problems, However, he could not be persuaded to co-operate with any medical examination. For one eye examination, eight staff accompanied Robert to the general hospital. Eventually, a general anaesthetic was given, and Robert remained in hospital for two days, with NIMROD staff present throughout the period. [. . .]

At the end of June 1984 Robert was admitted to Ely Hospital for a period of observation and assessment. This was with the aim of reviewing his medication (he was receiving increasingly large doses with little effect), to ensure his safety, and to give the staff and other residents in the house a break. While he was away, the staff planned for his return. They contacted the Rubella Association and learned about fingerspelling and other communication techniques from the headmistress of the local school for blind-deaf children. They planned routines for evenings, nights and mornings and arranged for night staff to 'double up' for one month in order to implement a night-time policy of confining Robert to the area of his bedroom.

Robert returned to the house at the beginning of August 1984. However, the problem behaviour and disturbance to neighbours and other residents continued. The eventual state of affairs was described by NIMROD's clinical psychologist:

> At the time, we were working on a programme to help Robert to stay in his room at night. If he came out of his room, he was to be gently turned round by a member of staff who was standing in the corridor and encouraged to go back into his room, but not forced. We wanted him to stay in his room because he tended to try and drag the other residents out of bed, or get in with them and people didn't want locked doors in the house. On one particular occasion, it was 3 o'clock in the morning and I'd gone to the house to check on the programme and the consistency of the staff in following it. We had a psychologist and two night staff standing in the corridor. One resident was crying in his bedroom and another was screaming downstairs. Robert was being encouraged to go back into his bedroom. He was pretty cross and the staff were on the point of giving up because he was determined to come out and was starting to injure himself. The neighbours' lights were on (new neighbours had just moved in with small children) and they were knocking on the wall from the other side. At that point the fourth resident got up to go to the loo. I looked at her and she looked at me – a psychologist standing in the corridor in the middle of the night with two staff, screaming and crying – and I thought, this is not my idea of community care – we must do something.

In September and October 1984 NIMROD staff, in conjunction with Robert's parents, began to explore alternative arrangements for Robert's care in the community. They also established contact with a representative of SENSE, an organisation particularly concerned with rubella-damaged people. (Robert's parents had been involved with SENSE since its inception.) They also visited a residential facility for rubella-damaged people. However, it appeared that Robert was presenting greater problems than most people who had been rubella damaged, and no ready solutions were apparent. [. . .] During this period, NIMROD staff were actively pursuing alternative premises and staffing for Robert, including the possibility of housing association property. In October 1984 Robert was again admitted to Ely Hospital for short-term care for two weeks. However, after his return to the house, he was clearly very distressed. He cried and screamed and clung to staff. He also became extremely angry at times, pulling down curtains, smashing lights and cutting himself with the glass, and put his head through one window which had not been fitted with strengthened glass. After two weeks of this, he was readmitted to the hospital, and has remained there ever since.

25.2   Living in a mental handicap hospital

Robert is still living in Ely Hospital, on a ward for twenty-four men who are described as severely mentally handicapped. The ward is divided into two halves, with a locked door connecting them. Robert lives and shares a dormitory with a group of fifteen of the more severely handicapped residents. He still goes home to his parents, for varying periods of time, at weekends.

NIMROD staff were concerned that Robert was losing some of the skills he had gained while living in the staffed house. Therefore, since March 1985, they have arranged for an additional person, paid for under South Glamorgan's flexicare scheme, to work with Robert on a one-to-one basis, for five hours each weekday. [. . .] In addition to the input provided by the flexicare worker, NIMROD workers continued to work closely with the hospital staff in the care of Robert. [. . .]

25.3   The future

At the present time, Robert's future is uncertain. Initial plans to move him into a specially prepared house with special staffing have not so far borne fruit. South Glamorgan's flexicare budget is stretched, and the time available for a flexicare worker for Robert has now been reduced to ten hours a week. In addition, the hospital asked that Robert's status, originally as a short-term care patient, should be categorised as an informal, long-term admission and this has now happened. As a consequence of this, it may be difficult for NIMROD to justify allocating any of its residential staff resources to Robert.

One future for Robert would therefore be for him to remain in hospital, with a reduction in the amount of extra staff available to him, and the continuing use of medication to restrain his violent behaviour. Most people agree that this is unsatisfactory. Robert's parents, NIMROD and the hospital staff are concerned that he will adapt to the day-to-day routine of the ward, which demands little of him and allows few opportunities for independence. [. . .]

In retrospect, it is perhaps not surprising that Robert had so much difficulty in adapting to life in the staffed house. He had developed a routine at home over nineteen years where his belongings were always kept in one place and the household routine was centred on him. Robert's parents explained that he had never slept for long periods and would often get them up early in the morning to have a bath. He was also never confined to one room and was able to move freely about the house. He was not accustomed to other people being around and generally had his own way in the house. Robert's parents feel that the move to the NIMROD house must have been a massive upheaval for him, added to which was the major trauma of his sight loss. They also wonder whether some of Robert's problem behaviour might have been caused by his drug regimes and possibly by withdrawal symptoms when his massive drug doses were changed. [. . .]

NIMROD staff have identified Robert's needs in three key areas:

> Robert needs an environment where everything is kept consistently in one place, e.g. household articles, personal possessions, clothes, etc. In neither the hospital ward nor the staffed house is it possible to leave items in one place, so that Robert can easily locate and use them . . .
> Robert needs a regime which can effectively contain his violent and self-mutilating outbursts. The presence of neighbours and other residents in the house, together with the extreme nature of Robert's problem behaviour, caused unprecedented problems for staff. In the hospital, these problems can be contained more effectively, but still at the expense of the staff, Robert and other residents . . .
> Robert needs enthusiastic teaching of new, useful skills, and the opportunity to use these. In particular, the house staff have identified communication as an area requiring major development. Opportunities are limited on the ward, by the numbers of other residents, staffing levels and the restricted availability of everyday experiences and objects.

There is still a strong desire to find an environment and the support for Robert which will meet these needs, and in which Robert will be content without a return to the major distress resulting from his stay in the staffed house. It remains to be seen whether the skills and resources necessary to provide for Robert, and people with similar problems, will become available.

25.4   Postscript

Since this story was written, NIMROD staff have continued their contact with Robert and still work with him. A comprehensive plan has been drawn up for Robert to move into a flat of his own. The flat has been allocated and additional funding is now being sought to provide the necessary support staff.

Acknowledgments

I am grateful to the many people including Robert's parents and NIMROD staff who spent time giving me information for this study and to Robert himself and the staff at Ely Hospital for allowing me to spend time on the ward. A great deal of the material presented here is direct quotation from reports prepared by other people and I am particularly grateful to Paul Clarke and John Williams for allowing me to quote extensively from their notes.

26 Ageing in the community: a matter of choice

Robert B. Edgerton

During the past few years, investigators have begun to describe the life circumstances of ageing persons with mental retardation and to explore the social policy implications posed by this growing population. Some important findings have emerged. One basic finding is that a very large percentage of ageing persons with mental retardation live in supervised and restricted residential settings, even though this need not be the case. [. . .] This study was designed to examine the lives of a small number of older men and women who had lived in the community for thirty years or more without receiving any services for persons with mental retardation.

26.1 The research: sample and method

Ethnographic field research describing the lives of forty-eight persons released from a large state hospital for mentally retarded individuals was originally carried out in 1960–1 (Edgerton, 1967). When a second follow-up study was conducted a decade later (1972–3), sample attrition had reduced the study population to thirty (Edgerton and Bercovici, 1976). A third follow-up study with a still further reduced sample of fifteen persons was carried out in 1982 (Edgerton *et al.*, 1984). The present follow-up research began in 1985. Two members of the 1982 sample had died before 1985, but three other persons who were previously inaccessible for intensive research were added to the sample, which currently consists of nine women and seven men. The mean age of the sample in 1987 was sixty-one; their mean IQ was sixty-two. [. . .]

26.2 The findings

During the five years since the last follow-up study of this sample (Edgerton *et al.*, 1984), there have been few dramatic changes in life circumstances of surviving sample members. Sadly, two sample members had died, both of heart disease, and one woman's non-retarded husband was now deceased. Although his death was traumatic for this woman, who had been heavily dependent on him, she soon displayed remarkable independence in a previously unexplored range of activities. The other sample members had avoided major changes in their lives. Five years earlier these older persons with mental retardation had demonstrated social competence, independence and indomitable optimism. Five years later they had increased their independence, social competence and zest for life still further.

Although there are some general attitudinal and behavioural patterns that characterise this population, there is also substantial variation. One of the dilemmas posed by long-term, intensive ethnographic research is that, as masses of detailed data accumulate, each person being studied comes to stand out from all the others as an individual, and generalisation about an entire sample becomes difficult. This is not to suggest that individual differences among sample members are only artifacts of the methods employed. For example, some members of the sample were in robust health, others had a smattering of minor physical complaints and a few suffered from serious medical problems. Similarly, some were so well dressed and groomed that they were indistinguishable from anyone else in their neighbourhoods, but a few were dishevelled, wore tattered clothing, or needed to bathe. [. . .] These men and women differed tremendously in personality, as one might expect, as well as in their knowledge of world affairs. For example, several members of the sample were quite well informed about local, national and even international events, whereas a few had no apparent interest in events that lay outside their own personal domains. Finally, although everyone had at least a few friends, acquaintances or relatives, three of the women and one man were nevertheless quite lonely. The others were so involved in multiple personal relationships that loneliness was rarely, if ever, an issue in their lives. These older men and women differed in many ways in addition to those that have been mentioned, but my focus here is not on these differences but on the ways in which all of these people, or almost all of them, were alike.

After thirty years of community living, these older mentally retarded people continued to display striking self-reliance. Only one person had ever been dependent on Supplemental Security Income (SSI) for her entire income. Two other people supplemented their SSI income with earnings from part-time jobs. In addition to these three individuals, a 66-year-old man had recently qualified for social security benefits, and another woman would become eligible in a few months. [. . .] It is fair to conclude that the people in this sample had made their way in the community by working. When these people were first discharged from what was then Pacific State Hospital (now Lanterman State Hospital), they and other members of their cohort believed that nothing was as important as their ability to work. They were right. They were selected for discharge because they were competent workers, and their ability to sustain themselves throughout the 1960s depended on their work skills. Although their virtual obsession with being able to work had weakened over the years as friends, recreation and other interests had grown in importance, they continued to be self-supporting and self-reliant.

When these people were originally studied in 1960–1, I concluded that these former patients succeeded in their efforts to sustain life in the community only as well as they succeeded in locating and holding a benefactor (Edgerton, 1967). Over the ensuing years, reliance on benefactors had weakened so markedly that now only one person relied on a benefactor, defined as someone whose assistance is necessary and not reciprocated. This one instance involved a 60-year-old woman who had been strongly dependent on her non-retarded husband for over thirty years. When he died over a year ago, she was unable to cope with details of the funeral and her husband's estate. A neighbour stepped in to see her through these difficult times, and this woman continued to take a strong interest in protecting her against exploitation.

The remainder of the sample was not only free from reliance on benefactors, but four men in the sample themselves acted as benefactors toward non-retarded friends to whom they gave money and other aid without any expectation of reciprocity. Seltzer (1985) suggested that this sample's decreased dependence on benefactors might increase once again as members of the sample grew older. That may well prove to be so, but the mean age of the sample at the present time is sixty-two years, and it has not happened yet.

All of the people in this sample were involved in the lives of others. Everyone in the sample had some meaningful personal relationships in which they both received and gave help and, with the exception of the one woman mentioned earlier who relied on SSI for her income, everyone in the sample had also had at least one meaningful and long-term sexual relationship. It is difficult to capture the quality of these many relationships in a few words, but it may be enough to say that they were complex. In addition to various kinds of friendship, eleven members of the sample had been married, and four had children (the other members of the sample had been surgically sterilised as a precondition for release from the state hospital). Seven sample members frequently made sizeable financial contributions to others, and although these people rarely joined organisations, even churches, five of them regularly volunteered their time to organisations that served elderly, infirm or handicapped individuals. [. . .] At the risk of being repetitive, these people gave to others every bit as much as they got from them and, as these men and women have grown older, they have developed many more resources to share with others. In addition to small sums of money, they have shared useful information, emotional support and affection.

Another central finding concerns social competence. First, it is important to note that these men and women have done nothing that is anti-social. Without exception, they have not created public disturbance, committed theft, used drugs or engaged in criminal acts. Only one man drank alcohol, but it has been several years since his drunkenness has led to personal injury or police action. Although some sample members had a shaky start in adapting to community life, these sixteen men and women have demonstrated impressive mastery over those home, work and public social settings that constitute their everyday worlds. [. . .] Evenings were not spent simply watching television but in conversation, card games, hobbies, listening to music and other varied activities. These people demonstrated comparable mastery over their work environment where they had done well for years, and they coped quite well with public places such as buses, coffee shops, shopping malls, bowling alleys, swap meets and public parks. Their behaviour was appropriate, and the difficulties they once had using money had been overcome. When they were invited to unfamiliar places, such as moderately expensive restaurants, expensive shops or relatively costly recreational events, they also behaved appropriately and almost always clearly enjoyed themselves.

Occasionally, a novel circumstance caused difficulty. For example, a man who could not read was asked by an ailing neighbour to buy groceries for her. She wrote a long shopping list that utterly baffled the sample member, who was too embarrassed to ask anyone at the market to read the list for him. There were also some recurring problem areas, including medical care. With one exception, no sample member had a personal physician. Instead, they went to clinics that served low-income patients, HMOs, or county hospitals, where the care provided was impersonal and bureaucratic. Under these circumstances, sample members often had difficulty making appointments, discussing insurance coverage and explaining the nature of their ailment. [. . .]

In general, bureaucratic institutions presented formidable problems for sample members, as they do for many persons who are not mentally retarded. For example, even with the assistance of a literate friend, the Social Security Administration can be intimidating. One woman in the sample spent over a year attempting to deal with the Social Security Administration's demand that she repay several thousand dollars that were allegedly overpaid to her. Without records of her own and with little understanding of the letters sent to her by the Social Security Administration, she was helpless without an advocate. [. . .]

These few difficulties notwithstanding, the older people in this sample did much more than 'get by'. They maintained their health, happiness and personal interests. They earned their living, made friends and looked forward to the next day, and the next year. By objective criteria, the quality of their lives was not substandard in comparison with other older, low-income, low-education people. Subjectively, they said that their lives were satisfying; close observation confirmed this. They seldom complained, often expressed happiness, and then anticipated the future with pleasure. To be sure, they had some concerns about the future, such as ill-health, loss of income, the death of loved ones and the onslaught of urban renewal projects that could force them to move, but no one dwelled on these problems morbidly. These people were not hanging on to life grimly, nor were they ignoring their impending physical decline. They were enjoying what they had, and who they were, and they continued to face life with confidence.

26.3   Conclusion

When the people in this sample are compared with persons of similar age, IQ and physical condition who live in restricted residential settings, there are some striking contrasts. Some of these contrasts are obvious. Older persons who live in restricted residential settings are less independent and less normalised in dress, speech, activities, responsibility and recreational interests. They also have dramatically less control over their lives because both routine and crucial life decisions are typically made for them by others. Although it may be possible to exert some influence over these restricted environments by indirect means, in general the lives of older persons in restricted residential settings are scheduled, regimented and supervised. The result can be learned helplessness (Rowe and Kahn, 1987).

This brings us back to our original question, namely, could a substantial number of older persons in these restricted settings live more independently? The research record strongly suggests that a majority of mildly and even moderately retarded young adults can adapt successfully to community living if they are given enough time and the help of others in doing so (Lakin, *et al.*, 1981). There is, therefore, no good reason to doubt that many individuals who have lived the majority of their adult lives in restricted settings could adapt as well as the members of my sample if they are given the same opportunity to do so. My years of research in restricted settings convinces me that many residents of these places have physical, psychological and intellectual attributes similar to those possessed by the people in my sample who live independently. How would their lives be different if they lived more independently like the members of my small sample? For one thing, both their public and private relationships would be primarily with non-retarded persons, and these relationships would be reciprocal, not asymmetrical. They would also have a far wider range of social competencies, and, although this is speculation, it seems likely that they would also have greater self-esteem as a consequence of their success in community living. It is certain that they would live richer, more exciting lives.

Would all of this make them happier? The answer to this ultimate question is problematic. It is a measure of human adaptability that people are able to find happiness in all manner of life circumstances, and it is true, in general, that older adults who live in restricted settings, including those with mental retardation, frequently express satisfaction with their lives

(Baur and Okun, 1983; Thurman, 1983). It is also true that when many older persons with mental retardation are offered opportunities to live more independently, they decline the offer, preferring their restricted and routine lives to the unknowns of a new life. They not only fear the unknown, they have had little experience making choices, and that may be the key difference. The sixteen men and women who have lived on their own have had the right and the obligation to make choices, large and small, for over thirty years. Their choices are often constrained in many ways, as they are for all of us, but they are choices nonetheless. They control their own lives. Like children, persons with mental retardation who live in restricted settings have choices made for them. Our culture makes the right to choose for oneself a fundamental value. The right – and the necessity – to make crucial choices about one's life must be a central definition of normalisation. By this definition, the older mentally retarded people in this sample are as normal as anyone among us.

Acknowledgment

I gratefully acknowledge support from the National Institute of Child Health and Human Development Grants No. HD–05540–02 to the author, HD 04612 to the Mental Retardation Research Center, UCLA, and NICHD Program Project Grant No. HD 11944–02, The Community Adaptation of Mildly Retarded Persons.

References

BAUR, P. A. and OKUN, M. A. (1983) 'Stability of life satisfaction in late life', *Gerontologist*, Vol. 23, pp. 261–5.

EDGERTON, R. B. (1967) *The Cloak of Competence*, Berkeley, University of California Press.

EDGERTON, R. B. and BERCOVICI, S. M. (1976) 'The cloak of competence: years later', *American American Journal of Mental Deficiency*, Vol. 80, pp. 485–97.

EDGERTON, R. B., BOLLINGER, M. and HERR, B. (1984) 'The cloak of competence: after two decades', *Journal of Mental Deficiency*, Vol. 88, pp. 345–51.

LAKIN, K. C., BRUININKS, R. H. and SIGFORD, B. B. (1981) 'Early perceptions on the community adjustment of mentally retarded people', in Bruininks, R. H., Meyers, C. E., Sigford, B. B. and Lakin, K. C. (eds) *Deinstitutionalization and Community Adjustment of Mentally Retarded People*, Monograph No. 4, pp. 28–50, Washington DC, American Association on Mental Deficiency.

ROWE, J. W. and KAHN, R. L. (1987) 'Human aging: usual and successful', *Science*, Vol. 237, pp. 143–9.

SELTZER, M. M. (1985) 'Informal supports for aging mentally retarded persons', *American Journal of Mental Deficiency*, Vol. 90, pp. 259–65.

THURMAN, E. M. (1983) 'Exploring the experiences of mentally retarded older adults in group home settings', unpubl. doctoral dissertation, University of Michigan.

27 For better, for worse?

Linda Ward

> Despite the disappointments – the mini-institutions, the nursing homes, the
> neglectful boarding homes – no one can legitimately claim that the lives of
> people with developmental disabilities are not better today than when the
> current wave of reform began in the early 1970s. It would take a cynical and
> uninformed outlook to suggest that deinstitutionalization has been an utter
> failure, that community settings are just as abusive as institutions, that the lot
> of people with developmental disabilities has not improved considerably over
> the past 15 years or so.
>
> Just as surely, though, it would be naive to think that the hopes and dreams
> of the 1970s have come to pass. Far too many people with the label of mental
> retardation remain segregated, isolated, and cut off from other people, both
> in places referred to as 'institutions' and those referred to as 'community
> facilities'.
>
> Over the past decade and a half . . . we have seen and heard much that
> gives us hope and much that gives us cause for reflection. The next wave of
> the movement to halt the exclusion of people with developmental disabilities
> from society will face new challenges. (Bogdan and Taylor, 1987)

The purpose of this chapter is to review progress within community
services for people with learning difficulties in the 1980s. Experiences in a
local service in Bristol provide a 'case study' illustration of some key issues.
Some possible strategies for ensuring good-quality services in the future
are outlined.

27.1 Introduction

> We do not know how to get complex service systems always to do what we
> think they should. We do not know how to take ideas developed in fertile
> environments and apply them to ones not so open to innovation and
> change . . . (Taylor *et al.*, 1987a)

The Wells Road Service was set up by Bristol and Weston Health
Authority in 1982. Its primary purpose was to establish whatever housing
and support was needed by adults with severe learning difficulties – and
their families – who lived in, or originated from, its catchment area. This
covered three square miles of south Bristol, and a population of 35,000
people.

The service was created as an alternative to existing health authority
provision in the area, and was inspired by the ideas within the influential
King's Fund document, *An Ordinary Life* (1980). Flexible residential
support would be offered to any adult in need of it within ordinary houses
in the community. Other kinds of opportunity and help would also be
made available to the many individuals still living with their families. In

contrast to most other services at the time, no one would be debarred from any part of the service on the grounds that they were too 'handicapped' or 'disturbed'. By Easter 1983 the service was well under way: initially supporting six people in two staffed houses, and beginning to offer other kinds of help to many more individuals living in their family homes.

More than five years have elapsed since then. In that time, national and local policies have increasingly endorsed 'community care'. All over the country, community living schemes have mushroomed. Now, however, there is some anxiety that the pressure to close hospitals and the ensuing scramble for community care could result in services where the search for quality which inspired many new community developments – like Wells Road – will be lost. The concerns about 'community care' expressed by the House of Commons Social Services Committee (1985) and by the Audit Commission (1986) – of inadequate funding, poor staff-training arrangements, confused organisation and management structures, and resulting low-quality services – are echoed by service providers on the ground. It seems timely, therefore, to review the progress and problems of an early service like Wells Road. What can be learned from experiences there which can help in the quest for better quality services in the future? How can we apply the lessons learned by services developed five or ten years ago – in more 'fertile environments' of innovation and change – to the different political and economic circumstances faced by services today?

27.2   The Wells Road Service: reviewing the evidence

In reviewing experience at Wells Road most of the evidence drawn upon is that arising from the evaluation of the service which was carried out from its inception in 1982. The evaluation focused on five key areas: the evolution and operation of the service overall; staffing issues – selection, training and support; the 'quality of life' enjoyed by residents and other service users; the social integration of service users within the local community; and the costs and quality of the residential service (as compared with other alternatives).

In weighing up the strengths and weaknesses of the Wells Road Service it is convenient to consider both its achievements and its failures from three different perspectives: as a residential service; as a community support service; and as a 'model' community-based service.

The residential service: successes and strengths

At the time that Wells Road was established there was still considerable scepticism in this country about the feasibility of housing people with *severe* learning difficulties in ordinary homes in the community. Wells Road – and the many services that have succeeded it – have given the lie to early critics of the 'Ordinary Life' movement. People who have lived in hospital for many years (including special hospitals like Rampton), people with 'difficult' or 'disturbed' behaviour, mental health or other acute problems, people with profound or multiple handicaps, people who have always lived hitherto in a comfortable, protected family environment – all have successfully managed the transition to a staffed home, and flourished there. It is easy to forget now that this in itself constitutes some degree of 'success'. Those who said of prospective residents of the new service 'You'll never manage it', 'He'll be back in hospital in a fortnight' and 'She'll never survive' were proved wrong.

There is now considerable evidence from this and other services that individuals who move to small domestic environments (particularly from institutions) may suddenly develop new skills – making the bed, a cup of tea or a snack, using a vacuum cleaner, answering the telephone, putting laundry in the washing machine, hanging clothes out on the line, digging the garden, shopping, participating appropriately in church services, making definite choices about how to look (for example, deciding to grow a beard), what to wear and what to do. This may be partly a result of increased staff attention and organised teaching. It is also a result of the sheer enrichment of the immediate environment, the ready access to and opportunities for carrying out day-to-day tasks which an institutional environment (or an understandably protective family) may have rendered difficult (Felce *et al.*, 1986). It was also clear at Wells Road that individuals had access to a far wider range of activities, experiences and relationships – ranging from holidays abroad to adult education classes locally – than previously. Particular individuals – with severe communication difficulties and health problems – were able to receive either more specialist or more consistent, caring help than previously in their lives. Several individuals who had been particularly unhappy in their previous environments were demonstrably more content in their new one. (Inevitably, one or two others found that living in this less regimented environment brought its own, and different, stresses.) Attempts to measure the 'quality of life' available to residents in the staffed houses suggest that it was higher in comparison both with individuals' past experience and with other residential alternatives in Bristol and the South West at the time (Davies, 1987, 1988). Measured against the yardstick of the Five Accomplishments – choice, competence, respect, community presence and participation (O'Brien, 1987b) – residents at Wells Road were certainly 'better off' in every respect.

The residential service: some weaknesses

Although the quality of life available to residents of the Wells Road Service was high in comparison with past experience and other residential alternatives, nonetheless there were areas of concern. Some of these have been reviewed elsewhere (Ward, 1988b, 1988d). They included problems of incompatibility arising from the establishment of *group* homes for three people, usually unknown to each other before the move; difficulties in relationships between individual staff and residents; problems over consistency in staff behaviour; and dilemmas surrounding staff behaviour in what is at once both their workplace and – more importantly – the residents' *home*, issues of freedom of choice (for example, to overeat or eat the 'wrong' food) and the 'dignity of risk', particularly in an urban environment with treacherous roads.

Recent research has confirmed more fundamental causes for concern – in particular, the amount of time spent by residents doing nothing, their lack of hobbies or personal interests, the desperately low quality of experience and opportunities offered by the local adult training centre, and the sheer social impoverishment and lack of relationships in most residents' lives – a disturbing finding confirmed increasingly by other researchers in this area (see, for example, Donegan and Potts, 1988; Bratt and Johnston, 1987; Cattermole *et al.*, 1988).

All of these issues are underpinned by the increasing recognition over the five years since Wells Road was established that the provision by community services of ordinary homes in ordinary neighbourhoods is no longer enough. Ordinary houses should be only a starting point – the springboard for a better, fuller life in the community. Services like Wells Road now have more complex issues to address on behalf of their users, like the pursuit of meaningful daytime activities and employment and the fostering of long-lasting social relationships with ordinary, non-handicapped members of the community.

By its own standards, the Wells Road residential service could be judged to have failed in some other respects too. For reasons largely beyond its immediate control (Ward, 1988c) it has failed to expand and create the number of houses intended: a total of twelve people have been housed over the period studied, in comparison with a projected target at the outset of 35–40. Within the homes created, moreover, there have been increasing external pressures – dictated by fire precautions, environmental health regulations and the requirements of the Registered Homes Act – to establish households and procedures far from the ordinary routines enjoyed by other, non-handicapped members of the population (Ward, 1988c). Most importantly, pressures on the local hospital to close have resulted in an exclusive focus now on hospital resettlement. Individuals living at home with their families in the local community but needing housing in the near future can no longer be assured that this will be available.

Meanwhile, there has been a sharp increase in staff turnover within the Wells Road houses over the last two years for a variety of reasons (Ward, 1987a) – with unsettling, often distressing effects on the individual residents with whom staff have been so closely involved. It is clear that even relatively 'good' residential services like Wells Road now have much to learn from experiences in some parts of the United States where people have realised that group living, the disruptions of a shift system and inevitable staff turnover work against the achievement of 'an ordinary life'. As Taylor *et al.* (1987b) comment: 'The problem with group homes is that they are almost never homes.' A better alternative is to start with individuals, help them to pick a housemate of their choice (if they want one) then add on compatible (maybe live-in) staff and other support – whatever is necessary to accomplish day-to-day living (Rucker, 1987). This seems to approximate much more closely to how other people in society go about organising the domestic foundations of their own 'ordinary lives'.

The community support service: successes and strengths

The community support service at Wells Road was particularly innovatory. Most 'Ordinary Life'-type services established at the time concentrated entirely on residential provision, in particular for people who were moving out of institutions, back into the community. From the outset, Wells Road made a very firm commitment to adults already living at home with their families in the community, in two ways. First, they too would be offered the chance of a home of their own in the locality, rather than taking second place to those currently living in hospital, as happens in most other services. In this way, it was hoped that precipitate, unplanned admissions to hospital or other residential provision at times of family crisis, death or sickness might become a thing of the past. Adults (and their families) might instead be able to prepare gradually for a planned move away from the family home, in the same way as their non-handicapped peers. For those adults and their families who were not interested in this prospect, the community service had other, no less important, possibilities to offer – support and opportunities for new experiences and relationships, friends, classes, introductions to local groups and activities, assistance with particular skills or contact with other local agencies and professionals who might be of help.

The idea of a community support service geared to enabling individuals already resident in the community to achieve a better 'quality of life' in these ways was unusual, if not unique. Most other community mental handicap services were either geared to a bare 'crisis intervention' approach or focused on meeting people's *residential* needs, in particular those brought about by hospital closures. One or two domiciliary care services were being set up at the time, but their emphasis was far narrower, focused on 'skill teaching' in the home.

Within the Wells Road Service, community workers were involved in a much wider variety of activities tailored to the particular individuals with whom they were involved. Key features of the community support

workers' activities are summarised elsewhere (Ward, 1986a). They include: the introduction (and regular review and improvement) of individual programme plans for consumers who wanted them; support to
families from the practical and small (help with benefits, respite care,
incontinence aids) to the complex and far-reaching (including preparation
for a relative to move away from the family home); the establishment of a
variety of educational opportunities, leading eventually to participation in
integrated adult education classes; the development of an independent
housing association to acquire and manage the large number of houses
required by the service; the pursuit of various avenues for developing
leisure interests and making relationships and friends; the establishment of
networks of support embracing other professionals, family members and
others in the local community; and attempts to develop worthwhile
daytime opportunities including employment and work experience. The
success of the service was evident in the fuller lives enjoyed by consumers –
a job, a home of their own, new interests, skills and experiences, a first
weekend away from home, a friend. After years without help, families
were deeply appreciative of the support and information now available
('Now you do feel as though you've got some support. You're not going it
alone' (Ward, 1987b)). They were pleased at the new opportunities
available to their relatives ('I can remember when he'd come home from
the Centre, sit in the chair, television on and that was it . . . But now, he's
got more than a full social life'). They commented positively on the
benefits that ensued – a growth in confidence for the individual concerned
('A year ago, I never thought I could do any of this') and a sense of relief
for themselves ('When they told me I was just inside the Wells Road area, I
couldn't believe it – I could have cried, well I did cry. It was the best thing
that happened to me all year'; 'Well, it's relieved us, hasn't it?').

The community support service: some weaknesses

Consumers of the new service could find few faults (Ward, 1988a). On the
contrary, the new service brought enormous relief and satisfaction to
individuals and families who in the past had received very little and for
whom the future had promised little but uncertainty and concern. Other
professionals in the patch (social workers, community mental handicap
nurses) were also, after an initial period of negotiating territory and
respective responsibilities, largely happy with the new service – aware that
there were were far more unmet needs in the local area than they could
hope to meet on their own.

From the point of view of key 'stakeholders' in the service, then, it was
an undoubted success. Its only real failure was, however, fundamental: its
failure to survive. By 1986 plans to reproduce the community support
service in the wider Bristol and Weston Health Authority had been
abandoned. Within the Wells Road patch itself the original community

support service had been phased out, its surviving worker becoming a (temporary) member of the new local community mental handicap team. The reasons for this change of fate are complex to unravel, and have been partly explored elsewhere (Ward, 1986a, 1987c). A key factor appears to have been the relative powerlessness of 'stakeholders' within the service (individuals, their families and friends, the service staff and its manager) to advocate successfully its continued existence within the Wells Road patch and its replication in the wider health authority area. Wells Road had failed to secure powerful allies in the wider world – allies who shared its vision and would be committed to safeguarding it. Changes of personnel in key positions within the health authority also had a significant part to play, as key advocates for the Wells Road Service were lost in the aftermath of the Griffiths reorganisation.

A 'model' local service?

From the outset Wells Road was seen as more than merely a small-scale, local service. In making available ongoing revenue to establish and run the service, the (area) health authority had made it clear that some evaluation of the proposed 'model' was required. 'Success' should mean replication of the project elsewhere in the district. The research which ensued was funded by the Joseph Rowntree Memorial Trust in the hope that lessons learned by this small service might be of use to others embarking on similar ventures elsewhere.

Overall, research and experience revealed the service to have many positive features. Attention was paid to providing a good, supportive work environment for staff, in the belief that this would maintain morale, encourage staff to do a better job and, hopefully, lead to a better quality of life for the individuals with whom they worked (Porterfield, 1985). Details of the efforts made by the service in this area have been reviewed elsewhere (Ward, 1989). They included: detailed job descriptions (subject to regular review in the light of experience); regular staff meetings (for residential and community staff separately, and for all the staff team); individual staff supervision; group support sessions; intensive initial training; ongoing service training; and involvement in reviews of the service's progress and forward planning.

Other strengths of the model service (in addition to those outlined earlier) were:

- the successful grading of all staff posts initially on the administrative and clerical scale, to ensure an open recruitment policy thus allowing the appointment of people with relevant experience in education, social services and voluntary organisations rather than restricting the field to qualified nurses only;

- the adoption of 'support worker' as a job title to convey the emphasis of staff's work, rather than the more usual, but less appropriate, 'care assistant';

- the support given to community staff to act as 'professional advocates' (almost case-managers, see below) for their clients – even where the chosen course of action conflicted with the established wisdom or practice of other agencies or professionals;
- the small patch base, which meant staff could get to know individuals well and help plan ahead with particular people in mind (as opposed to the more conventional, large-scale, 'top-down' planning for abstract numbers of people estimated to be in different 'dependence' categories);
- the service's commitment to flexibility and learning by doing and, where necessary, from its mistakes (for example, its shift away from the original 'core and cluster' model (Ward, 1986b) together with its constant reappraisal and refinement of the individual programme plan system that it operated to maximise its benefit and acceptability to individual consumers);
- attempts to involve users, families and other people in the service through regular meetings for relatives, the involvement of other members of the community such as volunteers, friends or advocates, and the first steps towards promoting self-advocacy within the staffed houses via resident house meetings (the importance of building a sense of 'ownership' of local services amongst those with a stake in their success, such as users, families, advocates, neighbours and staff, is returned to below: their 'empowerment' may be critical to the pursuit, and defence, of high-quality neighbourhood services in politically unfavourable climates and at times of economic constraint).

27.3   Lessons for the future?

A number of specific weaknesses or problems in the Wells Road Service have been outlined, alongside its undoubted successes and strengths. An underlying issue must now be addressed: how to sustain and improve a good service once it is established.

One important strategy is to ensure that community services are regularly reviewed, and reviewed by those with a 'stake' in their success – that is, by staff, users, families, advocates, neighbours and managers alike. A variety of vehicles for such evaluation exist. *Positive monitoring* is one possibility. Positive monitoring involves a number of steps: setting out clearly what should be done within a service, teaching staff how to do it, regularly checking on how things are progressing and giving *positive*, constructive feedback to individuals on their work (Porterfield, 1985). *Quality Action Groups* (Independent Development Council for people with mental handicap, 1986) by contrast place more emphasis on the equal involvement of *all* stakeholders in regular service reviews. Representatives of front-line staff, users, families, friends and management form a group which meets regularly to evaluate the quality of their particular service and to take practical steps to improve it.

Finally much remains to be done in strengthening the voice of consumers and other representatives in the quest for quality. The significance of *self-advocacy* (individuals learning to speak up for themselves and their peers) and *citizen advocacy* (individual members of the community forming a partnership with someone vulnerable or at risk and not able to speak out for themselves) is now widely accepted – though financial support for the latter is hard to come by. *Empowerment* of families and relatives so that they may play a constructive role in service developments affecting their relatives – rather than the more hostile and negative role into which they are so often cast – is, however, almost unknown in this country.

In conclusion, it is clear that work must be done at every level if community services are to develop, survive and, most importantly, improve. For this to happen, the voices of users, advocates, families and staff, and their sense of 'ownership' of the services in which they are involved, must be strengthened. A common vision of what life could be like for individual users must be agreed by them and those close to them, and steps for moving closer to that vision taken. The involvement of managers in this process is vital. Managers who 'get to know' (Brost and Johnson, 1982) individual users of their service, and spend time with them, their families and staff, are more likely to become committed champions of the service if it comes under threat. The importance of managers sharing in a vision of the 'desirable futures' (O'Brien, 1987b) that the service is striving to effect for its users must be underlined. If services are locally based, small scale and flexibly organised then they are more likely to be able to respond creatively to the needs of the known individuals whom they serve. Rigidity, uniformity and large-scale planning are likely to work against the quality of individuals' lives. Finally, services must admit their mistakes and learn from them. Good services will set a value on learning from the lessons of the past and trying to do new – and better – things in the future: 'We need the courage and the grace to learn the lessons of our collective ignorance and fallibility. There is much to learn in close attention to our errors and failings as we work to share and improve the lives of people with handicaps' (O'Brien, 1987a).

Acknowledgments

Grateful thanks are due to the Joseph Rowntree Memorial Trust for funding the evaluation of the Wells Road Service on which this chapter is based.

References

AUDIT COMMISSION (1986) *Making a Reality of Community Care*, London, HMSO.

BOGDAN, R. and TAYLOR, S. J. (1987) 'Conclusion: the next wave', in Taylor, S., Biklen, D. and Knoll, J. (eds) *Community Integration for People with Severe Disabilities*, London, Teachers College Press.

BRATT, A. and JOHNSTON, R. (1987) 'Changes in lifestyle for young adults with profound disabilities following discharge from hospital care into a "second generation" housing project', *Mental Handicap Research*, Vol. 1, No. 1, pp. 49–74.

BROST, M. and JOHNSON, T. (1982) *Getting to Know You: One Approach to Service Assessment and Planning for Individuals with Disabilities*, Wisconsin, Wisconsin Coalition for Advocacy.

CATTERMOLE, M., JAHODA, A. and MARKOVA, I. (1988) 'Leaving home: the experience of people with a mental handicap', *Journal of Mental Deficiency Research*, Vol. 32, No. 1, pp. 47–57.

DAVIES, L. (1987) *Quality, Costs and 'An Ordinary Life': Comparing the Costs and Quality of Different Residential Services for People with Mental Handicap*, London, King's Fund Centre.

DAVIES, L. (1988) *Cost Evaluation of Residential Services for People with Learning Difficulties*, University of Birmingham, Health Services Management Centre.

DONEGAN, C. and POTTS, M. (1988) 'People with mental handicap living alone in the community: a pilot study of the quality of their life', *British Journal of Mental Subnormality*, Vol. 34, No. 66, pp. 10–22.

FELCE, D., de KOCK, U. and REPP, A. (1986) 'An eco-behavioural analysis of small community-based houses and traditional large hospitals for severely and profoundly mentally handicapped adults', *Applied Research in Mental Retardation*, Vol. 7, No. 4, pp. 393–408.

HOUSE OF COMMONS SOCIAL SERVICES COMMITTEE (1985) *Community Care with Special Reference to Adult Mentally Ill and Mentally Handicapped People*, London, HMSO.

INDEPENDENT DEVELOPMENT COUNCIL (1986) *How Good are Your Local Services for People with Mental Handicap?* London, Independent Development Council for People with Mental Handicap.

KING'S FUND CENTRE (1980) *An Ordinary Life: Comprehensive Locally-Based Residential Services for Mentally Handicapped People*, London, King's Fund Centre.

O'BRIEN, J. (1987a) 'Embracing ignorance, error and fallibility: competencies for leadership of effective services', in Taylor *et al.*, (1987a).

O'BRIEN, J. (1987b) 'A guide to personal futures planning', in Bellamy, G. T. and Wilcox, B. (eds) *A Comprehensive Guide to the Activities Catalog: An Alternative Curriculum for Youth and Adults with Severe Disabilities*, Baltimore, Paul H. Brookes.

PORTERFIELD, J. (1985) 'After initial training, then what? In-service training, positive monitoring and staff support', in Ward, L. and Wilkinson, J. (eds) *Training for Change: Staff Training for 'An Ordinary Life'*, London, King's Fund Centre.

RUCKER, L. (1987) 'A difference you can see: one example of services to persons with severe mental retardation in the community', in Taylor *et al.* (1987a).

TAYLOR, S., BIKLEN, D., KNOLL, J. (eds) (1987a) *Community Integration for People with Severe Disabilities*, New York, Teachers College Press.

TAYLOR, S. J., RACINO, J., KNOLL, J. and LUTFIYYA, Z. (1987b) 'Down home: community integration for people with the most severe disabilities', in Taylor *et al.* (1987a).

WARD, L. (1986a) 'Alternatives to CMHTs: developing a community support service in South Bristol', in Grant, G., Humphreys, S. and McGrath, M. (eds) *Community Mental Handicap Teams: Theory and Practice*, Kidderminster, British Institute of Mental Handicap.

WARD, L. (1986b) 'Changing services for changing needs', *Community Care*, May 22, pp. 12–13.

WARD, L. (1987a) 'After induction – then what?', *British Journal of Mental Subnormality*, Vol. 33, No. 65, pp. 131–42.

WARD, L. (1987b) 'A bit more peace of mind? Families' views of a community mental handicap service', *Social Work Today*, 30 November, pp. 12–13.

WARD, L. (1987c) 'Pursuing quality in community support services', in Ward, L. (ed.) *Getting Better All the Time? Issues and Strategies for Ensuring Quality in Community Services for People with Mental Handicap*, London, King's Fund Centre.

WARD, L. (1988a) 'Developing opportunities for an ordinary community life', in Towell, D. (ed.) *An Ordinary Life in Practice*, London, King's Fund Centre.

WARD, L. (1988b) 'Thwarting ordinary lives', *Community Care*, 21 January, pp. 22–3.

WARD, L. (1988c) 'What price ordinary life?', *Health Service Journal*, 10 March, pp. 276–7.

WARD, L. (1988d) 'Whose home is it anyway?', *Community Care*, 14 January, pp. 23–5.

WARD, L. (1989) 'An ordinary life: the views and experiences of residential staff', *Mental Handicap* (in press).

28 Community care: the ideal and the reality

Gillian Dalley

28.1 Introduction

The nineteenth century was a period which saw considerable investment in the provision of institutional care for dependent members of society – notably those deemed to be suffering from mental illness and those born with mental handicaps; the building of large-scale hospitals or asylums was regarded as a social achievement (Thompson and Goldin, 1975) and an advance on the neglect or barbarity of treatment which had so often characterised the past. Too often, however, the improvements of one generation become the outmoded encumbrances of the next. By the middle of the present century, it was becoming clear that institutional care had become a euphemism for the negation of individual rights and the imposition of care and treatment which was frequently harsh and in-appropriate (Goffman, 1961; Townsend, 1962). The past forty years have thus seen a movement away from institutions towards 'the community', with the aim of seeking to redress the iniquities of the worst forms of 'incarceration' (Walker, 1982).

In 1971 the first of several influential White Papers – *Better Services for the Mentally Handicapped* – was published (DHSS, 1971). This set out the principles, philosophy and priorities of an improved service for mentally handicapped people based firmly on the principles of community care. It stressed the importance of mentally handicapped people being able to live at home with their families or, failing that, in 'home-like' surroundings with the 'understanding and support of the community at large'. A second White Paper, this time relating to services for the mentally ill (DHSS, 1975), was equally firm in stressing the importance of community-based services. It claimed that a 'philosophy of integration rather than isolation still holds good; . . . (the) main aims must continue to be the development of locally based services and a shift in the balance between hospital and social service care'.

From 1976 onwards there has been a series of policy documents setting out government policy (Labour until May 1979 and Conservative since then) for the health and personal social services (DHSS, 1976, 1977, 1981a, 1981b). The cornerstone of those services which deal with long-term care – for all relevant client groups: elderly, mentally ill and mentally and physically handicapped people – has been community care.

The most recent documents to be produced have been the report of the Audit Commission (1986) and the findings of the Griffiths review of community care (1988). These mark a stage beyond the laying down of principles and policy: they are both concerned with reviewing progress made towards the implementation of community care policies and with cataloguing the deficiencies and lack of progress made – in spite of a widespread and general acceptance of the principles propounded. Those principles, at their broadest, are about moving people from long-stay institutions into family or 'family-like' homes and hostels, and preventing people from entering the old-style hospitals and asylums. But those principles and community care policies in general require further scrutiny; there are, perhaps, conflicting perspectives bound up in the policy package labelled 'community care'.

28.2   Ideal models

There has been a widespread embracing of the concept of community care by diverse sections of the policy establishment – politicians and their civil servants, planners, professional practitioners and their academic counterparts, and health and welfare managers. This might be termed what Dunleavy (1981) has called a case of 'ideological corporatism'. Almost all of these different interests would claim a commitment to the concept, although their definitions of the concept and their motivations for adopting it might vary considerably.

A discussion document published by the DHSS in 1981 (DHSS, 1981c) noted the lack of consistency or agreement about the meaning of the term 'community care'. Broadly speaking, there are four separate models which can be identified, although none is entirely discrete. First, there is one which is essentially *client-focused* and is particularly concerned with the principles, quality and standards of service which clients receive. Second is the *managerial-planning model*, which is particularly concerned with the process of deinstitutionalisation, the closure of long-stay hospitals and the discharge of their inmates into the community. Third is the *professional practice model*, which centres on the development of professionally delivered community-based and domiciliary services. Last is the model which emphasises *informal care* as the central element in community care, and embodies the notions of 'community', 'self-help' and 'neighbourliness' in contrast to professionally based forms of care.

Client-focused model

The 1971 and 1975 White Papers mark an early stage in the success of the client-focused model in influencing policy. Basic to the principles underlying it is a concern that people who are dependent on long-term care should retain full rights of citizenship and not be subject to 'incarceration' in old-style institutions. At the same time, active protection of their rights is important, thus there is an emphasis on self-advocacy or advocacy by supporters wherever possible (Sang and O'Brien, 1984; King's Fund Centre, 1985). The principles of normalisation propounded by Wolfensberger (1972) have been incorporated into this perspective: every human being, regardless of physical and mental disability or infirmity, has the right to be a valued member of society and to live a life as close as possible to 'normal' life, as defined by most members of society.

Of equal significance is the 'ordinary life' approach developed in recent years (Towell, 1988; King's Fund Centre, 1980). This approach builds on the view that the rights of disabled people to live 'ordinary' lives – unremarkable lives, not distinguished by the fact of their mental or physical disability – should be central to any policy of care provision. Care should be tailored around the needs of clients rather than the convenience of service providers; care receivers should be able, wherever possible, to live in ordinary houses in local communities, supported where necessary in meeting their needs. They should be able to be integrated into local activity – in short, should enjoy an ordinary life rather than a life apart.

Managerial-planning model

In contrast to the client-focused model, the managerial-planning model is more concerned with the process of implementing community care policies than with defining underlying philosophy and principles. The expected rundown of the large psychiatric and mental handicap hospitals, determined by policy-makers in past decades, is at the heart of this approach. In fact, closures have taken longer than anticipated (Audit Commission, 1986) but most District Health Authorities now have firm plans. The model is one of logistics and operational strategies – moving patients out into suitable placements in the community; overseeing and arranging the redeployment of hospital staff, sometimes moving them into the community too; disposing of large buildings, often on valuable sites; ensuring that budgets designated for the long-term care sector are protected ('ringfenced') and move out with the patients (King's Fund Institute, 1987) in the transition from hospital to community – and accomplishing this under conditions of resource scarcity (Lister, 1988).

Professional practice model

If the development of community care has been in part caused by a rethinking of the philosophy relating to the rights of individual patients, this has also been paralleled by changes in the way in which professionals see their roles in the provision of care. Sociological studies of the professions (Freidson, 1970; Johnson, 1972) suggest that professions and professionals are concerned to establish and maintain dominance in whatever fields they operate. As the switch in thinking about long-term care has occurred – from institutions to community, from custodial approaches to care to open, rights-focused forms – professions have had to think about recasting their roles (Hill, 1982), perhaps in order to maintain dominance. They are able to do this, as Wilding (1982) suggests, in several ways: through their ability to define needs and solutions (through the notion of 'professional expertise'); through their control over the allocation of resources, especially at 'street level' (Lipsky, 1983); and through their control of individual professional–client relationships. Further, they are able to set the agenda for policy debate at national level (Dunleavy, 1981) in so far as it relates to the form and content of practice.

As the development of community care policies has progressed, the professions involved have increasingly claimed key roles within them. The importance of the role of the community psychiatric nurse has been stressed (Carr, Butterworth and Hodges, 1980); the Royal College of Nursing (1985) published a document promoting the role of the community mental handicap nurse. The health service union COHSE has stressed the key role of their members in the development of community care (COHSE, 1977). The Griffiths Report (1988) sees the role of the GP as gatekeeper to the variety of community care services as of central importance. There have been ideological and demarcation disputes between the health service and social work professions about the appropriate roles of each in the implementation of community care (Dalley, 1989).

Informal care model

The last model of significance in the community care movement is one which identifies the importance of the role of informal care. In his study of services for mentally handicapped people, Bayley (1973) was perhaps the first to make the distinction between care *in* the community and care *by* the community, seeing the latter as having the most far-reaching implications. Since then, increasing emphasis has been placed on the role of family, friends and neighbours in the provision of care, although evidence is mixed about the degree to which it is reasonably available and reliable (Ayer and Alaszewski, 1984; Wenger, 1984; Abrams *et al.*, 1986). Policy documents since 1979 have stressed the importance of informal care (DHSS, 1981a, 1981b) and there has been a growth in the public recognition of the role of informal carers – for example, with the establishment of the Association of Carers in 1981 and the Informal Caring Support Unit at the King's Fund Centre in 1985.

The philosophy on which the model is based places individual and family responsibility for caring at the centre of community care; as a consequence it tends to underplay the importance of professionally provided services. Volunteers and unskilled paid workers are seen as having an important part to play (Hadley and McGrath, 1984; Bayley *et al.*, 1987).

Community care: a coherent model?

It is convenient, for the purpose of analysis, to examine the movement towards community care in terms of the models described above, but it would be mistaken to regard them as mutually exclusive. Individuals or interest groups may claim or be shown to hold views which 'fit' more than one of the views at the same time. Indeed, there seems to be a growing consensus – or ideological corporatism (Dunleavy, 1981) – about the rightness of community care as a strategic policy; there is an increasing recognition of the importance of individual client rights in relation to the pattern and design of policy and services. In this sense, it is perhaps justifiable to talk in terms of a coherent integration of the ideal models.

Nevertheless, there are elements within the policies which are contradictory. The interests of professionals, though their pronouncements may be clothed in a rhetoric of 'consumerism' and respect for client rights, may well run counter to the interests of those for whom they provide services. Conversely, stress on informal, volunteer and unskilled care may run counter to the interests of professionally trained staff. The concerns of managers and planners to operationalise policy – at the lowest possible cost – may lead to a playing down and devaluing of individual client needs. Reliance on informal care may be attractive to hard-pressed service providers but detrimental to the informal carers themselves.

In addition, there have been changes in emphasis over time. The community care movement can be traced back clearly to changes in professional practice in the mental health field during the 1950s. But in subsequent decades, policy-makers have focused on different elements – for various reasons, some to do with economic constraints and others to do with changes in the ideology of central government during the past decade. Greater stress is now placed on the role of individuals and families rather than on the state; the state is coming to be seen as 'enabler' for private and voluntary action rather than as provider; economic recession has created greater concern for issues of efficiency and value for money (Pinker, 1985).

28.3　The reality of community care

The ideals underlying community care may be mixed, but community care policies have been established with the intention that they be implemented. It is pertinent to enquire how far the practice of community care matches any of its ideals. The picture from the field is one of variation (Hunter and Wistow, 1987; King's Fund Institute, 1987): there is evidence of progress towards professed objectives in some areas and scant success in others. Studies of case-management and attempts to achieve efficiency in long-term care conducted by the PSSRU at the University of Kent (Davies and Knapp, 1988) have argued that experimental schemes must be evaluated rigorously in the light of hypotheses which they have generated relating to how proposed benefits might be secured. Furthermore, they are concerned with how the relationship between successful innovation at the local level relates to higher-level arrangements: creative policy development and implementation must, they argue, be integrated to be successful.

Three major reports in recent years have reviewed progress towards community care. The House of Commons Social Services Committee (1985), reviewing services for adult mentally ill and handicapped people, was pessimistic in its conclusions: in particular, it noted that the families of service users were placed under great strain because of failures and deficiencies in provision. The reports of the Audit Commission (1986) and the Griffiths review (1988) were also concerned with the patchiness of progress. While they described successful innovatory schemes (and suggested criteria by which they could be identified), they also analysed some of the reasons for a general lack of progress. Of these, fragmentation and lack of co-ordination of services, together with unsatisfactory financial arrangements, were prominent.

Critiques of community care

Just as there are several models of community care, so there are a number of critical perspectives on it which relate to those models. The work of the PSSRU has tended to adopt the managerial-planning model as a framework in its emphasis on efficiency, value for money and policy development and implementation. Similarly, the criticisms lodged by Griffiths and the Audit Commission have been located within the same perspective.

Some critiques, however, focus on aspects relating to the other models. Those who are concerned with individual client rights and needs look at the standards and quality of the services as measures of progress. A number of research studies have criticised the levels and quality of community care provision (Glendinning, 1983; Baldwin, 1985; Abrams, 1977; Heginbotham, 1985, 1988; Campaign for Mentally Handicapped People, 1980); others have been concerned with establishing evaluative approaches (Robertson and Osborn, 1985). Lack of will, low levels of commitment to client-focused policies, and lack of resources have been given as reasons for failures to ensure good-quality care.

Other criticisms have centred on what the reality of community care policies means in practice for those who provide care informally. Although the principles of informal care, based on notions of 'community' (Durkheim, 1960; Joseph and Sumption, 1979) and 'neighbourliness' (Abrams, 1977), are lauded in recent policy documents (DHSS, 1981b), such forms of caring, in fact, place enormous burdens on those providing the care (Hicks, 1988; Briggs and Oliver, 1985; Wright, 1986). Evidence seems to suggest that, where informal care is available, statutory services are less likely to be forthcoming regardless of particular needs and circumstances (Hunt, 1970; Blaxter, 1976). Furthermore, financial penalties are actually incurred under current legislation (Supplementary Benefit (Requirements and Resources) Regulations, 1987), where attempts are made to provide small-scale, family-style care for mentally handicapped or mentally ill adults. Carers in such circumstances are ineligible to receive the same level of payment as those who provide board and personal care in larger, registered homes – and yet they are providing precisely the informal 'family model of care' that central government has consistently advocated. Care within the private, domestic domain, it seems, cannot and should not be assessed in terms of financial worth.

Perhaps the most trenchant critique has come from feminists who have not only pinpointed the failures of the policies at a practical level but have also begun to examine some of the fundamental ideological premises upon which elements of the policies are based. Taking the evidence of an undue burden being placed on carers, particularly women, as a starting point (Equal Opportunities Commission, 1982; Brody, 1981; Parker, 1985), they have gone on to suggest that this is not by chance (Finch and Groves, 1980, 1983; Ungerson, 1983). Rather, it is linked to the position and role which women are still expected to play in society – based on notions of 'familism' (Barrett and McIntosh, 1982; Dalley, 1988). These notions run deep and frame not only the social expectations of women's roles – altruistic concern for others, for example, at expense to themselves (Land and Rose, 1985) – but also the models of family or surrogate family care which community care policies offer as the ideal for disabled people living in the community. At a philosophical level, it has been suggested (Dalley, 1988) that these concepts are linked closely to the pervasive ideology of possessive individualism which increasingly dominates contemporary political thinking – at the expense of collectivist values which might offer a greater source of support and concern both for women and for those who are dependent on structured forms of care.

28.4   Conclusion

Community care as a *generalised* concept has dominated thinking in the field of long-term care for several decades. Because it has many meanings and conceptual frameworks, any evaluation of its success or failure is problematic. The need, however, for long-term care – for reasons of demography and improvements in society's ability to ensure disabled people's chances of survival (Illsley, 1981) – will remain a key policy issue into the next century. But whether progress towards effective and appropriate forms of community care will ultimately be achieved has yet to be determined.

References

ABRAMS, P. (1977) 'Community care: some research problems and priorities', *Policy and Politics*, Vol. 6, pp. 125–51.

AUDIT COMMISSION (1986) *Making a Reality of Community Care*, London, HMSO.

AYER, S. And ALASZEWSKI, A. (1984) *Community Care and the Mentally Handicapped: Services for Mothers and Their Mentally Handicapped Children*, London, Croom Helm.

BALDWIN, S. M. (1985) *The Costs of Caring*, London, Routledge & Kegan Paul.

BARRETT, M. and McINTOSH, M. (1982) *The Anti-social Family*, London, Verso.

BAYLEY, M. (1973) *Mental Handicap and Community Care*, London, Routledge & Kegan Paul.

BAYLEY, M. *et al.* (1987) *Practising Community Care: Developing Locally-Based Practice*, Sheffield, Joint Unit for Social Service Research, University of Sheffield.

BLAXTER, M. (1976) *The Meaning of Disability*, London, Heinemann.

BRIGGS, A. and OLIVER, J. (eds) (1985) *Caring: Experiences of Looking After Disabled Relatives*, London, Routledge & Kegan Paul.

BRODY, E. (1981) 'Women in the middle and family help to other people', *Gerontologist*, Vol. 21, pp. 471–80.

CAMPAIGN FOR MENTALLY HANDICAPPED PEOPLE (1980) *Even Better Services: A Critical Review of Mental Handicap Policies in the 1970s*, London, CMH.

CARR, P. J., BUTTERWORTH, C. A. and HODGES, B. E. (1980) *Community Psychiatric Nursing: Caring for the Mentally Ill and Handicapped in the Community*, Edinburgh, Churchill Livingstone.

COHSE, (1977) *Memorandum of Evidence to the Royal Commission on the NHS*, London, COHSE.

DALLEY, G. (1988) *Ideologies of Caring: Rethinking Community and Collectivism*, London, Macmillan.

DALLEY, G. (1989) 'Professional ideology or occupational tribalism: the health service-social work divide', in Taylor, R. and Ford, J. (eds) *Social Work and Health Care, Research Highlights*, No. 19, London, Jessica Kingsley Publishers.

DAVIES, B. and KNAPP, M. (eds) (1988) *The Production of Welfare Approach: Evidence and Argument from the PSSRU*, Oxford, Oxford University Press for the British Association of Social Workers.

DHSS (1971) *Better Services for the Mentally Handicapped*, Cmnd 4863, London, HMSO.

DHSS (1975) *Better Services for the Mentally Ill*, Cmnd, 6233, London, HMSO.

DHSS (1976) *Priorities for Health and Personal Social Services in England: A Consultative Document*, London, HMSO.

DHSS (1977) *The Way Forward*, London, HMSO.

DHSS (1981a) *Care in Action: A Handbook of Policies and Priorities for the Health and Personal Social Services in England*, London, HMSO.

DHSS (1981b) *Growing Older*, Cmnd 8173, London, HMSO.

DHSS (1981c) *Report of a Study on Community Care*, London, DHSS.

DUNLEAVY, P. (1981) 'Professions and policy change: notes towards a model of ideological corporatism', *Public Administration Bulletin*, Vol. 36, pp. 3–16.

DURKHEIM, E. (1960) *The Division of Labour in Society*, New York, Free Press.

EQUAL OPPORTUNITIES COMMISSION (1982) *Caring for the Elderly and Handicapped: Community Care Policies and Women's Lives*, Manchester, EOC.

FINCH, J. and GROVES, D. (1980) 'Community care and the family: a case for equal opportunities', *Journal of Social Policy*, Vol. 9, No. 4, pp. 487–514.

FINCH, J. and GROVES, D. (eds) (1983) *A Labour of Love: Women, Work and Caring*, London, Routledge & Kegan Paul.

FREIDSON, E. (1970) *Professional Dominance*, New York, Aldine de Gruyter.

GLENDINNING, C. (1983) *Unshared Care: Parents and Their Disabled Children*, London, Routledge & Kegan Paul.

GOFFMAN, E. (1961) *Asylums*, Harmondsworth, Penguin.

GRIFFITHS, R. (1988) *Community Care: Agenda for Action* (The Griffiths Report), London, HMSO.

HADLEY, R. and McGRATH, M. (1984) *When Social Services are Local: The Normanton Experience*, London, George Allen & Unwin.

HEGINBOTHAM, C. (1985) 'New problems, new responses: an overview', in Horobin, G. (ed.) *Responding to Mental Illness*, Research Highlights in Social Work, No. 11, London, Kogan Page.

HEGINBOTHAM, C. (1988) 'Mental health: "the revolution that is going wrong"', in Lister, J. (ed.) *Cutting the Lifeline: The Fight for the NHS*, London, Journeyman Press.

HICKS, C. (1988) *Who Cares: Looking after People at Home*, London, Virago.

HILL, M. (1982) 'Professions in community care', in Walker (1982).

HOUSE OF COMMONS SOCIAL SERVICES COMMITTEE (1985) *Community Care with Special Reference to Adult Mentally Ill and Mentally Handicapped People*, London, HMSO.

HUNT, A. (1970) *The Home Help Service in England and Wales*, London, HMSO.

HUNTER, D. and WISTOW, G. (1987) *Community Care in Britain: Variations on a Theme*, London, King Edward's Hospital Fund for London.

ILLSLEY, R. (1981) 'Problems of dependency groups: the care of the elderly, the handicapped and the chronically ill', *Social Science and Medicine*, Vol. 15A, pp. 327–32.

JOHNSON, T. J. (1972) *Professions and Power*, London, Macmillan.

JOSEPH, K. and SUMPTION, J. (1979) *Equality*, London, John Murray.

KING'S FUND CENTRE (1980) *An Ordinary Life: Comprehensive Locally-based Residential Services for Mentally Handicapped People*, London, King's Fund Centre.

KING'S FUND CENTRE (1985) *Advocacy and People with Long-Term Disabilities: Report of a Conference Held at the King's Fund Centre*, London, King's Fund Centre.

KING'S FUND INSTITUTE (1987) *Promoting Innovation in Community Care: From Small-Scale Developments to Mainstream Provision*, London, King's Fund Institute.

LAND, H. and ROSE, H. (1985) 'Compulsory altruism for some or altruistic society for all?', in Bean, P. *et al.* (eds) *In Defence of Welfare*, London, Tavistock Publications.

LIPSKY, M. (1983) *Street-Level Bureaucracy: Dilemmas of the Individual in Public Services*, New York, Russell Sage Foundation.

LISTER, J. (ed.) (1988) *Cutting the Lifeline: The Fight for the NHS*, London, Journeyman Press.

PARKER, G. (1985) *With Due Care and Attention: A Review of Research on Informal Care*, Occasional Paper No. 2, London, Family Policy Studies Centre.

PINKER, R. (1985) 'Social welfare and the Thatcher administration', in Bean, P. *et al.* (eds) *In Defence of Welfare*, London, Tavistock Publications.

ROBERTSON, A. and OSBORN, A. (eds) (1985) *Planning to Care: Social Policy and the Quality of Life*, Aldershot, Gower.

ROYAL COLLEGE OF NURSING (1985) *The Role and Function of the Domiciliary Community Nurse for People with a Mental Handicap: Report of a Working Party of the RCN Community Mental Handicap Nurses Forum*, London, RCN.

SANG, B. and O'BRIEN, J. (1984) *Advocacy: The UK and American Experiences*, King's Fund Project Paper, No. 51, London, King Edward's Hospital Fund for London.

THOMPSON, J. D. and GOLDIN, G. (1975) *The Hospital: A Social and Architectural History*, New Haven, Yale University Press.

TOWELL, D. (ed.) (1988) *An Ordinary Life in Practice – Developing Comprehensive Community-Based Services for People with Learning Disabilities*, London, King Edward's Hospital Fund for London.

TOWNSEND, P. (1962) *The Last Refuge: A Survey of Residential Institutions and Homes for the Aged in England and Wales*, London, Routledge & Kegan Paul.

UNGERSON, C. (1983) 'Women and caring: skills, tasks and taboos', in Gamarnikov, E. *et al.* (eds) *The Public and the Private*, London, Heinemann.

WALKER, A. (ed.) (1982) *Community Care: The Family, the State and Social Policy*, Oxford, Basil Blackwell and Martin Robertson.

WENGER, G. C. (1984) *The Supportive Network: Coping with Old Age*, London, George Allen & Unwin.

WILDING, P. (1982) *Professional Power and Social Welfare*, London, Routledge & Kegan Paul.

WOLFENSBERGER, W. (1972) *The Principle of Normalization in Human Services*, Downsview, Toronto, National Institute on Mental Retardation.

WRIGHT, F. (1986) *Left to Care Alone*, Aldershot, Gower.

Section V Our common humanity

Introduction

In this final section we draw together some of the overall themes of the book, looking at articles which grapple with the need for broadly based theoretical frameworks. Many shifts have been taking place, as the other sections have indicated: in terms of changes in 'Roles and relationships', in 'Recognising oppression' and 'Discovering a voice', and in developing different forms of 'Support in the community'. These all involve the adoption of certain perspectives and frameworks of thinking, whether consciously or otherwise, which influence the ways in which problems are defined, understood and tackled – and by whom.

We look at such frameworks, however, from a particular perspective: that of a common humanity. The circumstances of people with learning difficulties, however severe some impairments may be, can be seen and understood alongside the experiences of other groups in society who have been deprived of human rights. The struggle to understand common human experiences that is involved in moving towards greater emancipation, indeed the struggle simply to understand more about people, is reflected here in our shared concern to make those, essentially human, connections.

The interrelated concepts of emancipation, normalisation and oppression are woven through the arguments and the differing interpretations presented here, and it seems to us they are useful concepts to bear in mind in trying to make sense of what happens to people. There seem to be parallels also in the experiences of black people and women, and we have drawn on some accounts here which show the relevance of those experiences and analyses.

Wolfensberger and Tullman open the section with their summarising exposition of what is meant and implied by the normalisation principle. This most influential framework of thinking has had a powerful and positive influence on the nature of service provision and the attitudes of service providers. In this extract it is clear how their theoretical framework leads to direct implications for practice.

Some would argue that the strong emphasis on establishing people in 'valued social roles' risks repeating the errors of the past when 'other people' always seem to know best what is good for you. Perrin and Nirje set the discussion in a rather wider context by exploring some of the varying interpretations of the concept of 'normalisation', and suggesting that Wolfensberger diverges from some of the original and current thinking in Scandinavia.

The next two articles borrow from feminist and black perspectives in turn. First, Smith and Brown consider what we can learn from the women's movement and also raise the question of conflicts of interest as community care policies impact on women in particular. Secondly, Baxter draws attention to the parallel experiences of black people and people with learning difficulties and considers the double discrimination faced by those who have both labels to contend with.

Robinson takes us more explicitly into questions of common humanity, recognising the apparent contradictions between the messages normalisation seems to offer and the wish to value each human life in its own right. We may, he suggests, be closing our eyes to important alternatives. Perhaps 'difference' is sometimes to be celebrated.

Williams, in her article, draws out some underlying themes in a discussion of the nature and experience of oppression. This important article helps us to review and reinterpret some of the earlier contributions to the Reader. It offers a clear and helpful perspective to use in both recognising and understanding some of the processes at work, and also in considering some of the ways in which oppression may be resisted.

Finally, in a valuable review of approaches to the development of knowledge and understanding through research, Sidell reminds us that we cannot be too confident about what we think we know. In her account of the philosophies of knowledge that lie behind the methodologies of research and practice, she takes us into challenging new areas of questioning and uncertainty. This seems an appropriate enough way to end a book which seeks to expand our understanding and help us in 'making connections', but which does not expect to find straightforward answers to questions which were never simple.

29   A brief outline of the principle of normalisation

Wolf Wolfensberger and Stephen Tullman

Wolfensberger subsequently replaced the term 'Normalisation' with the concept of 'Social Role Valorisation' (SRV), (Wolfensberger, 1983), which he hoped would reduce misunderstanding of the original term. Normalisation is frequently taken to mean that people are to be 'normalised', rather than, as he intended, that services and opportunities should be normalised. The emphasis on Social Role Valorisation has not been entirely successful in shifting interpretations, and the term 'Normalisation' has become widely established.

29.1   Introduction

The principle of normalisation first appeared in North America in the late 1960s (Wolfensberger, 1980). Since then, it has evolved into a systematic theory that can be used as a universal guiding principle in the design and conduct of human services, but which is especially powerful when applied to services to people who are devalued by the larger society. [. . .]

In discussing the normalisation principle throughout this article, we use the following simple definition: 'Normalisation implies, as much as possible, the use of culturally valued means in order to enable, establish and/or maintain valued social roles for people.' Though very brief, this definition has a vast number of implications for human services, ranging from the most global to the most minute. The definition reflects the almost paradigm-breaking assumption that the goal of human services with the most impact is social role enhancement or role defence.

Obviously, this definition reflects the assumption that if a person's social role were a societally valued one, other desirable things would be accorded that person within the resources and norms of his or her society. Indeed, the attributes of the person, which might otherwise be viewed negatively by society, may now be viewed positively. [. . .]

In order to perceive the crucial function of role enhancement, it is necessary to understand the dynamics of deviancy making. A person can be considered 'deviant' or devalued when a significant characteristic (a 'difference') is negatively valued by that segment of society that constitutes the majority or holds norm-defining power. [. . .]

Obviously, how a person is perceived affects how that person will be treated, and has the following implications:

1   Devalued people will be badly treated. Others will usually accord them less esteem and status than non-devalued citizens. Devalued people are apt to be rejected, even persecuted, and treated in ways that tend to diminish their dignity, adjustment, growth, competence, health, wealth, life span and so on. [. . .]

2   The negative treatment accorded devalued persons takes on certain forms that express the way society conceptualises the roles of a devalued person or group. For example, if a group of children is (unconsciously) viewed as animals, then they may be segregated in a special class that is given an animal name – often even the name of animals that are seen as expressive of a devalued children's identity. Thus a class for retarded children may be called 'The Turtles'. [. . .]

In the habilitation area it is very common for the sick role and perception to be attributed to clients who certainly are no sicker than most of the population, and who really need a developmental approach, adult education, industrial apprenticeship training and the like. Instead, they are interpreted as sick by association with medically trained staff. [. . .]

3   How a person is perceived and treated by others will, in turn, strongly determine how that person subsequently behaves. The more consistently a person is perceived as deviant, therefore, the more likely it will be that he or she will conform to that expectation and emit the kinds of behaviour that are socially expected, often behaviours that are not valued by society. [. . .]

29.2   The normalisation principle as a means of preventing, minimising or reversing societal devaluation

The fact that deviancy is culturally defined opens the door for psychologists to effect a two-pronged strategy of enabling devalued persons to attain a more valued membership in society by (1) reducing or preventing the differentness or stigmata that may make a person devalued in the eyes of observers and (2) changing perceptions and values regarding devalued persons so that a given characteristic is no longer seen as devalued.

Social role enhancement is the ultimate goal, but both stigma reduction/ prevention and societal attitude changing can be pursued through two major subgoals: (*a*) the enhancement of the social image of a person or group and (*b*) the enhancement of the competence of the person or group, including bodily, sensory, intellectual and social performance, and the practice of valued skills and habits.

Image enhancement and competency enhancement are believed to be reciprocally reinforcing, both positively and negatively. A person who is competency impaired is at high risk of being seen as being of low value and of suffering from image impairment; a person who is impaired in image and social value is apt to be responded to in ways that reduce his or her competency. Both processes work equally in the reverse direction.

The definition of normalisation used here places emphasis on 'the use of culturally valued means'. Service structures, programmes, methods, technologies and tools are all means towards the normalisation goal, and their value in the eyes of society is determined largely by the degree to which these means are used within the larger culture with and for *valued* persons of the same age, sex and so on. For example, the culturally valued analogue for the schedules of an educational programme for handicapped children would be the daily, weekly and yearly schedules of a school for non-handicapped children of the same age. Culturally valued analogues for a vocational programme for young adults might include apprenticeship, vocational school, night classes in vocational subjects, on-the-job-training and adult education. It would not include 'job therapy', make-believe work (valued people who perform fake work are at high risk of getting devalued) or playing games.

The reason culturally valued means are so important is at least fourfold.

1   Images are very transferable phenomena, as the worlds of advertising and public relations know only too well. The value message that is contained in a human service approach is highly apt to become attached to the people served. If delinquent boys were disciplined by means of electric cattle prods, they would be apt to be seen as animal-like. Relatedly, if a programme utilises means that deviate widely from cultural standards and norms, the devalued persons whom the programme serves are apt to be seen as different and distinct from other citizens – and *not* in a valued sense. As a result, the stigmata already attached to devalued people will be accentuated rather than minimised. In the end, the means that a service programme uses will have a powerful long-term effect on public attitudes towards (devalued) people. If the goal is to increase the level of public acceptance of people who are seen as negatively different, the message sent by what a programme does is as important as the changes it tries to achieve in its clients – and sometimes even more so.

2   Clients who are 'recipients' of certain services are apt to relate much better to them, both attitudinally and competently, if the means by which these services are delivered are familiar to them and are positively valued.

3   The skills, habits and relationships that are prerequisites for a meaningful life in open society are difficult to acquire in settings that are culture-alien, that lack familiar cues, reduce opportunity, suggest or impose alien or devalued roles, and so on.

4   The public, including families and staff, are less likely to support and relate positively to a human service programme that is unfamiliar, culture-alien and perceived as 'outlandish'.

It is possible to schematicise the normalisation principle in a number of ways that can help one to understand it better, and that can form a basis for the formulation of a variety of specific implementive measures. One way to schematicise the principle is to classify its implications into different levels of social systems as follows:

1   Actions on the level of the person concerned, usually a client.

2   Actions on the level of the person's relevant *primary* social systems (e.g. family) and *secondary* social systems (e.g. neighbourhood, community, service agency).

3   Actions on the level of society as a whole – that is, society's values, language usage, laws, customs and so on.

Thus combining the second and third levels, all action implications could be represented by the schema in Table 29.1.

Table 29.1   Implications of the two major goals of the normalisation principle on three levels of social organisation

Levels of action	Major action goals	
	Enhancement of personal competencies	Enhancement of social images
The individual	Eliciting, shaping and maintaining useful bodily, mental and social competencies in persons by means of direct physical and social interactions with them	Presenting, managing, addressing, labelling and interpreting persons in a manner that creates positive roles for them and that emphasises their similarities to, rather than their differences from, other (valued) persons
Primary and secondary social systems	Eliciting, shaping and maintaining useful bodily, mental and social competencies in persons by adaptive shaping of such primary and secondary social systems as family, classroom, school, work setting, service agency and neighbourhood	Presenting, managing, labelling and interpreting the primary and secondary social systems that surround a person or that consist of persons at risk so that these systems, as well as the persons in them, are perceived in a valued fashion
Societal systems	Eliciting, shaping and maintaining useful bodily, mental and social competencies in persons by appropriate shaping of such societal systems and structures as entire school systems, laws and government	Shaping cultural values, attitudes, and stereotypes so as to elicit maximum feasible acceptance of individual differences

A second way to conceptualise the normalisation principle is to break it into seven major strategies or strategy-related dynamics called *core themes*. We have found that most people understand the normalisation principle best by reviewing these themes, which capture and express most of the goals and processes of the principle. These seven core themes are:

1   The role and importance of (un)consciousness in human services.

2   The relevance of role expectancy and role circularity to deviancy making and deviancy unmaking.

3   The 'conservatism corollary' of normalisation, with its implications of positive compensation for people's devalued or at-risk status.

4   The developmental model and personal-competency enhancement.

5   The power of imitation.

6   The dynamics and relevance of social imagery.

7   The importance of societal integration and valued social participation.

Each theme is explained below.

29.3   The seven core themes of normalisation

The role of (un)consciousness in human services

[. . .] Normalisation is concerned with the identification of the unconscious, and usually negative, dynamics within human services that contribute to the devaluation and oppression of certain groups of people in a society, and with providing conscious strategies for remediating the devalued social status of such people. Furthermore, such normalisation-based service evaluation instruments as Program Analysis of Service Systems (PASS) (Wolfensberger and Glenn, 1978a, 1978b) and especially Program Analysis of Service Systems' Implementation of Normalization Goals (PASSING) (Wolfensberger and Thomas, 1983) have been deliberately structured so as to reward consciousness of human service issues on the part of human service personnel.

The relevance of role expectancy and role circularity to deviancy making and deviancy unmaking

The social roles that people impose on each other or adopt are among the most powerful social influence and control methods known. As with unconsciousness, the dynamics of role expectancies and role circularities are ever-present. A person who holds certain expectancies about the behaviour or potential for growth and development of another person will create conditions and circumstances that have a high likelihood of eliciting the expected behaviour. [. . .]

In the case of socially devalued people, the role expectancies that are imposed upon them are commonly negative ones. These role circularities are very effective in that devalued people often live up to them. [. . .]

Thus, a human service for devalued people must do everything within its power to break the negative roles into which its devalued clients are cast, and to establish such clients in as many positive social roles as possible.

The conservatism corollary to the principle of normalisation

Many people have negatively valued characteristics, but these are usually so few or minor that they do not place a person into a deviant role or hinder his or her functioning. Unlike other citizens, however, devalued people exist in a state of heightened vulnerability to further devaluations and negative experiences. [. . .]

The conservatism corollary of normalisation posits, therefore, that the greater the number, severity and/or variety of deviancies or stigmata of an individual *or* the greater the number of deviant people there are in a group or setting, the greater the impact of (1) the reduction of one or a few of the individual stigmata, (2) the reduction of the number of deviant people in the group or (3) the balancing off (compensation) of the stigmata or deviancies by the presence or addition of positively valued manifestations. [. . .]

Thus it is not enough for a human service to be merely neutral in either diminishing or enhancing the status of devalued persons in the eyes of others; it must seek to effect the most positive status possible for its clients. For example, on occasions where either a suit and tie or a sports jacket and sports shirt are equally appropriate attire, the man at value-risk in society would fare better wearing the suit-and-tie combination.

The developmental model and personal-competency enhancement

[. . .] Normalisation requires that the personal competencies of devalued (or at-risk) people be enhanced for a variety of reasons, among them the fact that even the appearance of competency in a person tends to elicit other positive feedback from observers, and society will be more accepting of any devalued traits or behaviours of people who otherwise have valued skills and competencies. In addition, a lack of competencies may inhibit devalued persons in many areas of functioning, a crucial one being social interactions, especially with valued persons. [. . .]

The power of imitation

[. . .] The models that are available for devalued people to imitate are often negative ones. Devalued people typically are (1) segregated from valued society and models, (2) grouped with other devalued people who very frequently have socially devalued characteristics and exhibit socially devalued behaviours and (3) often served by less competent human service workers than are valued people. [. . .]

Normalisation requires that the dynamic of imitation be capitalised upon in a positive way so that the role models provided to devalued persons are people who function routinely in an appropriate and valued fashion. Furthermore, normalisation implies that one would increase the sense of identification of devalued people with valued models, because people are much more apt to imitate those people with whom they identify.

The dynamics and relevance of social imagery

The use of unconscious image association is another effective learning and behavioural control mechanism. Historically, devalued people have been attached to and surrounded by symbols and imagery that overwhelmingly represent culturally negatively valued qualities. While these image associations are often made unconsciously, they strongly influence the role expectancies for and the social valuation of the persons so imaged. [. . .]

The implication of normalisation is that, as much as possible, any features of human services that can convey image messages about clients at value-risk should be positive. The incorporation of the dynamic of image transfer has implications for every aspect of a human service. Such features would include the physical setting in which the service is rendered (location, cleanliness, beauty, what it is near, etc.), the name of the service and its administrative body, the agency logo, the sources of funds, how clients are grouped, what kinds of programming are provided, the appearance projected by clients, what the clients are called, and what the service activities are called. [. . .]

The importance of societal integration and valued social participation

[. . .] Because segregation tends to make people more devalued and more dependent, society pays a high price for it in many complex and deeply hidden ways.

Normalisation requires that a devalued person or group has the opportunity to be personally integrated into the valued social life of society. Devalued people would be enabled to live in normative housing within the valued community and with valued people; be educated with their non-devalued peers; work in the same facilities as other people; and be involved in a positive fashion in workshop, recreation, shopping and all the other activities in which members of a society engage. [. . .]

It must be emphasised that the type of integration implied by normalisation theory is very specific: personal social integration and valued social participation. 'Physical integration', which merely consists of the physical presence of devalued people in the community, is only a potential *facilitator* of actual individual valued social participation. Also, social integration is not the same as 'mainstreaming' and 'deinstitutionalisation', which often are not truly integrative. [. . .]

*.4 Additional perspectives on the normalisation principle

In respect of the goal of normalisation, one can say that a person is normalised if he or she has that culturally normative degree of personal autonomy and choice that society extends to its non-devalued members, has access to the valued experiences and resources of open society much as would be the case for a typical citizen, and is free to and capable of choosing and leading a life-style that is accessible to at least the majority of other people of the same age. These goals are not attainable for every person, so it is important to keep in mind the qualifying phrase 'as much as possible' in the normalisation definition. Normalisation strategies must take into account the particular individual concerned, the limits of our current know-how and the individual's own choice of his or her personal goals and means. Low expectations, inappropriate pessimism, stereotyping and the like can have a very destructive effect on the person involved. Consequently, an adaptive human management approach is to maintain a healthy scepticism when confronted with the assertion that a specific normative human service measure or interpretation is unattainable or unrealistic.

The normalisation principle has sometimes been criticised as imposing cultural uniformity. In truth, it (1) promotes social tolerance and bridge-building, (2) opens up an enormous range of valued options that are commonly denied to almost a third of our population and (3) enables (not coerces) many people who have been devalued and excluded *against their will* to participate more fully. Only a few people or groups can be said to truly and deliberately choose social marginalisation and devaluation of their own free will. Even when they say they do, they often do so only reactively in response to *prior* rejection by society. For example, there never existed a self-segregatory movement among elderly people until relatively recently, when ageing became a human condition that received strongly patterned rejection and discrimination. [. . .]

References

WOLFENSBERGER, W. (1980) 'The definition of normalization: update, problems, disagreements, and misunderstandings', in Flynn, R. J. and Nitsch, K. E. (eds) *Normalization, Social Integration, and Community Services*, Baltimore, University Park Press.

WOLFENSBERGER, W. (1983) 'Social Role Valorisation: a proposed new term for the principle of normalisation', *Mental Retardation*, Vol. 21, No. 6, pp. 234–9.

WOLFENSBERGER, W. and GLENN, L. (1978a) *PASS (Program Analysis of Service Systems): A Method for the Quantitative Evaluation of Human Services – Handbook*, 3rd edn, Toronto, National Institute on Mental Retardation.

WOLFENSBERGER, W. and GLENN, L. (1978b) *PASS (Program Analysis of Service Systems): A Method for the Quantitative Evaluation of Human Services – Field Manual*, 3rd edn, Toronto, National Institute on Mental Retardation.

WOLFENSBERGER, W. and THOMAS, S. (1983) *Program Analysis of Service Systems: Implementation of Normalisation Goals (PASSING)*, 2nd edn, Toronto, National Institute on Mental Retardation.

30 Setting the record straight: a critique of some frequent misconceptions of the normalisation principle

Burt Perrin and Bengt Nirje

While normalisation ideas evolved in Scandinavia during the 1960s, the normalisation principle as concept was developed and articulated by Bengt Nirje and given its first statement in print by him in 1969 (Nirje, 1969). Since then, normalisation very quickly has become one of the most influential and widely quoted concepts internationally in mental retardation and in other human services areas, and has played a major role in the movement, however slow, towards community living. The principle has major implications regarding the ways we view and act towards handicapped people and for the programmes we develop for them.

Yet the normalisation principle has been widely misunderstood, by many of its advocates as well as by its critics. In some cases it has been misinterpreted so perversely as to produce implications and programmes directly opposite to what is intended by the principle! The purpose of this paper is briefly to identify and discuss a few of the more common misconceptions. As well, the later statement of normalisation by Wolfensberger deviates dramatically from the principle as originally conceived and presented by Nirje. Some of the more significant of these differences, particularly those reflecting different values and views of people, will be discussed.

What is the normalisation principle? As defined by Nirje (1976, p. 231): 'The normalization principle means making available to all mentally retarded people patterns of life and conditions of everyday living which are as close as possible to the regular circumstances and ways of life of society.'

Bank-Mikkelsen (1976, pp. 27–8) describes normalisation as meaning the acceptance of the mentally retarded with their handicap, offering them the same conditions as are offered to other citizens, inclusive of treatment, education and training needed to provide for optimal development. Implicit in the principle of normalisation is the concept that mentally handicapped people are entitled to the same rights and opportunities as are available to others in their society, including opportunities to exercise personal preferences and freedom of choice.

30.1   Some common misconceptions

Eight of the most common misconceptions of the normalisation principle are briefly discussed below.

Misconception 1: 'Normalisation means making people normal'

Probably the most common misinterpretation of the normalisation principle is the mistaken belief that it means mentally handicapped people must be expected, indeed be forced, to act 'normal', to conform in all respects to society's statistical norms for all dimensions of behaviour. Normalisation frequently has been confused with normalcy.

No, no, no! Normalisation does *not* mean normalcy; it does *not* mean that people should be normalised; it does *not* mean that anyone's behaviour should be forced to conform to any particular standard (for example, what 51 per cent of one's neighbours do or what 'experts' feel is best); it does *not* mean that mentally handicapped persons are expected to be made normal or to act like other people. It *does* mean that opportunities and support should be provided to permit a life-style similar in nature to that of other members of society, including similar opportunities for individual variation and choice. Normalisation means the acceptance of persons *with* their handicap within 'normal' society, with the same rights, responsibilities and opportunities as are available to others.

Misconception 2: 'Special services are inconsistent with the normalisation principle'

The normalisation principle, on the contrary, supports, indeed insists upon, the provision of whatever services, training and support are required to permit living conditions and routines similar to that of others in the community. At a minimum, this would include appropriate housing, opportunities for some form of work (or education for children) and leisure. This will vary from person to person depending upon need and personal preferences.

Most 'normal' people as part of 'normal' life use specialised services when appropriate. For example, a person with heart trouble may consult a cardiologist. The purpose of this abnormal treatment is to permit the continuation of everyday living patterns (i.e. 'normal' living).

The normalisation principle indicates that mentally handicapped people similarly should have access to those forms of special or added assistance they require in order to take part in normal living in the same way that 'special' services are provided to other members of society. Where possible, generic services (for example, regular dentists) should be used. A word of caution: just as with some medical conditions where the treatment or cure may be worse than the disease, some special services, despite their benefits, may actually *detract* from, rather than enhance, normal living (for example, institutions).

It also has been falsely claimed that special administrative organisations to co-ordinate or facilitate needed services for mentally handicapped people are inconsistent with normalisation. Normalisation, rather, deals with conditions of life; administrative organisation is secondary. Those organisational forms and administrative structures that support the furthering of all facets of integration of handicapped people are consequently more appropriate than other, more restrictive, forms and structures (Nirje, 1980).

Misconception 3: 'Normalisation supports dumping people into the community without support'

The normalisation principle has been interpreted falsely to mean that mentally handicapped people should be placed in the community without any support or assistance, however essential it may be. On the contrary, physical placement in the community does not necessarily represent integration or normalisation: the pertinent question is how closely the lives of mentally handicapped persons approach those of other members of the community. Where they do not, in the case for example of someone isolated in a rat-infested boarding house, this represents false integration, *not* community living or normalisation.

As Nirje (1980, pp. 47–9) has discussed, normalisation involves six different forms of integration (for example, social integration). Physical placement in itself is insufficient and does *not* represent normalisation.

Misconception 4: 'Normalisation is an all-or-nothing concept'

A common misconception is that normalisation refers only to totally independent living. However, there are degrees of normalisation, and the principle implies provision of a *range* of support and structure, depending upon the individual's need and abilities (for example, a continuum of housing, including highly structured settings and various forms of co-operative living; work alternatives, including work stations, other low-support arrangements, as well as sheltered employment; etc.). Normalisation can be applied as well to improve conditions and programmes within an institutional setting.

Misconception 5: 'Normalisation is appropriate only for the mildly retarded'

On the contrary, the normalisation principle applies to all, and indeed its implications may be most far-reaching for people with more severe handicaps. As Nirje (1976) has indicated, some of the ideas which led to the development of the principle grew out of analyses of facilities and programmes for severely handicapped people, in the attempt to make their living situation and patterns of life more similar to that of others.

Misconception 6: 'Mentally handicapped people are best off with their own kind, protected from the rigours of society'

This myth, however well meaning, has led to the creation of large asylums and institutions where, in the name of 'protecting' people, they too often have been (and still are) subjected to inhumane treatment and living conditions. But even more significantly, this view is contrary to factual evidence. Dybwad (1982), for example, has pointed out that the abilities of mentally handicapped people have been grossly underestimated. Given appropriate training and opportunity, they can function at levels never considered possible (see, for example, Gold, 1972). Thousands of 'hopeless' cases, once freed from restrictive institutions, not only have demonstrated their ability to function more than adequately as people, but have expressed a clear preference for this life-style.

Misconception 7: 'Normalisation is a Scandinavian concept inapplicable elsewhere'

Normalisation does not mean the application of Scandinavian services elsewhere, and in fact is neutral regarding cultural values. The specific implication of normalisation will be different for every culture, as what constitutes normal living patterns and opportunities varies from society to society. Ironically, the principle may be easier to implement in many developing countries which do not have an entrenched infrastructure of facilities and programmes, along with a history of segregating handicapped people from the community.

Misconception 8: 'Normalisation is a humanistic concept, but idealised and impractical'

On the contrary, one of the major benefits of the principle is that it is practical, providing guidance for how we view and treat handicapped people, along with many specific action implications. [. . .]

30.2   The Wolfensberger deviation from the original concept of normalisation

Up until now, we have spoken of normalisation as originally defined by Nirje, with its emphasis on normal living opportunities, patterns and circumstances of life. However, in recent years Wolfensberger's (1972) definition also has received considerable attention, and as he (Wolfensberger, 1980b) notes, most discussions of the pros and cons of normalisation have failed to distinguish between the differing versions of the principles.

We wish to indicate clearly that Wolfensberger's version of 'normalisation' deviates in many significant ways from the original concept of the principle and thus, contrary to Wolfensberger's (1972, p. 28) claim, cannot be considered as a reformulation, refinement or operationalisation of the principle. Rather his version, with its focus on using normative means and on establishing normative behaviour, is built upon a fundamentally different value base and conception of people, with quite different implications for how we view and treat handicapped people.

The original concept of normalisation as articulated by Nirje and discussed earlier in this paper is really quite simple: mentally handicapped (and other handicapped) people should be given the opportunity to live a life as similar in nature as possible to that of others, with similar rights and responsibilities. Just as (within certain limits which vary from society to society) a 'normal' individual may engage in unpopular, nonconformist or even 'deviant' behaviours, the normalisation principle implies that the same right also should apply to mentally handicapped people. Normalisation emphasises clearly respect for the individual and his or her right to be different. As Dybwad (1982) has indicated in his own critique of Wolfensberger, it is normal to be different.

Wolfensberger (1972, 1980a), on the contrary, interprets normalisation as specifying various standards of behaviour to which a mentally handicapped person must conform. He speaks openly of 'normalizing' people through 'eliciting, shaping, and maintaining normative skills and habits' (Wolfensberger, 1972, p. 32; 1980a, p. 17) or even through the use of force: 'Normalizing measures can be *offered* in some circumstances, and *imposed* in others' (Wolfensberger, 1972, p. 28, italics in original).

Note that the above statements make no provision for a person's *own* preferences regarding his or her life-style. Wolfensberger is not *opposed* to the concept of self-determination, and indeed he does include this as one of the ratings in PASS (Program Analysis of Services Systems, a rating system developed by Wolfensberger's interpretations of normalisation). However, he (Wolfensberger, 1980b) indicates that this right to choose may be in conflict with what is defined as appropriate, normalised behaviour and he clearly indicates that the latter should take priority. [. . .]

The values and implications of the above are alien to those of the normalisation principle as originally delineated. Wolfensberger requires a mentally handicapped person to act in conformity to values chosen by *others*. To us, this authoritarian approach, however benevolent in its intentions, represents an unwarranted abuse of the powers of the therapeutic state, well documented elsewhere (for example, Kittrie, 1971). Normalisation as originally conceived indicates that individuals should be encouraged and assisted in expressing their *own* preferences and making their *own* choices; normalisation implies that opportunities and training should be provided to assist in this process.

Are mentally handicapped people capable of making any choices regarding their lives? As previously discussed under Misconception 6, the capacities of mentally handicapped people to do just this have been well documented elsewhere (for example, Nirje, 1972; Dybwad, 1982). While in some cases assistance with certain decisions may be required, this is no different in kind from the situation of 'normal' people when faced with unfamiliar areas (for example, medicine, the law, economics, plumbing).

Wolfensberger has recently (1980b) clarified that his specification of 'normative' behaviours does not necessarily refer to the statistical mean. However, his conservatism corollary is even more limiting: 'With a choice from among the continuum of options around the cultural value mean, the more positive (or conservative) option' should be chosen (Wolfensberger, 1980a, p. 16). This once again fails to consider the preferences of individuals by prescribing standards of behaviour which they must follow. We also note with no further comment the value base which automatically asserts that the more conservative options are by definition more positive!

A key element of normalisation as originally proposed is the provision of opportunities for mentally handicapped people so that they can live a life similar to that of others. Wolfensberger's conservatism corollary blatantly contradicts this by *setting* different standards than for 'normal' people. For example, he indicates that: a mentally handicapped person should not work with animals although he says it is perfectly acceptable for others; handicapped people should not wear their hair long, even though others in the community may do so; a middle-aged man should wear a necktie even though appearing in public with an open collar may also be normative in his community. If any handicapped persons associated with a programme under assessment by PASS refused to conform to the above (and to other similar examples), the programme would be downgraded in its assessment, irrespective of the personal preference of values of the clients.

At a PASS workshop held in Toronto in 1974, numerous examples along the above lines were presented. A black woman in attendance finally said: 'You aren't talking about normalisation; you are talking about making people into upper-middle-class whites!' Wolfensberger imposes solution whereas Nirje and the normalisation principle indicate proper ways to put questions concerning a situation and the development of solutions, allowing for individual preferences.

Wolfensberger's model of normalisation in our view is excessively concerned with the notion of mentally handicapped people 'passing' in society. As defined by Goffman (1963), passing refers to the ability of members of deviant groups to minimise their differences or signs of deviancy so that they can 'pass' undetected into society. For Wolfensberger, this means that mentally handicapped people must not do anything which will lead to them standing out or attracting attention to themselves and risking being labelled as deviant. Hence the conservatism corollary discussed above.

This applies to Wolfensberger no matter how appropriate the difference may be. To cite two examples, he argues that a mentally handicapped person should not wear a visible hearing aid, even if the hearing otherwise cannot be corrected (Wolfensberger and Glenn, 1975, Vol. 11, p. 31); a washroom in a residence would be downgraded in a PASS assessment if it has special gripbars, even though such modifications may be necessary for the convenience of disabled residents (PASS workshop referred to above). We note that, while likely unintentional, the acronym PASS is the same term used by Goffman (1963) to describe the process whereby minority and deviant groups attempt to hide or deny their differences.

This concern with passing and obsession with minimising deviancy leads to an emphasis by Wolfensberger on the *appearance* rather than the *reality* of normalisation. [. . .] It is contrary to the direction taken by most minority groups, at least in the Western world, which now are insisting upon their right to equality of opportunity without having to deny or hide their uniqueness. It is also contrary to the recent direction taken by self-help movements of handicapped people, including the mentally handicapped, such as People First, who are now demanding the services they need to enable them to participate on the same basis as do others in society. [. . .]

Wolfensberger also takes a narrow reductionistic approach to normalisation, focusing on specific behaviours which can be manipulated by others and easily measured. The original definition of normalisation involves the availability of and the freedom to choose among the normal range of options, life circumstances, patterns of life and opportunities, with the ability to participate on the same basis as do others in society. PASS and other such standardised devices are not suitable for measuring normalisation expressed in these terms. While the *appearance* of normalisation may be subject to measurement by PASS, this is far less significant than the *reality* of normalisation as defined above, including consideration of individual preferences and experience. This also is subject to scientific scrutiny (for example, Kebbon *et al.*, 1982).

Wolfensberger's narrow focus on observable behaviours has led him (and others) to create a meaningless distinction between means and ends. For example, he (Wolfensberger, 1980b) has labelled Nirje's definition of normalisation as means rather than ends oriented (presumably because it speaks of *making available* patterns and conditions of life rather than of *imposing* specific behaviours upon people). Yet he also has labelled Bank-Mikkelsen's statement of normalisation, which is essentially the same as Nirje's, as concerned only with outcome and not with means! This may be because Bank-Mikkelsen (as does Nirje) points out that normalisation is silent with respect to appropriate treatment modalities. As discussed earlier under Misconception 2, pedagogical methods such as precision teaching, early infant stimulation are no more or less inconsistent with normalisation than pedagogical methods in general. The criteria is the same: do they work?

30.3   Conclusion

The normalisation principle has been described by Dybwad (1969) as 'elegant in its simplicity and parsimony. It can be readily understood by everyone'. While we agree with the first part of Dybwad's statement, it is apparent that, in the intervening years, normalisation has been subject to numerous misinterpretations which this paper has attempted to address.

The normalisation principle has been misunderstood and misinterpreted for too long. It does not necessarily imply conformity, but rather the freedom to live a life based on the same values and on the same terms as others in society. Proper understanding of normalisation and its meaning can go a long way towards improving services, life conditions and the dignity of handicapped people.

References

BANK-MIKKELSEN, N. E. (1976) 'The principle of normalization', in Nielsen, B. (ed.) *Flash 2 on the Danish National Service for the Mentally Retarded*, Copenhagen, Personal Training School.

DYBWAD, G. (1969) 'Action implications, USA today', in Kugel, R. and Wolfensberger, W. (eds) *Changing Patterns in Residential Services for the Mentally Retarded'*, Washington DC, President's Committee on Mental Retardation.

DYBWAD, G. (1982) 'Normalization and its impact on social and public policy', in *Advancing your Citizenship: Normalization Re-examined*, Eugene, Oregon, Rehabilitation Research Training Institute.

GOFFMAN, E. (1963) *Stigma: Notes on the Management of Spoiled Identity*, Englewood Cliffs, N.J., Prentice Hall.

GOLD, M. (1972) 'Stimulus factors in skill training of retarded adolescents on a complex assembly task: acquisition, transfer and retention', *American Journal of Mental Deficiency*, Vol. 76, pp. 517–26.

KEBBON, L., HJARPE, J. and SONNANDER, K. (1982) Report of research findings on the evaluation of the normalization principle. Paper presented to the IASSMD Congress, Toronto.

KITTRIE, N. N. (1971) *The Right to Be Different: Deviance and Forced Therapy*, Baltimore, Johns Hopkins Press.

NIRJE, B. (1969) 'The normalization principle and its human management implications', in Kugel, R. and Wolfensberger, W. (eds) *Changing Patterns in Residential Services for the Mentally Retarded*, Washington DC, President's Committee on Mental Retardation.

NIRJE, B. (1972) 'The right to self-determination', in Wolfensberger, W. *The Principle of Normalisation in Human Services*, Toronto, National Institute on Mental Retardation.

NIRJE, B. (1976) 'The normalization principle', in Kugel, R. and Shearer, A. (eds) *Changing Patterns in Residential Services for the Mentally Retarded*, revised edn, Washington DC, President's Committee on Mental Retardation.

NIRJE, B. (1980) 'The normalization principle', in Flynn, R. J. and Nitsch, K. E. (eds) *Normalization, Social Integration and Community Services*, Baltimore, University Park Press.

WOLFENSBERGER, W. (1972) *The Principle of Normalization in Human Services*, Toronto, National Institute on Mental Retardation.

WOLFENSBERGER, W. (1980a) 'A brief overview of the principle of normalisation', in Flynn, R. J. and Nitsch, K. E. (eds) *Normalization, Social Integration and Community Services*, Baltimore, University Park Press.

WOLFENSBERGER, W. (1980b) 'The definition of normalization: update, problems, disagreements, misunderstandings', in Flynn, R. J. and Nitsch, K. E. (eds) *Normalization, Social Integration and Community Services*, Baltimore, University Park Press.

WOLFENSBERGER, W. and GLENN, L. (1975) *PASS – Programme Analysis of Service Systems*, Vol. I – Handbook, Vol. II – Field Manual, 3rd edn, Toronto, National Institute on Mental Retardation.

31   Whose community, whose care?

Helen Smith and Hilary Brown

A movement for change in mental health and mental handicap services to community based services has much to learn from the Women's Movement. Feminists, in their analysis of the oppression and discrimination experienced by one group in our society, have provided a useful framework within which to understand the 'second-class citizenship' accorded to people with disabilities. Lessons from women's experiences can help build bridges with the growing community care and self-advocacy/ user movements to negotiate creative ways forward in this area of social policy.

In this article we want to explore parallels between the oppression and discrimination experienced by women and by all people (men and women) who use mental health and mental handicap services. We also hope to question some basic and probably unconscious assumptions contained in the move to community care, and to look at how women in their role as both paid and unpaid carers are exploited by a society which has dominant male values as its norm.

The relationship between 'valued' and 'devalued' social groups is played out at all sorts of levels and the Women's Movement has much to offer in its analysis of oppression because of gender; in analysing the tensions between the world of private relationships (for example, caring) and public policy (for example, services) (Evans, 1979); and in its analysis of the way families, and by implication many small-group living situations, work for and against different members (Barrett, 1980). A feminist perspective, then, on the way 'community care' is being implemented is long overdue given the relevance of much feminist theory to this area of social policy.

The experience of being 'devalued' against standards which are taken to be universal is one area in which many groups in society – women, black people and service users among them – find common cause for concern. Aspiring to and in some cases taking on the values and roles of the dominant social group is a strategy which feminist women have rejected, leading as it does to changes for a few 'exceptional' women without affecting the way women as a whole perceive themselves or are perceived. Our experience suggests that it is preferable to reown and reassert some alternative ways of being in the world rather than be seduced by valued but not necessarily valuable roles.

31.1   The experience of being other than 'normal'

The slogan 'the personal is political' (Coedt, 1973 *et al.*) was a springboard from which women could develop an awareness of their position; issues which had previously been relegated to the personal domain, such as family relationships and domestic violence, were reclaimed as areas of political consequence. The analysis of the collective experiences of women asserted that the day-to-day life of individual women is governed by wider rules and regulations rooted in a male-centred definition of the world. Self-advocacy groups in both mental illness (Survivors Speak Out) (Barker and Peck, 1987) and mental handicap services (People First) are similarly looking to understand their individual experiences as having shared themes and political implications arising from their definition as a deviant social group. They too will need to develop a theoretical base which allows for the interplay of different factors (race, gender, sexual orientation, class), and does not create a false impression of homogeneity. Individual con-sciousness-raising is one route to empowerment but does not, in itself, create change in society.

Feminists such as Dworkin (1981) have analysed the power of patriarchy as being based on the metaphysical assertion of self. There is an 'I am' that exists a priori for men that women are not allowed to express. Men have firmly established themselves as the norm with women in counterpoint to them. People who use services share this secondary status and have their statements of self constantly eroded and ignored. Like women, who are the 'opposite' or 'second' sex in relation to men, service users exist in relation to a supposed norm and are described in terms that emphasise their deviation from it. Thus they are *dis*abled as opposed to able, *in*sane as opposed to sane, *sub*normal as opposed to normal. Many service users exist in relation to their diagnosis, being described and even introduced to others as 'a schizophrenic' or 'a Down's syndrome' until they have taken into themselves this spoiled identity. 'I'm spastic' someone might say in the same apologetic tone as women who are 'just housewives'.

People who have a disability are subjected to a series of stigmatising and further handicapping experiences. They are often separated from their friends and family (as women are in moving around following their husbands' jobs). They are often economically dependent (as many women are on benefits or 'allowances' from their husbands). The rhythms and routines of their daily lives set them apart from mainstream activities (as do those of women confined by children to the house). They become associated with children and child-like activities and talked to as if, because of their lesser status, they are themselves children and lack their full years' worth of valid human experience (the 50-year-old 'girls' in the office, for example, or the 'mums' on the committee of the local nursery). We are not drawing these parallels in order to play down the qualitative difference

between the lives of many women and the levels of deprivation experienced by people in long-stay human services. Rather we wish to indicate
the pervasiveness of these mechanisms in the processes which downgrade
whole classes of people in our society and establish the validity of looking
to women's experience and literature for debate about the structures of
oppression and strategies for withstanding them.

This shared experience of powerlessness is evidenced by the fact that
services have real physical power over people's lives which is masked by a
focus on individual pathology in the same way that responsibility for
violence against women, and the threat of it, is shifted on to individual
women. The popular view that women *cause* male violence through the
clothes they wear or by walking alone at night suggests that it is they who
are powerful and therefore to blame for initiating such behaviour. Similarly the devalued status and restriction of rights experienced by service users
is attributed to the effects of illness and not to contact with and the
practices of the psychiatric system. Yet despite the 'pathologising' of users'
experiences, the psychiatric language still implies blame: users are described as having weak super egos, inadequate personalities, poor life
adjustment. Moreover, the conditions in which individuals can be said to
be making meaningful choices are often absent in 'client' relationships, as
they are between men and women where an element of coercion is often
either stated or implied. Professionals may not only manipulate decisions,
but also avoid responsibility for the outcome by making a charade out of
the process of consent and consultation.

There are many further instances where both women and people who
rely on services are disempowered in similar ways. Just as women are
circumscribed by invisible and differential rules such as the amount they
are allowed to speak in meetings without being deemed to have spoken too
much (Spender, 1980), so are the possibilities for people who use services
limited by powerful assumptions about what is proper for someone who is a
'patient' or 'client' of the system. Relationships between women are
trivialised, just as links between people who have lived together on a
hospital ward for many years are disregarded. If either women or service
users are seen to be too skilled to be contained within the stereotypes to
hand, they are split off so that women who think logically are described as
being masculine in their approach and people with learning difficulties who
speak out for themselves are said to be 'hardly handicapped at all'.

Relationships between people who come together on the basis of
alienation or a shared history of oppression are complex and ambivalent.
People whose identity is fragile are vulnerable to competition and envy and
may find it difficult to identify with each other. They see in the stigma of
the other their own degradation. They may apply the same oppressive
categories as professionals to lift themselves out of the class of the 'worst
cases', the 'low grades', the 'undeserving poor'. Many women also
internalise the view that their relationships with other women are unimpor-
tant and gravitate towards men. Like people with disabilities they come to

believe what the dominant ideology says about them.

Alternatively victimisation may become the characteristic identity which binds a group of women together (Raymond, 1986), tying them to a history of pain, anger or depression with the result that success or autonomy can seem to jeopardise this one lifeline of support. Service users are also in danger of seemingly gaining power through relationships forged by a common enemy – psychiatry – and a shared negative identity as victims. This is ultimately self-defeating as the personal growth of individuals is sacrificed in order to maintain the integrity of the group, leading to dissatisfaction, resentment and splitting.

The common theme running through these analogies is the existence of a more powerful group which states that it is the norm against which others are measured. The effects of this process on service users are that they are caught in a vicious circle whereby their deviation from this supposed norm deprives them of the personal power and authenticity which they need to challenge legitimately the validity of the whole process. Just as women's experiences are sanctioned and redefined by men, so are service users' experiences constantly translated and interpreted by professionals. The dominant social group will allow labels to be changed or sanitised (as in 'subnormal' to 'with learning difficulties') and may even concede real improvements in material conditions (as in allowing women to take credit in their own names). However, power to move the boundaries around (even if this leads to more leniency) merely highlights the basis of control. Rights which are *given* can equally be taken away.

The recent move to limit the availability of abortion illustrates this process. The 1967 Abortion Act enabled women to seek abortion on certain grounds, adjudicated by the medical profession. Twenty years later we see a move to restrict severely these concessions. What is never given is a once-and-for-all decision that women should have control over their own bodies and over major decisions in their lives. For people who use services the same is true. Thirty years ago parents of children with disabilities were told to put their children in hospital; now they are told that hospitals are closing. It is politically expedient at this particular time to replace long-stay hospitals and provide services for people in the community. However, the commitment to pursue valued life-styles for disadvantaged people will never seriously challenge the status quo or hide the fact that service users are not in control of their own lives. A government decision in twenty years' time could reverse the situation and people in dispersed community services would be powerless to resist. The hope is that community integration will increase the potential for members of the public to become advocates against such encroachment on the rights of people with disabilities. Whether such patronage would be offered or sufficient is a matter of conjecture.

31.2   Living in the community: happy families for all?

The analysis of the position of people who use services as being one of continued oppression and discrimination in the community may seem too theoretical in the face of the very real improvements in the lives of people who have left long-stay institutions. However, the types of service being set up in the community are based on many unconscious assumptions about what is a 'normal' way of living; these services may do little, therefore, to challenge dominant values. In replicating situations which oppress women, services may unwittingly render women users doubly vulnerable to discrimination, and perpetuate the exploitation of women as carers.

Goffman (1961) fired the opening gambits in the campaign to break up institutional models of services:

> A basic social arrangement in modern society is that the individual tends to sleep, play and work in different places, with different co-participants, under different authorities, and without an overall rational plan. The central feature of total institutions can be described as a breakdown of the barriers ordinarily separating these three spheres of life.

The issues had already been cast from an exclusively male point of view. This basic social arrangement advocated by Goffman may indeed be the most valued (and hence the most 'normal') pattern but it is not the most socially cohesive, belonging primarily to men, and to employed men at that. It is a life-style which is supported by, indeed *relies* on, servicing by women who are themselves rarely afforded the luxury of compartmentalising their lives in this way (as evidenced by their shopping in the lunch hour or taking annual leave to look after sick children).

It is no joke that marriage qualifies as an institution, 'within which women are reduced to a common social type' (Oakley, 1974). Because the issues are not addressed in terms of power and powerlessness, in terms which challenge the invisibility of women's different life experiences and the unequal value placed on women's work, most progressive caring services have sought to replicate for everyone some notion of what a valued, idealised (and usually asexual) life-style might look like – a notion which is riddled with hidden assumptions. As Wolfensberger (1972) asserts:

> One thing that can be very bad about our ideologies is that more often than not, we are not aware of them. Sometimes we take them so for granted that we lose sight of their existence. [. . .] There are few things more vicious, more maladaptive, more inimical to individual and collective well being than unconscious ideologies.

He goes on to review how ideologies have forged '*man*'s patterns of response to devalued groups of fellow *men*' (our emphasis). Services not aware of these dynamics will continue to disempower people, especially women, in the new community settings.

31.3 Women as carers: paid and unpaid

How can any movement advocate 'care' in the community without acknowledging how and why women hold together other people's fragmented lives? 'The ethos of female care for others is not simply an alternative to the predominant male values of a strategic intelligence and abstract moralizing; rather it emerges from a context that assumes female inferiority and powerlessness' (Westkoff 1986).

The 'maintenance' role ascribed to women is one of those things which is so taken for granted that we lose sight of its existence; it remains hidden as long as it is functioning properly, and because it is a 'given' in most situations it is neither planned for nor properly recompensed. It is most successfully masked when subsumed under the umbrella of a personal or familiar relationship when the work will be lost in a blur of duty and sentiment. An alternative position, and one which does not undermine the rights of women to be paid for the work they do, is that articulated by Dalley (1988):

> By collectively taking on responsibility for the provision of care, the tensions, burden and obligation inherent in the one to one caring relationship, which are the byproduct of the family model of care, are overcome. Particular individuals are not forced into particular caring and cared for roles, dictated by their social and biological relatedness; for it is in those relationships that dependence becomes a warped and unhealthy pressure on the actors involved.

When care is offered within the context of family relationships, the needs and rights of unpaid carers are neither acknowledged nor respected. Thus our services for adults with learning difficulties continue to assume that mothers will be there at the end of the arbitrarily short working day which their sons and daughters are offered. Relatives' views on major life changes or new service models are not sought or much taken into account on the grounds that they are not the legitimate client of the service. Yet the frequency with which carers become clients in their own right as a result of stress and distress demonstrates the inadequacy of adhering to this simplistic formulae.

For paid carers, the vast majority of whom are women, the close identification between caring as women's work and its subsequent relegation to the category of low-paid, low-status work is glaringly clear. Hierarchical health service structures, particularly in residential establishments, mirror and often distort traditional patterns of power and dominance within the family. The segregation of women in their roles at home is reflected throughout human services with its predominantly male management and female workforce.

Normalisation principles deal with issues about the status of workers in terms of their low status or deviant image rubbing off on the client to his or her further detriment. The close identification between caring as women's work and its subsequent relegation to the category of low paid, low status work, make this level of analysis derisory.

While caring is a function which does not attract status, authority or decent pay, collective routes are more likely to achieve change. An alternative strategy would be to use equal opportunities policies and structures, where they exist, to bring test cases using the principle of equal pay for work of equal value; to re-establish the complexity and demanding nature of caring for people with special needs; and to renew a political struggle for funding which is equal to the task. Users of the service and staff might find common cause if they became aware of the effects of being ghettoised together and worked jointly on tackling these issues.

Ambivalence stalks behind the jargon of community care and the best carers come saintly and cheap. Being defined by other people is as damaging if that definition is idealised as it is if derogatory (Dworkin, 1981). The process we see in the vision of twentieth-century motherhood (Dally, 1982) has resulted in mothers being put on a pedestal while their real needs and those of their children are not addressed. This generalises to women's work in the caring professions, nurses being a prime example of 'angels' who cannot afford to pay the mortgage. While caring continues to be work done by women, organised by men, to be mystified as a kind of *natural* outlet for women rather than as skilled and physically demanding work, carers, paid and unpaid, will continue to be simultaneously scapegoated and flattered while their need for a decent standard of living and proper resources is ignored or redefined.

31.4   Conclusion

Service users, like women, need an accurate and clear analysis of the reality of the world and of their oppression within it. Feminist scholarship has much to offer in its analysis of the way values are expressed through social relationships and social structures, and in its subjective exploration of 'otherness'. People who wish to change the caring services for the betterment of the lives of those who use them need to foster a far-sighted and open-minded vision of how things might be – a vision which, because it is grounded in reality and fairness, inspires people towards action. Women have been grappling with these issues for centuries (Wollstonecraft, 1792; Spender, 1982), although their voices have only recently been heard or put on record. As users find themselves on the brink of a major change in the way they receive services, and start to discover a collective voice, the least we can do is share what we have learned.

Acknowledgment

The views expressed in this chapter are those of the authors as individuals and as feminist women. Thanks are due to the many friends and colleagues who have helped to sharpen and influence our thinking.

References

BARKER, I. and PECK, E. (1987) *Power in Strange Places: User Empowerment in Mental Health Services*, London, Good Practices in Mental Health.

BARRETT, M. (1980) *Antisocial Family*, London, Verso.

COEDT, A., LEVINE, E. and RAPONE, A. (eds) (1973) *Radical Feminism*, New York, Quadrangle.

DALLEY, G. (1988) *Ideologies of Caring: Rethinking Community and Collectivism*, London, Macmillan.

DALLY, A. (1982) *Inventing Motherhood*, London, Burnett Books.

DWORKIN, A. (1981) *Pornography: Men Possessing Women*, London, The Women's Press.

EVANS, S. (1979) *Personal Politics*, New York, Vintage Books.

GOFFMAN, I. (1961) *Asylums*, Harmondsworth, Penguin.

OAKLEY, A. (1974) *The Sociology of Housework*, Oxford, Martin Robertson.

RAYMOND, J. (1986) *A Passion for Friends: Toward a Philosophy of Female Affection*, London, The Women's Press.

SPENDER, D. (1980) *Man Made Language*, London, Routledge & Kegan Paul.

SPENDER, D. (1982) *Women of Ideas and What Men Have Done to Them*, London, Routledge.

WESTKOFF, M. (1986) *Feminist Legacy of Karen Horney*, New Haven, Connecticut, Yale University Press.

WOLFENSBERGER, W. (1972) *The Principles of Normalisation in Human Services*, Toronto, National Institute on Mental Retardation.

WOLLSTONECRAFT, M. (1792) *A Vindication of the Rights of Women*, reprinted 1978, London, Penguin.

32 Parallels between the social role perception of people with learning difficulties and black and ethnic minority people

Carol Baxter

Sociological analyses demonstrate that the response to difference in our society has produced many devalued and disenfranchised groups of people. Because of their different intellectual capabilities, people with learning difficulties find themselves cast into negative social roles. This produces a process of devaluation and discrimination which results in their being denied their full rights as citizens (Wolfensberger, 1975).

One area which has not been given much attention is the situation in which a person possesses more than one socially devalued characteristic. Historically, black and ethnic minority people have been on the fringe of society. In the field of health and social welfare, the issue of colour and ethnicity is therefore an important one because it cuts across all other devalued groups to produce double and even multiple levels of discrimination.

Wolfensberger (1972) identifies eight social role perceptions that are particularly damning to people with learning difficulties. This paper sets out to draw parallels between these eight social role perceptions and the way in which black and ethnic minority people are evaluated in British society. It aims to demonstrate that both groups have been historically attributed identical social roles with the effect that people with learning difficulties who are also from black and ethnic minority communities experience double discrimination.

Paul Williams (1985) has presented an overview of Wolfensberger's eight perceived roles of people with learning difficulties. What now follows are quotations from Paul Williams' overview, followed by a discussion of how they relate to black and ethnic people. Since these social role perceptions are only notional categories for describing people's experiences, there will inevitably be some overlaps.

32.1 As subhuman

Historically, mentally handicapped people were considered to be less than fully human. Institutions were built without the ordinary comforts of a home because mentally handicapped people were not considered to have the same human feelings as other people (Wolfensberger, 1975). Even today, we have managed to coin the term 'subnormal' – perilously close to 'sub-human'. Only a few years ago a working party of the Anglican Church in Canada, considering church policy on euthanasia, talked of 'the grave mistake of treating human-looking shapes as if they were human' (Shearer, 1981). (Williams, 1985)

Black and ethnic minority people have similar experiences. Slavery and other forms of imperialism against black people were excused and justified on the grounds that black people were not only unchristian but also not human beings. By the height of the slave trade these views seem to reflect prevailing attitudes. In 1760 the 23-volume, London-published *Universal History* expressed the view of Africans as subhuman: 'It is hardly possible to find in any African any quality but what is of the bad kind, they are inhuman' (cited in Fryer, 1984). Edward Long, a popular historian of that period, developed this view: 'When we reflect on . . . their dissimilarity to the rest of mankind, must we not conclude that they are different species of the same genus' (cited in Fryer, 1984). Scientific explanations were sought and Social Darwinists put forward the theory that the white races were becoming dominant because of their 'natural' superiority and that the elimination of inferior races would strengthen humanity (Alexander, 1987). Science was soon used, therefore, to justify not only imperialism and domination but the oppression and even genocide of black people. It is from this basis that racism in British society developed its roots. This form of racism is based on the belief in the superiority of the white race.

Today, partly as a result of this history, prejudices may be directed against black and other, particularly non-white, ethnic groups in this country. Even well-intentioned people (including professionals who provide services for people with learning difficulties) may, as a result of their education, experience and environment, hold negative, patronising and stereotyped views of black and ethnic minority groups. These may subconsciously affect their attitude and behaviour towards them. Service providers are likely to make assumptions about the needs, wants, feelings and capabilities of black and ethnic minority people.

One area in which racist assumptions are evident is in the area of housing – one of the largest documented areas of discrimination and disadvantage affecting both people with learning difficulties and black people. People with learning difficulties living in the community are more likely to live in poor housing in a poor-quality environment (Flynn, 1989). Black people are likely to occupy upper stories of high-rise blocks. For a larger proportion, the available space and amenities are worse than for whites (Brown, 1984).

32.2   As sick

> We very strongly encourage a 'sickness' perception of mental handicap in
> Britain, where 50,000 mentally handicapped people are cared for in places
> called 'hospitals' by people called 'nurses', under the supervision of 'doctors'
> and within the management of the 'health service'. At the trial in England in
> 1981 of Dr Leonard Arthur, at which he was found not guilty of the
> attempted murder of a baby with Down's syndrome, a witness for the
> defence described Down's syndrome as 'a timebomb of disease'. (Williams,
> 1985)

Despite resettlement from large hospitals into the community, many
services for people with learning difficulties are still largely the responsibility of health services and involve medical and nursing staff.

The notion of black people as not being physically wholesome has been
and to a large extent still is commonly held. The image is one *not* of being
ill and physically frail, but of being the source and means of spread of
diseases and a threat to world health. Those infectious diseases and other
conditions which are associated with poor personal and social hygiene and
habits are often identified with black people. For example in the past,
unfounded scare stories published in the press about diseased immigrants
(for example, with smallpox) have been used to support racist campaigns
for immigration control.

There has also been a tendency to present black people as the cause of
those diseases which are least socially acceptable and which are associated
with unhealthy sexual habits. For example, the discovery of AIDS
(Acquired Immune Deficiency Syndrome) has generated considerable
public anxiety and the widespread dissemination, via the mass media, of
various theories attempting to locate the origins of the virus in Africa:

> Whilst the general scapegoating of minority groups and foreigners is a well
> known historical practice (the extermination of Jewish communities blamed
> for the 'Black death' in 1348; the identification of American Indians as the
> source of the new mysterious disease syphillis in the 16th century), it is to the
> peculiar institution of slavery and its racist legacies still with us today that one
> must refer in order to place the current theories about AIDS in the proper
> historical perspective. (Yearwood and Amooquay, 1987)

Even black people's reactions to racism have been medicalised. On the
slave plantation, runaways were diagnosed as suffering from 'drapetoma-
nia' – 'the running away from home sickness'. Today, the medicalisation of
black people's normal responses to racism and the stresses of poverty and
alienation is one reason for the disproportionate numbers of Asian and
Afro-Caribbean people who are being treated for schizophrenia and
paranoia (Littlewood and Lipsedge, 1982).

32.3   As a holy innocent

> In some cultures mentally handicapped people are revered as holy 'children of God', being regarded as without original sin. They still usually end up deprived, rejected and segregated from the mainstream of social life. A letter in another British newspaper, the *Daily Mail* recently, following a television series called *Horace* – an attempt to dramatise the adventures of a supposedly mentally handicapped person – gave an insight into the way this unhelpful social role perception can easily be evoked in the public's mind: 'The programme can surely only help the more fortunate among us to a greater understanding of these truly lovely innocents' (*Daily Mail*, 3 May 1982). (Williams, 1985)

There is very little historical evidence to suggest that the role of 'holy innocent' was ever generously applied to black people. Despite the fact that racist and other stereotypes are usually surrounded by contradictions (for example, clichés such as 'work like a black', and 'lazy like a black' exist alongside each other), it would still appear that being viewed as a holy innocent would pose too much of a contradiction when applied to people who have been haunted by the mythology of mostly physical, subhuman and evil qualities. The image of the saintly and innocent Uncle Tom in Harriet Beecher Stowe's pro-abolitionist *Uncle Tom's Cabin* must be one if not the only such historical image of black people.

Media portrayals of black people in situations of natural disasters such as famines, earthquakes and floods in Third World countries often present the image of them as innocent victims of a divine plan. This kind of emphasis inevitably serves to focus attention away from the exploitative relationship between the Western nations and these Third World countries.

32.4   As an eternal child

> In keeping with the role of holy innocents, people with learning difficulties are often viewed and treated as perpetual children. The notion of 'mental age' may have had some technical scientific use, but as a more generally used idea it has been disastrous. It has led people to perceive mentally handicapped people as eternal children, looking 40 years old but 'really a two-year-old inside'. Some leisure clubs for mentally handicapped *adults* are actually called 'Peter Pan Clubs'. (Peter Pan was, of course, the boy who never grew up.) Many mentally handicapped adults have always been treated in every aspect of their lives, even including clothing in some instances, as children. They have the behaviour, possessions and experiences of children; and they are only accorded the same rights, responsibilities, dignity and respect as small children. (Williams, 1985)

Under the system of slavery and imperialism as well as in the present capitalist systems, workers are expected to give the principal part of their production, the fruits of their labour, to someone else and in turn be taken care of. Colonialists therefore cast themselves as father and mother who had a moral duty in taking care of their spiritual and mental well-being – to Christianise the natives, who did not know what was best for themselves. This philanthropic explanation made their gross exploitation appear less distasteful. The forced dependency role could then be explained in terms of the inherent child-like nature of black people. This view was summed up in 1889 by Rudyard Kipling:

> Take up the white man's burden.
> Send forth the best ye breed
> Go bind your sons to exile
> To serve your captains' need;
> To wait in heavy harness
> On fluttered folk and wild –
> Your new caught sullen peoples,
> Half devil and half child.

The relationship between black and white people today is still paternalistic and patronising. Adult black people are often referred to as 'boys' and 'girls' and in endearing terms such as 'sunshine'. Black communities are denied the economic resources and political and social power to determine their own direction. Meanwhile white-managed organisations can still not resist the temptation of applying for and receiving funds to set up projects on behalf of the black community – and employing token members of these communities.

32.5   As an object of pity and burden of charity

A common historical response to the problems of handicapped people has been for religious groups or others to 'take pity' on them and provide some basic services out of a sense of charity. A recent editorial in the British newspaper, the *Daily Star*, following a report of a group of mentally handicapped people being denied admission to a pub in Cornwall, described the people concerned as 'these pathetic charges and their saintly helpers' (*Daily Star*, 7 July 1982). Voluntary organizations often portray handicapped people as pathetic in order to gain charitable money through evoking a sense of pity. The Royal Society for Mentally Handicapped Children and Adults has a logo depicting a pathetic, sad-looking child. The Spastics Society makes extensive use of a pathetic doll-like model of a child with calipers and crutch, situated outside shops to raise money. (Williams, 1985)

The 'burden of charity' image of black people is one which is widely perpetuated by television, a medium which is increasingly playing a major role in fundraising charity activities. Although they are grossly underrepresented on television, these communities tend always to appear when there are disasters or problems. The classic appearance of the naked body, protruding ribs, distended abdomens and fly-swarmed mouths of black children is one such prevalent image.

There is substantial evidence that black people (particularly those who are handicapped) are not claiming the social benefits to which they are entitled. Despite this, the image of black people as merely passive recipients of charity as well as being a burden to the state – living off its social programme to a greater extent than white people – is allowed to predominate. The tremendous amount of self-reliance, hard work and determination which are features of many people's lives, both here and in other countries, goes ignored.

32.6 As an object of ridicule

> The mentally handicapped person as a jester is a well-known historical image; the 'village idiot' was often an object of fun and teasing. Even today the environments in which mentally handicapped people find themselves often have a high proportion of clown images or 'silly' images in them. A series of posters is available showing monkeys in various humorous situations – wrapped in toilet paper, cleaning their teeth in a toilet bowl, etc. An extremely large number of establishments where mentally handicapped people live or work have these posters prominently displayed – reflecting an often unconscious role perception of the handicapped person as 'fool'. For some mentally handicapped people the major content of other people's conversation with them may consist of jokes or supposedly humorous remarks. (Williams, 1985)

In the 1920s and 1930s openly laughing at and insulting black people was commonplace, as is evident in art and drama. White people blacking up in caricatures of black people was popular – as in *The Black and White Minstrel Show*. The rhyme

> Eenie, meenie, minie, mo
> Catch a nigger by his toe
> If he hollers, let him go
> Eenie, meenie, minie, mo

and the song about 'Ten Little Indians' are examples.

Black people's chances of success are largely limited to areas in which they have to place themselves on display – for example, as performers and entertainers and in sports. The image of them as comedians, jokers and simple fun-loving people is still prevalent. Popular caricatures of both Afro-Caribbean and Asian people reflect this. American movies depicting the excitable obese 'black mama' still form part of television film entertainment. The golliwog ('grotesque ugly doll' – *Concise Oxford Dictionary*, 5th edition) is still produced as a child's toy today.

32.7   As a menace

Early this century, mentally handicapped people were considered a eugenic threat and large numbers of relatively mildly handicapped people were placed in institutions where the sexes were segregated. Today, many attempts to establish new community residential services for mentally handicapped people are met by objections, often based on erroneous notions of the 'danger' to local people, children, pets, property or property values. (Williams, 1985)

Traditionally, a common response to those people whom society considers a menace is to have them removed. Prisons and mental hospitals are the two main places where 'deviants' in society are locked away.

The National Association for the Care and Resettlement of Offenders (1986) highlighted the fact that people from this section of the community are more likely to be victims of robbery and assault than the rest of the population. However, the process of criminalising the black community finds its clearest expression in the disproportionate numbers of black people held in prisons. For example, the NACRO report also demonstrated that offenders from these communities are significantly underrepresented in terms of probation orders and are therefore more likely to receive custodial sentences. It revealed that black people were less likely to receive bail than whites and were given longer sentences for similar crimes, yet tended to have fewer previous convictions.

Black people stand a higher risk of being diagnosed as mentally ill (particularly as schizophrenic). Research has indicated that a large proportion are misdiagnosed, their normal signs of distress being misinterpreted as mental illness (Littlewood and Lipsedge, 1982).

Outside of prisons black people are still often viewed with a great deal of suspicion and as a danger to people and property. Indeed, this has contributed to the difficulties black people have in obtaining reasonable housing in the private sector, because people have at times operated under the pretext that their presence poses a threat to the 'British (white) way of life'. Petitions to keep black people out of white neighbourhoods are not uncommon, and racial harassment in housing is a constant cause for concern within black communities.

32.8   As an object of dread

Throughout history the birth of a handicapped child has been seen as the result of evil forces. The 'dreadful' perception of handicap was often encouraged by public exhibition (Fielder, 1981; Howell and Ford, 1980; for an alternative perception see Drimmer, 1976). Most handicapped people today will have experienced people crossing over to the other side of the road rather than meet them. (Williams, 1985)

One of the effects of racism is that black people have been seen as socially undesirable and unattractive and are often dreaded by people in white society. Words such as 'cannibals', 'barbaric' and 'dirty' were commonly used in reference to black people. Many white people today will admit to profound feelings of fear and anxiety in the presence of large numbers of black people.

Much of the dread of black people is a result of their supposedly predominantly sexual orientation. The prevalent characterisation of black men in many American and an increasing number of British films as 'the buck' demonstrates this: 'The buck is the only black stereotype that is sexual. He is brutal, violent, virile, tough, strong – finds white women especially appealing. He is the personification of the black threat to white womanhood and more importantly to white male authority and dominance' (Wallace, 1978). In communities where black men are present, comments such as 'What could happen to English girls?' and 'Would you want your daughter to marry one?' may still be heard.

Similarly, there is a very prevalent view of mentally handicapped people having strong and uncontrolled sexual urges (Craft, 1987). It is commonplace in large mental handicap institutions for people routinely to be given sexual suppressants. The idea of respecting and positively educating people with learning difficulties about socially acceptable ways of expressing their sexuality is very slow to catch on even within the present more humane ideology behind models of services (Craft, 1987).

32.9   Conclusions

As with all struggles against oppression, the campaign to improve policies and services for people with learning difficulties and the campaign for better race relations share a common target and a common language. Health and social welfare agencies have been challenged for their failure to recognise the human value of these sections of our communities. There are cries against segregation, violation, congregation and containment of people, and there are calls for consultation, representation and equal opportunities policies to redress these inequalities in society.

Services to people with learning difficulties are not developed or provided in a social vacuum. Their policies and practices are a reflection of beliefs about what are appropriate responses in society, although service providers are often not aware of the ideologies which shape their beliefs and responses to the people whom they care for and support. There has been an increasing appreciation of the sociological analysis of the position of people with learning difficulties, which has led to continued developments in service. However, there is still much to be done to tackle the issue of racism as an integral part of services.

This article has tried to demonstrate that racist stereotyped images are prevalent in our society. As with views about people with learning difficulties, they exist mainly as part of our unconscious ideology – a factor which makes them less open to challenge. This leaves black and ethnic minority people with learning difficulties doubly disadvantaged and at risk of being kept on the fringes of society. Awareness of the issue of racism and a commitment to challenging it in our personal, professional and organisational practices are essential to the development of services in a multiracial society. The issue therefore has urgent implications for equal opportunities policies in general and anti-racist policies in particular. Without this determination, the common humanity of all people will continue to be violated.

Acknowledgment

This chapter was prepared in the course of carrying out a research study on services for people with learning difficulties and their families from black and ethnic minority communities. The study, to be published under the title *Double Discrimination?* in 1990, was funded by the King's Fund Centre and the Commission for Racial Equality.

References

ALEXANDER, P. (1987) *Racism, Resistance and Revolution*, London, Bookmarks Publishing Corporation.

BROWN, C. (1984) *Black and White Britain*, the third PSI survey, Aldershot, Gower.

CRAFT, A. (1987) *Mental Handicap and Sexuality*, Tunbridge Wells, Costello.

DRIMMER, F. (1976) *Very Special People: The Struggles, Loves and Triumphs of Human Oddities*, New York, Bantam Books.

FIELDER, L. (1981) *Freaks: Myths and Images of Secret Self*, Harmondsworth, Penguin.

FLYNN, M. (1989) *Independent Living for Adults with Mental Handicap: A Place of My Own*, London, Cassell.

FRYER, P. (1984) *Staying Power: The History of Black People in Britain*, London, Pluto Press.

HOWELL, M. and FORD, P. (1980) *The Live History of the Elephant Man*, Harmondsworth, Penguin.

LITTLEWOOD, R. and LIPSEDGE, M. (1982) *Aliens and Alienists: Ethnic Minorities and Psychiatry*, Harmondsworth, Penguin.

NACRO (1986) *Black People and the Criminal Justice System: Summary of the Report of the NACRO Race Issues Advisory Committee*, London, NACRO.

SHEARER, A. (1981) *Disability: Whose Handicap?*, Oxford, Basil Blackwell.

WALLACE, M. (1978) *Black Macho and the Myth of the Super Woman*, East Grinstead, Dial Press.

WILLIAMS, P. (1985) 'The nature and foundations of the concept of normalisation', in Kracas, E. (ed.) *Current Issues in Clinical Psychology 2*, New York, Plenum Press.

WOLFENSBERGER, W. (1972) *The Principle of Normalisation in Human Services*, Toronto, National Institute on Mental Retardation.

WOLFENSBERGER, W. (1975) *The Origin and Nature of our Institutional Models*, New York, Human Policy Press.

YEARWOOD, S. and AMOUQUAYE, E. (1987) *Aids and Racism*. Cited in a Joint Report of the Race and Equality Unit, Women's Unit and Environmental Health Service, Haringey Local Authority, London.

33 Normalisation: the whole answer?

Tim Robinson

The normalisation principle has played an important and influential part in recent developments in services for people with mental handicaps. In particular, it has added considerable force to the rediscovery of optimism and to the attack on a hundred years of underestimation of their potential. It has been even more central in efforts towards reintegration into the mainstream of society, rather than hiding people away in large hospital complexes or ignoring them in the privacy of their family homes. For the most part, these effects have been clearly beneficial and have provided considerable impetus to the attack on the vested interests behind earlier, often damaging, approaches.

However, as the principle has taken root in the English-speaking world, its character has changed in important ways and some worrying tendencies have become apparent. In its Scandinavian beginnings (for example, Nirje, 1976), it was first and foremost an issue of human rights based on a recognition of people with a mental handicap as our fellow human beings and citizens. In North America and Britain, under the dominating in-fluence of Wolfensberger, normalisation has been converted into a tech-nology to transform the image and capabilities of people with mental handicaps so that they will be more accepted within society.

Wolfensberger has made great claims both for the scientific basis and for the potency of this technology (for example, Wolfensberger, 1972, 1983). At one point he described it as 'a scientific theory that is universal, parsimonious and congruent with social and behavioural science' (1983, p. 234). In large measure, the social and behavioural science to which he is referring consists of the labelling theory of deviance and related arguments about the powerful effects of social expectations on people's performance and behaviours. In each case, he has adopted early, very strong statements of these perspectives. He has then drawn on these in a very imaginative way to suggest mechanisms to reverse some of the vicious circles which can lock people with a mental handicap into a marginal and stigmatised role in society. There is much that is original and of value in his proposals. In all this, issues of human rights and of choice have not been lost, but they have receded into the background and their role within normalisation has become somewhat ambiguous.

As this has happened, the principle has begun to take on some of the characteristics of a dogma, even a prison. The practical implications of normalisation have been elaborated in ever finer detail, in particular in the evaluation instruments (PASS and PASSING) which have been developed to assess how closely a service approximates to the principle (Wolfensber-ger and Thomas, 1983). The whole framework is treated as so self-evidently valid (Wolfensberger's own words, 1972, p. 42) and morally right that there is strong resistance to any kind of open debate about the issues. Internal tensions and ambiguities have been glossed over and obscured, rather than being properly addressed. Above all, the closest possible approximation to normalisation is seen as always offering the optimum solution for everyone.

The purpose of this chapter is not to overturn normalisation, but to address some of these dangers so that the potential, and also the limitations, of the principle can be clarified. Central to this is the need for an acceptance of open debate in which people can question aspects of normalisation without being treated as unprincipled fools or moral lepers. Above all else, there is a need to take some of the rhetoric out of the debate and replace it with reasoned argument. Tyne's (1985) reference to all options other than life in an ordinary house in the community as 'the new apartheid' is a classic example of this use of morally loaded rhetoric to foreclose debate. Who could possibly support apartheid? There are, sadly, plenty of other examples in a similar vein (for example, Williams, 1986; Brandon, 1985).

Within this debate we need to acknowledge that we are on the horns of a dilemma. In many respects, society as it exists provides a very unwelcoming and hostile environment for anyone with a mental handicap. Unfortunately, this is directly related to some of our core values and central institutions. For example, the emphasis on maximising economic growth; on individualistic competition; on literacy, numeracy and performance in formal education; on the importance of independence and standing on one's own feet, all ensure that life is made difficult for many people with a mental handicap. It also ensures that they frequently face problems of stigma and low status.

As Wolfensberger (1983) has rightly pointed out, there are two ways in which we can proceed. First, however reluctantly, we may acknowledge the massive reality of society as it is and choose to work largely within the framework provided by its dominant values and institutions. This, basically, is the route which the technological variant of normalisation chooses to follow. The aim is to use our knowledge of the social sciences in order to engineer a greater acceptance of people with mental handicaps on society's terms. This involves enhancing their social image and competencies to a point at which they are accepted and acceptable in terms of existing values.

If we accept this approach, the problem is whether normalisation as a technology is sufficiently powerful, or likely to command sufficient resources and support, to achieve an acceptable degree of real integration for all those involved. If it does not, then some people may find themselves in a painful no man's land. Unfortunately, there does not appear to be a lot of good systematic evidence on precisely how effective normalisation programmes are and what there is is sometimes rather ambiguous (for example, Eyman *et al.*, 1979).

There are grounds also for questioning some of the more extravagant claims made about the scientific basis of normalisation. In particular, a substantial critical literature has now developed reassessing both labelling and social expectation theory (for example, Gove, 1980; Nash, 1976). This re-evaluation does not discount the importance of the processes involved, but it does suggest that they are often less powerful and less easy to control in the real world than Wolfensberger's black and white accounts would suggest.

Further, we must ask how likely a full-blooded commitment to normalisation is, given the nature of the society we live in. Some of Wolfensberger's own recent writings have begun to express considerable pessimism on this score (1984, 1987). None of this suggests that we should abandon normalisation, but it does point to real dangers in relying on it as the only route to salvation.

The alternative Wolfensberger points to is to challenge and seek to alter society's values so that valuation and respect for people with a mental handicap becomes possible on a different basis. This Wolfensberger rejects as a hopeless, if morally admirable, exercise and, given how heavily the dominant values are entrenched, one can understand his pessimism.

Despite this, one has to ask why he and others are so passionately concerned with normalisation in the first place. It does not seem to be simply a question of the missionary zeal of the technocrat wedded to a belief in his own powers. There is certainly something of this in what has been written but, in addition, there also seems to be a burning sense of injustice, a concern to right wrongs done to people with mental handicaps in society. The problem is on what philosophical base this rests – on what view of the nature of man, on what theory of distributive justice, on what ultimate values. We have to turn away from the preoccupation with the technological facets of normalisation and address these more fundamental issues if normalisation is not to lose its way.

Fundamentally, we need to develop a philosophy which provides a sound basis for valuing and respecting all human beings, including those with a mental handicap, regardless of their capabilities, performance or appearance (see, for example, Bayley, forthcoming; Vanier, 1982). It may be unrealistic to expect to convert the whole of society to such a value system or to restructure all our major institutions around it, but it is not unrealistic to seek to widen the circle of those within society who are influenced by it. At the very least, it would seem crucial to provide such a basis for everyone in the welfare services working directly with those with a mental handicap. Otherwise, within the dominant values, they are only left with a basis for respecting and valuing those people for whom normalisation has proved a successful technology.

Starting from such a deeper basis, normalisation appears in a different light. It becomes one very important way in which we may express our respect and valuation of people with mental handicaps – by offering them the maximum opportunity using our best knowledge to participate in and benefit from society as it currently is. For many, maybe most, this will represent what they want and what offers them the prospect of the best quality of life. However, such a philosophy should also provide a basis for developing other alternatives based more centrally on the counter-philosophy itself. Some may prefer these alternatives and they may offer them a better quality of life than 'maximum feasible normalisation'. These alternatives have to be judged against the philosophy itself and not just against how closely they conform to some measure of normalisation. Sometimes such alternatives will involve a measure of segregation judged in normalisation terms. However, it will be a segregation necessary to produce a counter lifestyle which may offer a better quality of life to some people, rather than a segregation to hide people with mental handicaps away.

The problem is well illustrated in two short articles which Hazel West has written about her anxieties for the future of her daughter Lucy (1983; 1986). Lucy is quite severely impaired with 'little understanding of language or the world'. She is, though, friendly, fun-loving, gregarious, full of spontaneity. West graphically describes one occasion when they encountered a busker in town. 'Suddenly, into the circle came running a slight girl, betrousered, anoraked, woolly hatted. In the centre [of the circle of onlookers] she gave out a great roar of excitement, raised her arms high above her head and began to dance. She danced from sheer joy which sprang spontaneously in response to the music, swaying her body, waving her arms, tapping and stepping, twisting her head now this way, now that, before the silent crowd' (West, 1986, p. 12). Lucy was twenty-two. Her behaviour would hardly score well on any measure of normalisation. She would seem in dire need of some 'social image enhancement' or her prospects of meaningful social integration will be severely affected.

It is, of course, possible that a comprehensive programme of normalisation from birth would have avoided these difficulties. However, we need to ask what the costs of this might have been for Lucy and whether it would necessarily have offered her a better quality of life. Her mother's comment tinged, as she admitted, by a mixture of guilt and pride was: 'How could I suppress her? . . . The sheer joy and jubilation she conveyed must be meaningful, infectious, even important in these fractious and, for some, depressing times. Surely she must remind many of us of the joys we neglect to register and express in our own lives.' Provocatively, she ends her article like this: 'Lucy cannot talk at all and understands little verbal language, but her every smile and action communicates a clear message: "Love me as I am – not for what you hope to turn me into. Respect me as I am – I merit your respect"' (ibid, p. 12). Are these just the projections of a guilt-ridden and overprotective mother who, as she made clear elsewhere (West, 1983), seeks a sheltered community for her daughter as the only place she can be herself? Well, maybe; but there again maybe some of the advocates of normalisation ought to look a little more closely at the kind of society in which they are advocating normalisation. Maybe its values need questioning and the damage this can do to some people needs acknowledging.

One challenging and exciting development in recent years, which begins to address some of the dilemmas identified in this chapter, is the creation and spread of L'Arche communities around the world. Their underlying religious philosophy is not easy to summarise briefly, but it does offer a significantly different basis for valuing people – even people with a very severe degree of mental handicap (for example, Vanier, 1982). This starts from a radical acceptance that we are all of equal importance in the eyes of God. People with a mental handicap are just as much children of God as anyone else. As children of God we have an obligation to love one another. This involves not simply doing something which will benefit the other person but, more fundamentally, being with them and fully open to them as human beings. Further, Vanier (the founder of L'Arche) stresses that in such a relationship, we can learn and receive from the person with a mental handicap – no matter how severe their impairment may be. Whilst there are differences of role within each community, everyone is first and foremost a member of the community. L'Arche communities, therefore, can be just that – communities and not merely services provided for clients.

This is not a passive orientation – there is a strong belief in the capacity of all people to grow and develop. Nor is it antithetical to normalisation. For some, the L'Arche community is a way station towards fuller integration into the community; for some it is a base from which to participate in the wider society to the degree they choose; for others, something of a haven from a hostile world. The person, though, not the normalisation principle, is at the centre. Such communities offer both a valuable option in the spectrum of possibilities for people with a mental handicap and also act as living proof that a more humane basis for life is possible. Interestingly there is no shortage of 'so-called normal people' who wish to live in these communities. For them it is a valued option too.

I would like to end with some challenging words from Jean Vanier. 'Handicapped people, particularly those who are less able, are frequently endowed with qualities of heart which serve to remind so-called normal people that their own hearts are closed. Their simplicity frequently serves to reveal our duplicity, untruthfulness and hypocrisy. Their acceptance of their own situation and their humility frequently reveals our pride and our refusal to accept others as they are. So often so-called normal people have interior barriers that prevent them from relating with others in a simple way.' (Cited in Ryan and Thomas, 1980, p. 150.) Romantic twaddle? Maybe, but maybe that simply shows how far we have been corrupted by the values of our society.

In all this, normalisation is most certainly not dead, but its precise meaning and significance must be opened up to real debate. This is not likely to be comfortable. Clear and definite frameworks are always easier to work within. However, we are on the horns of a real dilemma and this dilemma cannot be neatly massaged away. We need to tolerate some uncertainty and dispute, while we return to basics and address the underlying philosophical issues involved. This may not produce one neat solution but, without it, we shall certainly get some of our answers wrong.

References

BAYLEY, M. (forthcoming) 'Normalisation or social role valorisation: an adequate philosophy?', in Baldwin, J. and Hattersley, J. R. (eds) *Mental Handicap: Social Science Approaches*, London, Routledge & Kegan Paul.

BRANDON, D. (1985) 'Honesty, wisdom and crass ignorance', *Community Care*, 28 March 1985.

EYMAN, R. K. *et al.* (1979) 'Relationships between community environments and resident changes in adaptive behaviour: a path model', *American Journal of Mental Deficiency*, Vol. 83, No. 4, pp. 330–8.

GOVE, W. (ed.) (1980) *The Labelling of Deviance*, London, Sage.

NASH, R. (1976) *Teacher Expectation and Pupil Learning*, London, Routledge & Kegan Paul.

NIRJE, B. (1976) 'The normalisation principle', in Kugel, R. and Shearer, A (eds) *Changing Patterns of Residential Services for the Mentally Retarded*, Washington, President's Commission on Mental Retardation, revised edition.

RYAN, J. and THOMAS, R. (1980) *The Politics of Mental Handicap*, Harmondsworth, Penguin.

TYNE, A. (1985) 'The new apartheid', CMH Newsletter, No. 41, Summer.

VANIER, J. (ed.) (1982) *The Challenge of L'Arche*, London, Darton, Longman & Todd.

WEST, H. (1983) 'Care in whose community?', *Parents Voice*, September, pp. 22–3.

WEST, H. (1986) 'Love me as I am', *Parents Voice*, Spring, p. 12.

WILLIAMS, P. (1986) 'Comments made in passing', *Community Care*, 7 August 1986.

WOLFENSBERGER, W. (1972) *The Principle of Normalisation in Human Services*, Toronto, National Institute on Mental Retardation.

WOLFENSBERGER, W. (1983) 'Social role valorisation: a proposed new term for the principle of normalisation', *Mental Retardation*, Vol. 21, No. 6, pp. 234–9.

WOLFENSBERGER, W. (1984) 'Holocaust II?', *Journal of Learning Disabilities*, Vol. 17, No. 7, pp. 439–40.

WOLFENSBERGER, W. (1987) 'Values in the funding of the social services', *American Journal of Mental Deficiency*, Vol. 92, No. 2, pp. 141–3.

WOLFENSBERGER, W. and THOMAS, S. (1983) *Program Analysis of Service Systems, Implementation of Normalisation (PASSING)*, 2nd edition, Toronto, National Institute on Mental Retardation.

34   Mental handicap and oppression

Fiona Williams

34.1   Introduction

This article offers a framework for understanding the lives of people with
learning difficulties as an oppressed group in society. The concept of
'oppression' has emerged as a useful analytical tool to understand the
processes through which certain groups in society find themselves in
subordinate positions, for example, women, the poor, black people or
disabled people.

The emergence of the use of 'oppression' to describe relationships of
power between different groups in society has stemmed from two developments. The first has been a recognition of the experiences of movements
struggling against oppression – for example, the Women's Movement, and
the Civil Rights movement in the United States in the early 1960s. The
second has been an acknowledgement that existing theories of social
divisions based on 'class', whilst important, were inadequate in themselves
in providing an account of why and how these different forms of subordination take place. 'Class' denotes divisions in society based on *economic*
relationships. However, not all forms of inequality can be reduced to
unequal economic relationships even though economic deprivation may
play an important part in reinforcing the inequality of the oppressed. At
the same time, acknowledging the existence of other forms of oppression
does not deny that class exists as a major division in society. What it does
do is force a more complex understanding of the processes by which
different groups in society exercise power over other groups.

34.2   Disability and oppression

The rise of a social and political movement around the issue of disability
has been important in generating social theories of disability. These can
provide us with some helpful concepts for a social understanding of mental
handicap. For example, in his classification of different approaches to
disability, Oliver (1986) distinguishes between 'personal tragedy' theory
and 'social oppression' theory. The 'personal tragedy' approach sees the
characteristics of the disability itself as the cause of the problem and
requiring some form of intervention or help. This may include, for
example, medical treatment, charity, custodial care, day care, professional
help or targetted state benefits. What characterises this approach is that it

takes for granted the dependency of disabled people (or people with learning difficulties) upon the able-bodied world: it does not question the extent to which society itself (rather than the characteristics of disability or mental handicap) is responsible for creating that dependency.

By contrast, the 'social oppression' approach shifts the focus away from the characteristics of the individual's disability and on to the 'social restrictions imposed on them by society' (Oliver, 1986, p. 6). Within the field of mental handicap there have been significant, if tentative, moves in this direction. There has, for example, been more emphasis on hearing what people with learning difficulties have to say about their lives, upon exposing, examining and challenging the labels and stereotypes imposed upon people with learning difficulties. In short, the 'problem' has been turned on its head and the question asked: 'Whose problem?'

However, these developments do not, in themselves, constitute a social theory of oppression: they merely point in that direction. Also, it would be mistaken to push the comparison between mental handicap and disability too far. As forms of oppression, each gives rise to its own histories, social issues, ideologies and subjective experiences. Indeed, the usefulness of the concept of oppression is that it allows us to understand the very specific experiences of subordination of particular groups.

34.3   A framework for understanding oppression

The following section outlines a framework for analysis drawn from theories of other forms of oppression. This points to some of the issues to be explored if we wish to build up a coherent analysis.

Alison Jagger (1983) makes three observations about the meaning of oppression. First, it is 'the imposition of unjust constraints on the freedom of individuals or groups'. Second, it is systematic: 'oppression is the imposition of constraints; it suggests that the problem is not the result of bad luck, ignorance or prejudice, but is caused rather by one group actively subordinating another group to its own interest'. And third, 'Liberation is the correlate of oppression. It is release from oppressive constraints' (p. 6).

We can reduce these observations to three points which encompass the issues a social theory of mental handicap needs to explore: discovering *how* the oppression operates; explaining *why* the oppression takes place; exploring *what strategies* exist to eradicate the oppression.

How does the oppression operate?

Five areas of exploration are suggested here:

1 Accounts of their lives and their histories from people with learning difficulties themselves The rewriting of a history from the viewpoint of an oppressed group has been an important step for many other groups. For example, in her book *Hidden from History* (1973), Sheila Rowbotham says, 'the women's movement has made us ask different questions of our past' (p. x). The documentation of the experiences of people with learning difficulties is gaining recognition through the publication of various auto-biographies (for example, Joseph Deacon's *Tongue-Tied*, 1974), through 'People First' and the Campaign for People with Mental Handicaps, and other research works (for example, Bogdan and Taylor, 1982; Atkinson and Williams, 1989, *Know Me As I Am*).

2 Empirical evidence of disadvantage and injustice One example here comes from research which has shown that people with learning difficulties experience significant poverty by being denied access to paid work or, if in paid work, by being badly paid (see Flynn, 1989; Sumpton, 1988). Furthermore, they often have very little direct control over money that is theirs. Thus this poverty and financial dependency reinforces any real or assumed dependencies people in this group might have, and it mitigates against their being able to live 'normal' lives.

Other evidence can be drawn from the areas of legal, political and civil rights (see Chapter 14). Many social policies for people with learning difficulties have effectively denied them rights normally afforded to others, for example the right to integrate with others, the right to marry and to be a parent, the right to vote, and the right to freedom from harassment, violence and abuse.

3 Stereotypes and labels Stereotyping is a process experienced by all oppressed groups. Sets of characteristics are deemed to be held by all members of the group, and often these characteristics are seen in highly negative terms. People with learning difficulties are often described as volatile, child-like, incapable of deep emotion and so on. Such stereotyping effectively denies people any individuality of their own. Wolfensberger (1988) is one writer who has attempted to counter negative stereotypes with the documentation of positive 'assets' belonging to people with learning difficulties – spontaneity, joy, etc.

The process of attaching labels ('imbecile', 'moron', 'subnormal', 'mentally handicapped' . . .) represents an important dimension in the social creation of mental handicap. Such labels, and the definitions which accompany them, reflect the social and political values and conditions of the society which creates them. The terms 'moron' and 'feeble-minded' were created at the beginning of this century as catch-all labels for those whose behaviour displayed characteristics deemed most inappropriate to the progress of society – slowness, promiscuity, alcoholism, criminality (see Abbott and Sapsford, 1987). Bogdan and Taylor (1982) exemplify this point further by reference to the American Association on Mental Deficiency's redefinition of 'mental retardation' in 1973 which, at the stroke of a pen, 'reduced the incidence of mental handicap and "cured" thousands of persons overnight' (p. 12).

4   Institutions, policies and practices which reinforce subordination (as well as those which do not)   There has been, since the 1960s, increasing documentation of the ways in which, for example, institutional care or policies of segregation and protection have led to oppressive and dehumanising outcomes. Some writers have focused on the impersonal aspects of routinised, large-scale care (Goffman, 1961); others have seen the relationships of power between the carer (professional or otherwise) and cared-for as the source of oppression, whether institutional or not. Writers have looked to the way particular policies are imbued with conflicting and contradictory meanings. 'Community care', for example, to some is the door to normalisation; to others it is a cost-cutting exercise (see Chapter 28).

5   Ideology   Policies and practices are themselves influenced by prevailing ideologies. For instance, ideologies about the nature of intelligence and social competence attribute importance to people's abilities in a very particular way – by regarding particular verbal skills as important but not particular forms of emotional maturity. Educational ideologies of competition and selection may well reinforce this partial view. Professional ideologies may fail to recognise the individual's need and capacity for autonomy, and ideologies of family life may give rise to unreasonable expectations being placed upon women's commitment to care.

Since people with learning difficulties are not a homogeneous group, all these different aspects may well impact in different ways. Men and women with learning difficulties experience family life differently (Noonan Walsh, 1988); black people with learning difficulties may well suffer racism on top of harassment (see Connelly, 1988).

Why does the oppression exist?

Many 'commonsense' explanations or justifications of forms of oppression like racism or sexism suggest that oppression exists because of a 'natural' inferiority or 'essential difference' the group bears in relation to the rest of society. This notion of 'essential difference' needs to be scrutinised. Even if some differences do exist we need to understand why they carry such significance.

One starting point is to document the variations in treatment of people with learning difficulties through histories and across cultures. From this we could see that different societies give mental handicap different meanings according to their different beliefs and social and economic structures. In our own society, for example, one explanation might look to the development of industrial capitalism to explain the significance of devaluation of people with learning difficulties. This particular development put a premium on the classification and selection of the workforce in terms of speed and literacy and numeracy skills, and also upon the qualities deemed necessary for competent motherhood. Since people with learning difficulties failed on both counts, they have been largely excluded from the rewards and status of paid work and parenthood, and rendered marginal to society.

What strategies for liberation exist for people with learning difficulties?

Drawing from the experiences of other oppressed groups, three possible strategies are suggested here. First, however, I look at two issues which, some argue, make strategies for the liberation of people with learning difficulties *not* comparable with those of other groups.

One important strand in the struggle against oppression is the formation of *autonomous groups*. Women-only, black-only, disabled-only groups, it is argued, provide an important setting within which to share experiences, raise consciousness and develop strategies. For people with learning difficulties this development is represented by self-advocacy groups which increasingly are stressing their right to exist without the presence and permission of people who are not so labelled (Crawley, 1988). However, for people with severe learning difficulties this development may seem more problematic. They may require intermediaries to give them a voice that the wider world can understand. However, this problem could be resolved by the development of imaginative strategies of communication. One example is the way Joseph Deacon (1974) wrote his autobiography with the assistance of members of his household, who were themselves labelled as having learning difficulties.

A further issue is the emphasis many oppressed groups give to 'becoming powerful'. Of all people in society, people with learning difficulties have probably the least experience of exercising power over others. Wolfensberger (1988) has seen this as one of their 'assets' as a group. 'Becoming powerful' is thus seen as an inappropriate and possibly corrupting demand. However, the process of 'empowerment' should not mean the capacity to exert power over others: rather it implies taking control over one's own life. The objective of empowerment is to lead to greater independence, but not *total* independence. Paradoxically, the path to greater independence is one which reinforces the idea of interdependence and co-operation.

Strategy 1: Integration into the world as it is

This can be seen as encompassing integration into mainstream schooling, into the community, and into the rights of a normal life-style. The strength of this strategy lies in its insistence that *all* people have certain fundamental rights as human beings. This emphasises the similarities we all, as people, share; it helps dispose of stereotypes and claims about 'essential differences'.

Its limitations lie in the implications of the strategy – especially in its stress on the individual changing to fit the rest of society, rather than on society changing to fit the needs of the individual. In relation to women this strategy has been criticised by the Women's Movement as 'competing with men on their terms'. In common with policies for 'integration and assimilation' aimed at black immigrants in the 1950s and 1960s, such a strategy begs the question of integration into *whose* norms, *whose* values, *whose* culture? Integration policies may, intentionally or otherwise, serve to devalue rather than enhance the characteristics of those whose integration is sought. They may put undue pressure on people with learning difficulties to adapt, and infer that those who fail do so because of their own incapabilities.

By stressing the rights of an oppressed group to have access to the opportunities and life-styles of mainstream society, this could lead to an underrating of the *specific* needs the group may have and, perhaps, their right to be different.

Strategy 2: Withdrawal from society into a separate culture

The practice of setting up 'alternative communities' is widespread. Within the Women's Movement there is a strand of political and cultural separatism, as there is in some organisations of black groups, especially in the United States. In the context of people with learning difficulties these are represented by the therapeutic communities such as L'Arche and the Steiner villages (see Vanier, 1982).

The importance of these forms of alternative living is that they vigorously assert the *positive attributes* which they, as an oppressed group, share against the negative attributes of the outside world. Wolfensberger (1988) stresses the gentle, non-materialistic characteristics of people with learning difficulties as against the hard greediness of the outside world. As such, these communities provide important sources of validity and esteem.

Secondly, their importance lies in their visionary or prefigurative contribution. That is to say, they are able to give practical recognition to new ideas, practices and values previously thought of as Utopian. They thus defy the pessimists and cynics and act as an inspiration to others.

One problem associated with this as a long-term strategy is that, to some extent, it can be said to let society 'off the hook', particularly in the case of the majority of those in the oppressed groups who are unable to withdraw with the separatists. More important, however, is the fact that it encourages mainstream society to think that essential biological or cultural differences *do* exist between them and the oppressed group. It allows society to think that people with learning difficulties are better off away from the hurly-burly of life. And it does not require of society that it confronts its own prejudices.

Strategy 3: Enter the world and change it

This is probably the most challenging of the three possible strategies. It means that the oppressed group has to identify those groups and organisations in mainstream society in which it can intervene, not just on the organisations' terms, as in the first strategy, but in order to raise in their *own* terms the changes which they want to bring about. In relation to women, for example, one of the strategies of the Women's Movement in Britain in recent years has been to get traditionally male-dominated organisations, like the trade unions, to prioritise issues concerning the care of children, equal opportunities or sexual harassment at work.

The importance of this strategy is that it puts the onus of change on the wider society, and it spells out what such changes might be. It also requires that the oppressed group is sufficiently collectively organised to articulate its demands. In this respect some organisations of people with learning difficulties, such as People First, are beginning to do this (Crawley, 1988). By, for example, asserting their right to make choices, to live independently and to have greater say in the provision of welfare services, such groups challenge society in a number of fundamental ways. They challenge the notion of dependency, and in doing this they challenge the way welfare services are provided, especially the hierarchical relationship between welfare user and welfare provider, and also the low levels of benefits available to those who have no paid work. Such demands challenge the idea that families, particularly mothers, should bear the major financial and social responsibility for the care of their dependents. At the same time, demands for the recognition of the specific needs of particular groups challenge the ideology of independency and individualism by insisting upon co-operation and interdependence.

A society which valued people with learning difficulties would have to question seriously the primacy it gives to cognitive skills at the expense of other attributes, such as emotional wisdom, insight and imagination. In turn it would have to examine the institutions of education, paid work and financial rewards which sustain these priorities.

The clear difficulty with these challenges, never mind the articulation of them, is that they present a Herculean task. They appear to strike at the very root of the social and economic organisation of most industrialised societies. On the other hand, whilst they may not be achievable in the here and now, they provide signposts to the goals we might be aiming towards; they provide, like the second strategy, a framework within which more short-term but achievable goals, like the representation of people with learning difficulties on relevant Social Services committees or the right to a minimum wage, can be placed.

Perhaps also the voicing of any such demands indicates those who are the allies of people with learning difficulties – other groups who are moving in the same direction. The demand for a fair day's pay for a fair day's work, the wish to have greater say over welfare services and the people who provide them, the right to walk down the street without fear of harassment or abuse – these are demands common to women, the poor, black people and disabled people. In addition, if some of the more far-reaching demands were realised, such as a reappraisal of the hierarchies of intelligence, competence and skill, it may lead to a better world for everybody, not just people with learning difficulties.

References

ABBOTT, P. and SAPSFORD, R. (1987) *Community Care for Mentally Handicapped Children*, Milton Keynes, Open University Press.

ATKINSON, D. and WILLIAMS, F. (1989) *Know Me As I Am: An Anthology of Prose, Poetry and Art by People with Learning Difficulties*, Sevenoaks, Hodder & Stoughton.

BOGDAN, R. and TAYLOR, S. (1982) *Inside Out: The Social Meaning of Mental Retardation*, Toronto, University of Toronto Press.

CONNELLY, N. (1988) *Care in the Multiracial Community*, London, Policy Studies Institute.

CRAWLEY, B. (1988) *The Growing Voice: A Survey of Self-Advocacy Groups in ATCs and Hospitals in Great Britain*, London, Campaign for People with Mental Handicaps.

DEACON, J. (1974) *Tongue-Tied*, London, MENCAP.

FLYNN, M. (1989) *Independent Living for Adults with Mental Handicap: A Place of My Own*, London, Cassell.

GOFFMAN, E. (1961) *Asylums*, New York, Doubleday,

JAGGER, A. (1983) *Feminist Politics and Human Nature*, Brighton, Harvester Press.

NOONAN WALSH, P. (1988) 'Handicapped and female: two disabilities?', in McConkey, R. and McGuiley, P. (eds) *Concepts and Controversies in Services for People with Mental Handicap*, Dublin, Woodlands Centre and St Michael's House.

OLIVER, M. (1986) 'Social policy and disability: some theoretical issues', *Disability, Handicap and Society*, Vol. 1, No. 1, pp. 5–17.

ROWBOTHAM, S. (1973) *Hidden from History*, London, Pluto Press.

SUMPTON, R. (1988) 'Poverty and mental handicap', in Becker, S. and MacPherson, S. (eds) *Public Issues, Private Pain: Poverty, Social Work and Social Policy*, London, Social Services Insight.

VANIER, J. (1982) *The Challenge of L'Arche*, London, Darton, Longman & Todd.

WOLFENSBERGER, W. (1988) 'Common assets of mentally retarded people that are commonly not acknowledged', *Mental Retardation*, Vol. 26, No. 2, pp. 63–70.

35 How do we know what we think we know?

Moyra Sidell

This article ends the Reader by asking questions about the very process of asking questions itself. In doing so, the author draws links with this book's sister volume Know Me As I Am: An Anthology of Prose, Poetry and Art by People with Learning Difficulties *which was described in the General Introduction. The collection of material for that book provides a valuable illustration of the excitement, the difficulties, and the moral dilemmas involved in the quest to know more about others – and more about ourselves.*

35.1 Introduction

A discussion of research methodology may seem to shelter uneasily under the umbrella of 'Our common humanity'. But in fact research methodology in the social sciences is concerned precisely with how we can know and understand this common humanity.

Happily, the barriers between research and practice, particularly in the field of mental handicap, are breaking down. Practitioners, especially nurses and social workers, are carrying out their own research, and research methods are being adopted in 'practice'. Methods which involve face-to-face, in-depth interviewing techniques, giving the respondents or clients the opportunitity to 'have their say' and reveal themselves and their ideas and opinions, appear to be favoured. These methods are known as qualitative and are appealing because they seem to focus on the respondent or client in the respondent–researcher or client–worker relationship. Similarly, biographical interviewing such as in *Know Me As I Am* is considered therapeutic and links can be made between this approach and counselling.

But research methods properly should be based on methodological considerations that take account of alternative methodologies. Research methods are the tools and techniques used to carry out and analyse a piece of research: tools such as questionnaires and techniques such as interviewing. Research methodology, on the other hand, is the theoretical assumption upon which the choice of a particular research method is made. Methodology is a philosophical matter concerned with both theories of knowledge and, in the social sciences, theories about the nature of social reality and the relationship between human beings and society. So before we can decide how to find out about social life – that is, which methods to use – we have to work out how we know what we know and what it is we want to know about. Methodological issues crucially affect that decision.

This chapter is an attempt to relate these methodological issues to research methods and to clarify, for the reader, what assumptions are being made about the nature of social life and how we can understand it when a particular research method is adopted.

Firstly, quantitative and qualitative research methods will be related to their respective philosophical traditions: positivism and phenomenology. But to stop there would be to ignore the enormous challenge made to these philosophies since the 1960s by structuralism and its later ramifications, which present very different ways of looking at 'reality' and may lead us to a different kind of analysis of 'Our common humanity'. The material in *Know Me As I Am* will be used to illustrate the methodological traditions discussed.

35.2   What is positivism?

It was Comte who first brought the 'scientific method' to bear on the study of the social world. He believed that the 'positive science' of society was at the top of a hierarchy of sciences and represented the zenith of knowledge. For Comte, positivism is a theory of knowledge based on the idea that the only kind of sound knowledge available to humankind is that of science grounded in observation. It is empirical in that it relies on observation of facts but it excludes from the boundaries of knowledge all that cannot be observed. It was founded on the belief that there is only one reality which is observable, and everything else fails the test of knowledge. Anything that was not observable was relegated to the realms of metaphysics, which meant not only that it could not be known but that such knowledge was meaningless. Much of psychology for Comte, writing in the 1830s, was merely metaphysics. Behaviourism, the more modern movement in the psychology of the 1930s, satisfied the demands of positivism in that it claims that human behaviour, in so far as it can be observed, is as much a part of factual reality as any other events in the physical world.

Since Comte, there have been many developments and refinements to positivism in the social sciences. These have been concerned with statistics and consequential issues of measurement as well as meaning and theory-testing. Whilst positivism is essentially empirical, it does not deny the importance of theory. However, if theory is to be more than mere speculation then it must be verified by empirical evidence. How to collect that empirical evidence has been a constant theme in the positivistic tradition. The most familiar instrument of positivism in the social sciences is the sample survey, where data is collected usually by administering a questionnaire. Various statistical techniques are then applied to analyse the data. It is the demands of these statistical techniques which dictate the design of the sample survey.

Broadly, statistical analysis falls into two categories: descriptive and inductive. Descriptive statistics measure and count certain characteristics of populations or groups of people or institutions. Inductive statistics use the laws of probability to infer from a sample of a population to the whole in order to be able to generalise and predict, provided that each unit of the population has an equal chance of being included into the sample, which then becomes a random sample.

Clearly these exercises were not purposeless and this process of observing, counting and describing was to provide an analysis of social affairs from which to formulate laws or law-like generalisations similar to those found in the natural sciences, with the ultimate purpose of controlling social life in the way that the natural sciences were controlling nature. It was found that regularities occurred in the social world in much the same way as regularities occurred in the natural world, leading to the assumption that there must be an underlying cause to these regularities. The bell-shaped frequency distribution of measurement known as the 'normal curve' indicates the strength of these regularities, the average or mean value being the true value, with irregularities due to error. These statistical procedures promote the importance of norms and regularities in human life and activity and clearly have profound implications for those with learning difficulties. They justify the labelling of 'abnormal' to someone who does not measure up to the norm in, say, IQ tests. It is thus possible to criticise the normalisation movement on the grounds that it is influenced by these notions of averages and normality.

To sum up the positivist position on 'Our common humanity', the 'what we want to know about' only has meaning if it can be observed. How we can know about it is by observing, measuring and analysing it statistically to produce laws which would enable us to understand and control it. The implications need not be sinister: social reformers such as Booth and Rowntree used these techniques to attempt to affect social policy on behalf of the urbanised poor.

How can we relate these procedures to *Know Me As I Am*? Clearly the material in that book was not gathered to positivistic specifications. No statistical sampling techniques were used or standardised instruments of measurement. So, strictly speaking, the material in it is not amenable to statistical analysis. But if for the sake of illustration we assume that all those who told their 'stories' represented a large enough random sample on which to perform statistical analysis and that they had all been prompted to provide standardised information on a number of specific variables – and if one of these variables was the number of friends each person had, and another the frequency of contact with these friends – it would then be possible, using various statistical techniques, to generalise and predict the amount of social contact that the 'average' person with learning difficulties has. Similarly one might try to measure and categorise the types of transition that such an 'average' person might have, and then predict the likely transitions that other similar 'average' persons might encounter. Clearly there are many difficulties with this type of analysis, but the task before us is not to attack or defend any of the methodologies discussed but to provide an understanding of the philosophical bases of these methodologies. It so happens that the quantitative method has in recent years been largely rejected in favour of the qualitative methods based on the principles of phenomenology.

35.3   Methodology in the phenomenological tradition

Phenomenology entered the forbidden territory of positivism by attempting to know the unknowable, that which positivism designates as metaphysical – the subjective experiences of individuals. Phenomenology asserts that only by studying the 'actors' in the social drama can the drama be understood. It is only the actors' consciousness of social reality which is important and worthy of study. A powerful influence on modern thinking has been the notion of the 'social construction of reality'[1] which has its roots in phenomenology. This asserts that reality is constructed by human beings in the process of thinking about it and is sometimes misconstrued in the belief that this 'Socially Constructed Reality' is less than real, is not natural. But the Social Constructionist position is that natural man/woman is social man/woman, there is no other reality.

Two major methodological strands have emerged in the phenomenological tradition: Symbolic Interactionism and Ethnomethodology. Both can be traced back to the German philosopher Kant. His basic idea was that history, culture and even the self are created by human beings and that these creations or constructions have to be understood by different methods from those appropriate to understanding nature. He would not disagree with the Positivist approach of observing the natural world but, unlike the Positivists, he acknowledged that there were other ways of understanding and knowing social (human) beings which were not directly observable.

Symbolic Interactionism derives from Kant's interest in unravelling the meanings of the world created by human beings. Its methodology was strongly influenced by the idea that man can act toward himself; that he is a reflexive being;[2] human beings interpret their world and are constantly engaged in acting and responding to symbols and gestures. Human action, therefore, is not simply the stimulus response mechanism of Pavlov's dogs, but a constant complicated interaction based on a shared understanding of the meaning of the symbols and gestures learnt through the process of socialisation. The implications of Symbolic Interactionism have been drawn out as:

> ... the peculiar and distinctive character of interaction as it takes place between human beings. The peculiarity consists in the fact that human beings interpret or 'define' each other's actions instead of merely reacting to each other's actions. Their 'response' is not made directly to the actions of one another but instead is based on the meaning which they attach to such actions.[3]

Interactionism sees all human action as collective action and methodologically requires close attention to be paid to that collective element. It entails the researcher taking a role in the acting unit, becoming involved in the drama so that he/she can come to know at least all the main actors.

Another strand of Phenomenology is Ethnomethodology. This concentrates on consciousness of the world, and is interested in the world of everyday life, the commonplace:

> Ethnomethodological studies explore the influence of people's standpoints (or perspectives) on their thought and action in great detail. To explain why people act as they do, ethnomethodologists examine their physical and social circumstances, their habits and the habits of those around them, their background knowledge, and their practical motives. These factors influence how people make sense of their environment and respond to it.[4]

How people make sense of their environment/situation is their account of it. Ethnomethodologists are interested in how these accounts are made.

Qualitative methods such as participant observation, in-depth unstructured or semi-structured interviewing, biographical and 'life history' construction are all drawn from these forms of Phenomenology. These methods have clearly attracted researchers in the field of mental handicap who feel that it is vital to listen to individuals so categorised to get their version of their situation. D. Atkinson[5] has drawn attention to this and there are other examples in this Reader, for example, R. Bogdan and S. J. Taylor[6] and the superb study of D. A. Goode[7] who made extraordinary efforts to understand how Christine made sense of her world in spite of not having any verbal accounts to draw on. And J. Wilkinson's concept of 'Being there' is an attempt to have a role in the acting unit.[8]

The anthology *Know Me As I Am* represents an attempt to understand the social reality of a group of people categorised as having learning difficulties. It does so by getting them to give accounts of themselves and their lives and so stands squarely in the qualitative/phenomenological domain. But one of the major problems in reaching an understanding of these accounts lies in the contextualising of them. Whilst we may be interested in certain features of the person's life, such as 'friendships' or 'transitions', we can only understand these features in the context of the individual's whole life. We certainly do not need stereotyped labels, but we do need to know a good deal about the person's background and significant others.

Provided with this background information, the Ethnomethodologist would claim only to try to understand how each individual accounts for his/her situation; how it is that they have many or few friends; or how the transitions occurred in a person's life; and why this was experienced in the way it was. The Interactionist might go further and look for common patterns between different people's accounts in order to explain the shared meanings that either friendships or transitions have for this group of people with learning difficulties.

The purposes of phenomenological analysis of *Know Me As I Am* would not be to seek generalisations about the social world of people with learning difficulties, but to understand the social world of the particular group of people whose accounts are given. Such an analysis might indeed give us insights into the social world of other people with learning difficulties, but this method does not pretend to yield hard evidence from which we can predict the likely experiences of people with learning difficulties in general. D. G. Goode's immense efforts to understand Christine would only help him to interact more meaningfully with Christine, but his methods provide an example of how to attempt to understand others with similar difficulties.

'Our common humanity' for the Phenomenologist is of our own creation and we only know it and communicate it to ourselves and to each other by the use of collectively understood symbols. Social reality is constructed and apprehended by human beings mainly through the symbol of language. Language is the prime means of communicating;

> ... through language I can transcend the gap between my manipulating zone and that of the other; I can synchronise my biographical time sequence with his; and I can converse with him about individuals and collectivities with whom we are not at present in face-to-face interaction.[9]

And language is also the means by which we communicate with ourselves in solitary thought, we 'live in a world of signs and symbols every day'.[10]

There are two worlds on offer to us, the Positivistic one which is objectively perceived by the senses as 'real' which we can know firsthand, and the Phenomenological world which is the world we create in the process of thinking about it and which we know symbolically. Structuralism offers yet another world to us – the world of signs which may not at first sight seem too far removed from the 'symbolic' world of the interactionist.

35.4   Structuralist reality

The Structuralist also lives, not only in a world of signs, but in a world of signs about signs, but there is an important difference between them and the Phenomenologists. For the Phenomenologist it is the individual who uses the signs and symbols as the means by which he/she subjectively experiences the objective world. For the Structuralist, and more particularly the Post-Structuralist, it is the language or sign system (and this includes gesture, dress, perfume, posture, etc.) which exists prior to and creates the subject and subjective experience.[11] It inverts the base/superstructure model and asserts a primacy of society over the self.

For the purposes of this chapter, the importance of Structuralism is that it raises doubts about our ability to understand human experiences using the qualitative methods which the Phenomenologists promise can yield such insights. These doubts arise because Structuralism maintains that people's accounts of their experiences can no longer be taken as direct, original experience because language lies outside their control. As Michel Foucault puts it:

> Expressing their thoughts in words of which they are not the masters, enclosing them in verbal forms whose historical dimensions they are unaware of, men believe that their speech is their servant and do not realise that they are submitting themselves to its demands.[12]

Language operates on experience through 'myth' and 'discourse'. Myths are not just concerned with 'classical' mythology but, as the anthropologist Levi-Strauss[13] points out, with the system of images and beliefs which all cultures, both primitive and sophisticated, construct. Myths convey cultural messages, often unconsciously, and Levi-Strauss believed actually form, as well as reflect, men's/women's thinking. He was concerned with 'how myths think in men, unbeknown to them'.[14]

Bogdan and Taylor, in this volume, rightly claim that mental retardation is a myth, 'a socially created category which is assumed to have an existence independent of its creators' minds'.[15] Mental retardation exists as myth and conveys a whole set of messages about what it means to be mentally retarded which do not directly describe any concrete reality. But myths exist in this way and exert a powerful influence on men's/women's thinking.

It was Roland Barthes who maintained that myth was not the innocent conveyor of a culture's beliefs, but that myths always convey the messages of the dominant culture which then help to maintain that culture. Myths are not merely untruths, they are much more subtle. To quote Barthes, 'Myth hides nothing and flaunts nothing; it distorts; myth is neither a lie nor a confession: it is an inflexion.'[16]

For Michel Foucault, the power of language lies in 'discourses' which are bodies of knowledge. Discursive fields are structured around social organisations and processes such as the education system, the media, the law, the political system, the family, etc. Legal discourses, for example, are concerned with crime, punishment, legal practice, etc. Within one discursive field there will be many competing discourses; some will advocate capital punishment, others the rehabilitation of offenders. The discursive field also defines what can be considered a legal matter. For instance, domestic violence used to be confined to the discourse on the family, but it is now entering the legal discourse as crime.

It would be a useful and ambitious exercise to explore all the competing discourses in the field of mental handicap, both from a historical and a cross-cultural perspective.

Foucault was interested in the relationship of discourses and power and the way in which one set of discourses becomes dominant.[17] For him, discourses are a reflection of particular values and are based on the 'interests' of different groups, of which class, gender and race are the obvious ones. How a discourse exerts power is through individuals who become its carriers by adopting the forms of subjectivity and the meanings and values which it propounds. This theory provides an understanding of where our experience comes from and can explain why so many of our experiences and opinions are sometimes incoherent and contradictory. It also asserts that there is no 'true' or 'right' discourse, there are only different discourses. It thus prevents us from searching for the 'truth' of the matter.

How would this thinking based on Structuralism affect our reading of *Know Me As I Am*?[18] A Structuralist reading would pay little attention to the author and his/her background. It would only be interested in what is said and the way in which it is said. There are highly technical ways of analysing the accounts in Structuralist terms using techniques which I have neither the space nor the expertise to demonstrate here. For our purposes, what structuralism can alert us to is the presence of myths and competing discourses, not only in the life stories presented but also in the creative work of fiction, poetry and drawings. We might look for evidence of competing discourses on institutions and community care; or versions of the myth that 'people like us don't get married and have children'. Myths and discourses do not remain fixed or static. They are constantly being retold, and each retelling reinterprets, that is, adds to or subtracts from them. We would then also be interested in comparing versions. This analysis ultimately tells us more about the discourses and myths than the people uttering them. For those of us who cherish a sense of the individual, the full impact of Structuralist thought and its assault on the self and the value of subjective experience is a bleak and unpalatable proposition. Even though we may wish to reject its full implications, we should, if nothing else, be mindful of the doubts it raises about how we can know and understand human experience.

35.5   Conclusion

This chapter has argued not for one methodology rather than another in the quest for knowledge, but an awareness that the different ways of pursuing knowledge make different assumptions about the status of that knowledge. It is tempting to advocate a kind of methodological pluralism in research on learning difficulties, which to some extent now exists in relation to Positivism and Phenomenology. Indeed, many studies happily combine a qualitative and quantitative element in their work, but Structuralism and Post-Structuralism offer not so much an alternative as a challenge to the basic assumptions of the other two traditions, which ought to shake any tendency to methodological complacency.

Notes

1 P. Berger and T. Luckman (1987) *The Social Construction of Reality*, London, Pelican Books.

2 G. H. Meade (1934) *Mind, Self and Society*, Chicago, University of Chicago Press.

3 H. Blumer (1962) 'Society as Symbolic Interaction', in A. M. Rose (ed.) *Human Behaviour and Social Processes: an Interactive Approach*, London, Routledge & Kegan Paul.

4 W. Handel (1982) *Ethnomethodology – How People Make Sense*, Englewood Cliffs, New Jersey, Prentice-Hall.

5 D. Atkinson (1988) 'Research interviews with people with mental handicap', *Mental Handicap Research*, Vol. 1, No. 1, pp. 75–90. Reprinted in this Reader.

6 R. Bogdan and S. J. Taylor (1982) *Inside Out: The Social Meaning of Retardation*, Toronto, University of Toronto Press. An extract is reprinted in this Reader.

7 D. A. Goode (1979) 'The world of the congenitally deaf-blind: towards the grounds for achieving human understanding', in H. Schvarte and J. Jacobs (eds) *Qualitative Sociology: a Method to Madness*, New York, The Free Press. Reprinted in this Reader.

8 J. Wilkinson, '"Being there": evaluating life quality from feelings and daily experience'. Specially commissioned for this Reader.

9 P. Berger and T. Luckman, op. cit., p. 54.

10 Ibid., p. 55.

11 There is much diversity, complexity and many conflicts within the Structuralist and Post-Structuralist tradition, but most forms can be related to Saussure's linguistic theory of signs and signifiers. It is beyond the scope of this chapter to give a thorough account of the theory and its implications but, for the reader who would like to pursue this, I would recommend they use Richard Harland's *Superstructuralism* (Methuen, 1987) and Terence Hawkes' *Structuralism and Semiotics* (Methuen, 1977).

12 Michel Foucault (1970) *The Order of Things*, London, Tavistock Publications.

13 Claude Levi-Strauss (1968) *Structural Anthropology*, London, Allen Lane.

14 Claude Levi-Strauss (1970) *The Raw and the Cooked*, London, Jonathan Cape.

15 R. Bogdan, and S. J. Taylor, op. cit.

16 Roland Barthes (1982) *Mythologies*, New York, Hill and Way.

17 Michel Foucault (1980) *Power/Knowledge*, Brighton, Harvester Press. Also, by the same author, *The History of Sexuality, Volume 1, an introduction* (1981), Harmondsworth, Penguin.

18 D. Atkinson and F. Williams (1989) *Know Me As I Am: An Anthology of Prose, Poetry and Art by People with Learning Difficulties*, Sevenoaks, Hodder and Stoughton.

List of contributors

Diane Amans is a senior lecturer at Stockport College and a tutor on the Open University course, 'Special Needs in Education'. She runs an evening class in 'Independent Living Skills' and trains people to work with adults who have learning difficulties. She is particularly interested in leisure and vocational opportunities.

Dorothy Atkinson is a lecturer in the Health and Social Welfare Department at the Open University and member of the K668 course team. Her background is in social work, and social work education, and includes several years' experience of working with people with learning difficulties and their families. She has published widely, basing her publications on practical experience and on research findings.

David Barron has retired from work on health grounds. As well as running his own home, he does voluntary work at Trafford General Hospital and lectures at schools and at Manchester University.

Carol Baxter is a freelance researcher, trainer and consultant in the area of health, race and equal opportunities. For twelve years she worked as a nurse, midwife, health visitor and health promotion officer. Carol is the founder of the Manchester Community Health Group for Ethnic Minorities and has been a research assistant at Bristol University on the Double Discrimination Project. Originally from Jamaica, she now lives in Salford with her family.

Roger Blunden is Director of the Community Living Development Team at the King's Fund Centre. He was previously Director of the Mental Handicap in Wales – Applied Research Unit, based in Cardiff, and has been associated with a number of major innovations in community-based services including the All-Wales Strategy for the Development of Services for People with Mental Handicap.

Robert Bogdan received his PhD in sociology from Syracuse University in 1971. He is the author of several research method texts. His latest book, *Freak Show: Presenting Human Oddities for Profits and Amusement*, is a social history of sideshows. Dr Bogdan is presently a professor of sociology, special education and cultural foundations of education at Syracuse University in New York, USA.

Ann Brechin lives with her husband and three children in Milton Keynes, where she has worked with the Open University for ten years. Previously a clinical psychologist she also worked closely with self-help family groups. She chaired the course team which developed 'Mental Handicap: Patterns for Living', and the course for which this Reader was compiled.

Hilary Brown is a Senior Lecturer in the Centre for the Applied Psychology of Social Care, at the University of Kent. She has been responsible, in recent years, for the development of training materials for staff in the priority care services, including 'Lifestyles' and the Bringing People Back Home video assisted packages. Hilary is married with one son.

Beverley Bryan was born in Jamaica and came to England at the age of ten. She has taught at all levels of the education system and now works in teacher education at Thames Polytechnic. She has been active in black community and women's politics, was a founder member of the Brixton Black Women's Group in the early 1970s and also of OWAAD, the first national black women's network. She is currently working on a history-fiction project. She has two sons and lives in South London.

Sybil Charnock, Pam Dennis, Hilary Lang, Mary MacLachlan and Jill Osman are all housewives. Their sons and daughters still attend Fairwinds Special Development Centre. Hilary, Jill, Pam and Sybil are at present running a 10 Session Workshop for eight professionals arranged through the training department.

Stella Dadzie was born in London of Anglo-Ghanaian parentage. She has taught for fifteen years in Secondary, Community and Further Education, most recently teaching Afro-Caribbean History and Popular Culture and co-ordinating Access and Return to Study courses in Further Education. She was a founder-member of the national Black women's organisation OWAAD (Organisation for Women of Asian & African Descent). She lives in North London with her eight year old son, working as a freelance trainer/consultant while completing her second book.

Gillian Dalley is a social anthropologist whose research interests include the working relationships between health and social work professionals involved in community care and the impact of community care policies on women. She has worked in the voluntary sector and currently works at the Centre for Health Economics, York University. She wrote *Ideologies of caring: rethinking community and collectives* (Macmillan) in 1988. She has three children.

Christine Darbyshire successfully completed a two-year 'Learning for Living' course at Stockport College and subsequently attended an evening class in 'Independent Living Skills'. She has recently begun six months' trial at a local sheltered workshop and hopes to remain in work in the future.

Hilton Davis is a Senior Lecturer in Clinical Psychology at the London Hospital Medical College. He works in the area of Child Health developing frameworks and methods for helping families of children with chronic illness and disabilities. A central assumption of this work is that respectful support for parents is the most effective ingredient of successful intervention.

Robert Edgerton is a Cultural Anthropologist in the Departments of

Anthropology and Psychiatry at the University of California. He is also an Associate Director of that University's Mental Retardation Research Centre. Although maintaining a broad interest in anthropology, his research involvement in mental retardation spans 30 years, focussing on the everyday lives of persons with mental retardation.

David Felce studied residential provision for people with severe and profound mental handicap as a member of the Health Care Evaluation Research Team. His work has involved evaluation of the Wessex Community Units and research on housing for adults with challenging behaviours. He was Director of the British Institute of Mental Handicap and moved to take up the Directorship of the Mental Handicap in Wales Applied Research Unit.

Margaret Flynn works with the National Development Team and is an Honorary Research Fellow at the Hester Adrian Research Centre, University of Manchester. Her background includes psychology and social work. Her PhD examined the decision-making skills of adults with learning difficulties. She has since been involved in research examining services and the experiences of young people and adults with learning difficulties.

David Goode. I live with my wife and son in New Jersey. I teach sociology and disabilities courses at the college. I have an interest in ethnomethodological studies of basic social processes through the examination of the lives of persons with severe disabilities. I also have a strong interest in social policy in the disabilities field and especially in quality of life as a social policy concept.

Lorraine Grindrod (formerly Eastwood). Since leaving the group home I have continued to work within the community. At the moment I am taking 'time-out' in order to reassess my personal goals. I am getting to know my grandchildren, and do all those enjoyable things which have been neglected over the years of caring for others. Undoubtedly, I shall return to 'community' based work, but in which direction remains to be seen.

Michael Gunn has been a Lecturer in Law at the University of Nottingham since 1978. He has a keen interest in the law as it affects people with mental handicap. This interest has resulted in contributions to conferences, courses and some writings. He also has developed an interest in mental health law and criminal law.

Kenneth Harrison (on behalf of People First of Plymouth) is aged 44. I left home at 21 years of age and spent the next 23 years in Hospitals, private or 'service' residential homes. For the last nine months I have lived independently, with support of home helps. Why did it take 23 years?

Dr A. Jahoda, Mr M. Cattermole and Professor I. Markova with the support of the Scottish Home and Health Department, have carried out research into training for independent living and quality of life of people with learning difficulties. Dr Jahoda is now working for Strathclyde

Regional Social Work Department and Mr Cattermole works for the MENCAP Homes Foundation in Hertfordshire. Their major interest concerns the quality of life of people with learning difficulties. Professor I. Markova works in the Department of Psychology at the University of Stirling and her main interest concerns communication between people with learning difficulties and professionals.

Richard Jenkins is Senior Lecturer in Sociology at the University College of Swansea. Having previously done research on the transition to adulthood and unemployment in Northern Ireland and South Wales he is currently engaged in a study of mental handicap and the transition to adulthood, funded by the Joseph Rowntree Memorial Trust.

Bengt Nirje is the Executive Director of the Swedish Parents Organisation and the originator of the Principle of Normalisation. He has worked in Canada and Sweden in direct services and is at present a research consultant in Uppsala.

Parent (anon). I have six children between the age of three and 14. Hazel (Hazel is not her child's real name), my youngest child, who is autistic, will be starting full time education in September. I have just completed the H.F.F.C. in Social Science and will be studying for the CQSW. My interest in a career in social work developed before I knew my daughter was autistic, but Hazel's autism has had some influence on my interest in working with the mentally handicapped.

Burt Perrin is based in Toronto where he works for the Ministry of Community and Social Services of the government of Ontario. In the 1980s he has been prominent in providing legal services to people with disabilities. He continues to be involved in social research and evaluation.

Louisa Reynolds was educated at a girls Grammar School, read history at University and later completed a teacher training course. She has worked in many different jobs but teaching has mostly paid the grocery bills. She has always taught in the area of special needs, most recently in adult education.

Ann Richardson, formerly a Senior Fellow at the Policy Studies Institute, now works as an independent researcher. She has published two books (with Jane Ritchie) about parents: *Making the Break* (King's Fund, 1986) and *Letting Go* (Open University Press, 1989). Their most recent book is on friendship and people with learning difficulties (*Developing Friendships*, PSI 1989).

Tim Robinson is a lecturer in Sociological Studies, Sheffield University. Recently qualified as a social worker and currently working part time with a family based respite care scheme for children with learning difficulties. Father of a child with spina bifida and hydrocephalus and, for ten years, secretary of a parent support group.

Suzanne Scafe was born in Jamaica. She has taught in secondary schools in both London and Jamaica and she now teaches at a college in South London. She has worked with the committee of Women for Progress in Jamaica and with London based black women's groups. She has recently published *Teaching Black Literature* (Virago). She lives in South London.

Moyra Siddell is a researcher by trade but also a trained nurse and the mother of two grown up daughters. Research experience has been in the field of health and social welfare though she claims not in mental handicap. Her interest however has been stimulated by being a reader on the K668 course and working with the course team on the development of a research strategy.

Valerie Sinason is a Senior Child Psychotherapist at the Tavistock Clinic. She is Psychotherapist Convenor of the Mental Handicap workshop and specialises in mental handicap and sexual abuse. She is on the ACCP Abuse Research Committee and Mental Handicap Convenor of the APP (Association for Psychoanalytic Psychotherapy in the NHS). A poet and writer, she is married and has two teenage children.

Helen Smith has a background in clinical psychology in a number of health service settings. Her work at the King's Fund Centre has focussed on developing comprehensive community-based services for people with mental health problems. She has recently joined the Institute of Social and Applied Psychology at the University of Kent.

Michelle Stanworth has researched and written extensively on issues related to gender and to reproduction. Her books include *Gender and Schooling, Women and the Public Sphere* (with Janet Siltanen) and *Reproductive Technologies*. She is Senior Lecturer in Sociology at the Anglia Higher Education College in Cambridge and Chair of the Women's Studies Panel there. She has two children.

John Swain lives with Jade and their four children in Newcastle-upon-Tyne where he lectures in special educational needs at the Polytechnic. He has been a consultant on the Open University 'Patterns for Living' and 'Changing Perspectives' courses, wrote *Changing Relationships* with Ann Brechin, and is conducting a research study of pupil participation in decision making.

Steven J. Taylor is Director of the Center on Human Policy and Professor of Special Education at Syracuse University. He has authored numerous publications, including *Inside Out: The Social Meaning of Mental Retardation*, with Robert Bogdan. Interests include community integration, social policy and disability, and social relationships between people with and without disabilities.

Sandy Toogood is Team Leader of the Intensive Support Team, Clwyd. He worked in community-based residential services before joining SETRHA's

(South East Thames Regional Health Authority) Special Development Team. His interest lies in developing high quality, community-based, residential services for people who exhibit challenging behaviours.

Linda Ward is Adviser to the Joseph Rowntree Memorial Trust's Disability Programme. Based at the University of Bristol's Norah Fry Research Centre, she has a particular interest in the development of better services for people with learning difficulties from black and ethnic minority communities. She was previously a member of the Open University course team which produced 'Mental Handicap: Patterns for Living'.

Julie Wilkinson was born in 1961 near Liverpool. At Keele University she read psychology and sociology and completed a Masters Degree. She later completed a PhD and a period as a Research Associate at Bristol University, evaluating aspects of challenging behaviour and quality of life in the field of learning difficulty. She now works as a Clinical Psychologist in the NHS, living in Bristol with her partner and her dog Billy.

Fiona Williams is a lecturer in the Department of Health & Social Welfare at the Open University. She has a background in social policy and is the author of *Social Policy, A Critical Introduction: Issues of Race, Gender & Class*.

Wolf Wolfensberger PhD was born in Germany and has lived in the United States since 1950. He was one of the earliest promoters in North America of community services for handicapped persons that would be systematic and based on what was then called the principle of normalisation. He has become an internationally known leader in services to handicapped people, but especially in mental retardation.

Index

AAMD (American Association on Mental Deficiency) 78, 256
'abnormality' (as concept) 263
abortion 90–91, 93, 103, 232; *for* handicapped women 105, 106
Abortion Act 1967 232
adaptive behaviour, 'measurement' of 78
adulthood 11, 100–107; *see also* social attitudes
Adult Training Centre *see* ATC
advocacy 106, 200–201; citizen advocacy 196; *see also* self-advocacy
ageing *see* elderly
AIDS (Acquired Immune-Deficiency Syndrome) 239
Albert 32–3
allowances *see* financial allowances
American Association on Mental Deficiency (AAMD) 78, 256
amniocentesis 89–93
Appleby, Fiona 68
ARC (Association for Retarded Citizens) (US) 126
Arthur, Dr Leonard 239
artificial insemination 89, 91
Asians (in Britain) 34–40
Association of Carers 202
ATC (Adult Training Centre): rights-denying 32–3; stigma/self-concept 149–55; users' comments 131–2
attitudes (to handicap) *see* social attitudes
autism 86–8

B., *Mrs* 35–40
Bainbridge, Vera 68, 69
Bangladeshi families (in UK) 34–40
Barry 140–46
Barthes, Roland 267
behaviourism 262
behaviour-modification 29–30, 111
'being there' approach 54–61, 265
benefactors 184
Better Services for the Mentally Handicapped (DHSS) 199
Black Power movement 83
blacks *see* ethnic minorities
Black and White Minstrel Show (television series) 242
blindness *see* deaf-blind
Boland, Roger 68
Bolton Community Health Council (1987) 54
Booth, Charles 263
bottom-up approaches 55–61, 195
Bourlet, Gary 116
Bowland, *Mr* 16
Boyson, Rhodes, MP 90
Bubwith hostel 123

Canadian Association for Community Living 126
carers: *as* oppressors 256; associations 202; continuity 26–7; informal 202, 203; low status 234–5; *see also* families;

professionals *etc.*
Carter, Edgar 69
Central Statistical Office: *Social Trends 14* (1983) 17
cerebral palsy 140–46
child development centre 86–7
Child Development Teams 34–40
children (of handicapped) *see* parenthood
choice 30–31, 112–15, 187, 225; categories model 114; reactive environment 114–15
Chris/Christine 133–9, 265, 266
citizen advocacy 196
citizenship 102; *see also* adulthood
client-focused care 200–201
CMHERA (Campaign Community and Mental Handicap Education and Research Association) 46
Coard, Bernard 84
cohabitation 101; *see also* marriage
community care *see* community living; families *etc.*
community living: adulthood 104–6; ageing 182–7; Associations for 126; care by/in community 202; choice 112–13; community as monitor 26–7; family attitudes 18–21; future planning 195–6; historical overview 199–205; interviews 13–21, 54–61, 63–71; L'Arche communities 251, 258–9; marriage/partnerships 15–18; models 200–203; normalisation 222; personal comments 127; policy 199–205, 256; resource control 201–2; Steiner villages 258–9; success/failure 188–9; women's care role *see under* women
community nurse 25; mental handicap 202; psychiatric 202
Comte, Auguste 262
Cooke, Miss 16
co-residency 18
counselling 50; Parent Advisers 34–40
culture, and norms 134, 223, 225, 233

Daily Mail (newspaper) 240
Daily Star (newspaper) 241
day nurseries 38
day services 130–32, 191, 234; *see also* ATC
Deacon, Charles 68
deaf-blind 115, 133–9, 175–81
decision-making skills 115
'defective' (as legal term) 94
deinstitutionalisation *see* community living
dentists 167–8
Department of Health and Social Security *see* DHSS
dependency 43, 45
desirable futures 196
'developmentally delayed' (as term) 104
DHSS (Dept of Health and Social Security) White Papers: (1971) 199; (1975) 199; (1976) 199; (1977) 199; (1981a) 199, 202; (1981b) 199, 202, 204
dignity 11, 29–33; *see also* adulthood *etc.*

directive therapy 113
disability theories 253–7
discourse theory 267–8
divorce 97
doctors 25, 43, 178; community living (US)
185; euthanasia 103, 239; GPs' care role
202; misdiagnosis 86–8; *see also*
professionals
Down's syndrome 7–12, 35–9, 105, 154, 239
drugs/medication 31–2, 169, 177, 178, 180–
81; medical approach 43; 'zombie-drug'
31–2

ECHR *see* European Convention *etc.*
education, special schools 84, 175
educationally subnormal (ESN), blacks 83–5
elderly 18, 182–7; care provision, general
199–200, 218
Ellis, *Mrs* 17–18
Ely Hospital 178, 179, 180–81
employment 16, 17, 122, 127, 183–4, 255;
role enhancement 213; users' comments
131–2
empowerment 196, 257
environment, learned helplessness 109–116
epilepsy 18, 122–3, 127, 160, 177
ESN (educationally subnormal), blacks 83–5
ethnic minorities 237–45; blacks 82–5, 91;
mental illness 239, 243; multiple
discrimination 237, 245, 256; non-English-
speaking 34–40
ethnomethodology 264, 265–6
eugenics 243; 'new' 89–93
European Convention on Human Rights
(ECHR) 94–7
euthanasia 103, 239

families 24–8; *and* learned helplessness 110;
as carers 7–12, 159–61, 175–6, 178, 180; *see
also under* women; choice 113, 114;
community living 18–21; constraints 27;
deprived 34–40; handicap acceptance 24–
5, 159–60; informal care systems 202, 204;
leaving home 7–12, 26–7, 192;
misrepresented 86–8; mothers as primary
carers 25; non-English-speaking 34–40;
Parent Advisers 34–40; professionals
assessed 24–8; reproductive choice 91, 93;
stigma/self-concept 149–55; 'taken
advantage of' 27; Wells Road project 188,
192–3
familism concept 205
'feeblemindedness' (as term) 77, 255–6
Field, Douglas 69
financial allowances 38; attendance
allowance 38; community care 'penalties'
205; Family Fund 38, 39; ignorance of 26;
not taken up 242; SSI (US) 183, 185;
Supplementary Benefit Regulations 205
finger-spelling 179
Five Accomplishments 55, 59, 190
Foucault, Michel 267–8
friends 14
Furniss, *Mrs* 124

genetic engineering 91–2
genetic screening 89–93
Gill, Beryl *and* Keith 68
Gilmore, Doreen 70

government (UK): care policy 199–205;
'enabling role' 203
GP (general practitioner) *see under* doctors
Graham, Robert K. 91
Greaves, *Miss* 17
Grey, Philip 69
Griffiths, Robert 175–81
Griffiths (R.) Report (1988) 194, 199–200,
202, 204
group homes 64–71, 191–6; landlady scheme
162–6
Guardian, The 90
'Guide to Personal Futures Planning, A'
(O'Brien) 55

handicap: approaches/models 42–51, 103,
237–45, 253–4; 'assets' 255, 257, 258;
behavioural approaches 103; *compared
with* black status 237–45; *compared with*
unemployment 100–107; *compared with*
women's status 229–35; denied/declared
147, 149–55; disability theories 253–7;
educational approach 43–5; gender
differences 256; incidence 78–9; medical
approach 42–3, 45, 103, 239; misdiagnosed
14, 86–8; multiple 115; personal tragedy
theory 253–4; physical, care provision 199–
200; poverty 255; psychological
approaches 103; social oppression theory
254; terminology 76–80, 94–5, 97, 103–4;
see also labelling
Hardcastle, Joyce 69, 70
Harlow, *Mr* 17
Harper, Robert 69
Hayes, Edward 69
Hazel 86–8
health visitors, misdiagnosis 86–8
Heart of the Race, The (Bryan *et al.*) 73
Heaton, *Mr and Mrs* 15–16
helplessness *see* learned helplessness;
powerlessness
*Helplessness: On Depression, Development
and Death* (Seligman) 109–10
Hidden from History (Rowbotham) 255
Hitler, Adolf 89
holidays 7, 27, 159, 160, 172; *for* carers 7; *see
also* short-term care
Horace (television series) 240
hospitals 25, 38, 180–81, 191, 232;
emergency care 176; flexicare workers 180;
misdiagnosis 86–8; short-term care 159,
160–61; *see also* institutions
hostels, entering 7–12
House of Commons Social Services
Committee (1985) 189, 204
household skills 15–17
houses, staffed *see* staffed homes
housing 238
housing project, district 188–96
*How the West Indian Child is Made
Educationally Subnormal . . .* (Coard) 84
human agency 154–5

IDC (Independent Development Council)
(1986) 195
ideological corporatism 203
'idiot' (as term) 77, 79, 103, 104, 126
illness, misdiagnosed 32
'imbecile' (as term) 79, 103, 126

'impairment' (as term) 104
independence, 'unattainable' 44
informal care 202
Informal Caring Support Unit 202
insemination, artificial 89, 91
Inside Out (Bogdan *and* Taylor) 73
institutions 180–81, 256; *as* protection 223;
    budget protection 201; choice 30–31, 112–
    13; historical overview 199–200; learned
    helplessness 186; medical approach 43;
    normalisation in 222; 'outside society' 106;
    personal comments 121–4, 127, 132;
    punishment ward 121; rights-denying 29–
    33; total 233
intelligence (as concept) 78
interactionism 264–5, 266
interviews 54–61, 63–71, 261, 265;
    'intersubjectivity' 133–9; stigma/self-
    concept 148–9
isolation 14, 16, 17
Ivan 30

Jeanette 105
Jensen, Arthur 82
Jones, Norma 69
Jordan, Marjorie 18
Joseph Rowntree Memorial Trust 194

Kallikak Family, The (Goddard) 77
Kant, Immanuel 264
key workers 132
King's Fund Centre 202; (1980) 55, 188, 201;
    (1985) 201
King's Fund Institute (1987) 201, 203
Kipling, Rudyard 241
Know Me As I Am (Atkinson *and* Williams)
    261–2, 263, 265–6, 268

labelling 73, 76–80, 125, 126–7, 132, 255–6;
    and norm-deviation 230; staff 194; theories
    of 249, 267–8
landlady/supervisor scheme 162–6
L'Arche communities 251, 258–9
law 32, 104–6; Criminal Law Revision
    Committee (CLRC) (1984 report) 95–6;
    sexuality 94–7, 104–5
learned helplessness 109–16, 186; 'taught'
    111–12; theories 109–10
letting go 7–12, 26–7
Lévi-Strauss, Claude 267
Long, Edward 238
Longton, Joe 16

M., Mary 167–74
Madoc, *Miss* 16
Makaton sign language 177
'managerial-planning' care model 201, 204
managers, empowerment 196
marriage/partnerships 15–18, 184; failed 17–
    18; legal aspects 94, 97; voidability 97
Martin 7–12
Mary M. . . 167–74
masturbation 95
Matrimonial Causes Act 1973 104
medical model 42–3, 45, 103, 239
medication *see* drugs
Mencap organisation 106
'mental age' (as concept) 103–4, 105, 240
'mental disorder' (as legal term) 97
Mental Health Act 1959 96

Mental Health Act 1983 104
Mental Health (Amendment) Act 1982 94–6
mental illness: care provision 199–200; ethnic
    minorities 239, 243
'mental retardation' (as term) 76–80, 126–7,
    256, 267
Miriam 32
'moron' (as term) 77–8, 79, 126, 255–6
mother-and-child groups 36
myth theory 267–8

NACRO (National Association for the Care
    and Resettlement of Offenders) (1986) 243
'named persons' 39
National Association for the Care and
    Resettlement of Offenders (NACRO)
    (1986) 243
networks *see* social support
NIMROD organisation 176–9, 180, 181
normal curve 263
normalisation 42, 46–9, 104, 211–18, 247–51;
    'abnormal' 31, 33; adulthood 104–6; *and*
    self-advocacy 45–8; appearance/reality
    225–6; choice 187; conservatism corollary
    216, 225–6; core themes 214–15; critiques
    of 247–51; defined 211–12, 220, 224;
    degrees of 222; friendships 14; 'image-
    changing technology' 247, 248; imitation/
    identification 216–17; imposed 224; in
    institutions 222; integration 217; means/
    ends differentiation 226–7; misconceptions
    220–27; 'people-changing' 258;
    philosophical issues 249–51; policy
    implementation 201; pragmatism 227;
    schemata 214–15; segregation 250; special
    services 221–2
'normality': culture-bound 134; inaccessible
    44
norms, statistics-defined 263
nurses: community 25; community mental
    handicap 202; community psychiatric 202;
    general hospital 25; idealised 235

Oaklands Housing Project 55–61
'obedient passivity' 134
O'Brien, Joan 16
opportunity-giving 115
oppression 73–116, 253–60; liberation
    strategies 257–9; *see also* rights *etc.*
'ordinary life' 55, 188, 190; adulthood 106;
    policy implementation 201
Ordinary Life, An (King's Fund Centre) 188

Pacific State Hospital (Lanterman State
    Hospital) 183
Parent Advisers 34–40, 74
parenthood 15–18, 105; right to 94
parents (of handicapped) *see* families
Parker, Denise 69
participant observation 56, 59–60, 147, 265
Participation Forum 116
partnerships *see* marriage
PASS (Program Analysis of Service Systems)
    46, 215, 224, 225–6, 247
PASSING (Program Analysis of Service
    Systems' Implementation of
    Normalization Goals) 215, 247
People First organisation 119–20, 226, 230,
    255, 259; conference 125–9; day service
    130–32

phenomenology 264–6
play 37, 38; deaf-blind 134–8
positive monitoring 195
positivism 262–4
post-structuralism 267–9
posture 143, 144, 167
'potential-reaching' 44
powerlessness 59, 60, 76, 257; *see also*
  learned helplessness
'professional-practice' care model 201–2
professionals: *as* 'legislators' 106; day
  services 132; deaf-blind children 133–4,
  135, 137–8; derogation of handicapped 79;
  educational 43–5; ethnic minorities 238;
  family support 24–8; medical 42–3, 45;
  normalisation 47–51; norm-deviation 231–
  2; rights-denying 29–33; role preservation
  201–2, 203; stigma/self-concept 149–55;
  value-changing 249; 'working alliance' 42–
  51
Program Analysis of Service Systems *etc. see*
  PASS; PASSING
prostitution 20
'pseudo-feeblemindedness' 77
PSSRU (Personal Social Services Research
  Unit) (University of Kent) 203–4
psychotherapy 140–46

quality action groups 195–6
questionnaires 263

Rangecroft, *Mr* 16
Registered Homes Act 1984 191
Representation of the People Act 1949 104
Reproductive Technologies (Stanworth) 74
reproductive technology 89–93
research methodology 54, 67, 182, 183, 261–
  9; interviews 261; participant observation
  147; questionnaires 263; users' conference
  130–31; *see also* interview *etc.*
rights, human/civil 29–33, 43, 200–201, 203,
  255; given, not innate 232; normalisation
  247; sex 94–7
'ring-fencing' (of budgets) 201
Rita, *Aunty* 17
Road Traffic Act 1960 104
Robbins, N. (1963) 136
Robert (Griffiths) 175–81
role circularity 215
role enhancement 211–18
role expectancy 215
Rose, Hilary 93
Rowntree, Benjamin Seebohm 263
Royal College of Nursing (1985) 202
Royal Society for Mentally Handicapped
  Children and Adults 241
rubella 175; *see also* deaf-blind
Rubella Association 179

Salvation Army 123–4
Sanger, Margaret 89
Saunders, Melanie 69
segregation: normalisation 250; self-concept
  148
Seguin, Edouard 44
self-advocacy 32, 42, 196, 230, 257; *and*
  normalisation 45–8; 'changing the world'
  259–60; choice 115–16; learned

helplessness 115–16; People First
  conference 125–9; press coverage 128–9;
  'right to differ' 226; writings 255, 261*ff*
self-concept 147–55
self-fulfilling prophecies, medical approaches
  43
self-help groups *see* self-advocacy
self-help scales 167
SENSE organisation 179
'severely mentally handicapped' (as legal
  term) 94–6
Sewell, *Mr and Mrs* 16–17
sexual abuse 20
sexuality 14–15, 244; 'abnormal' 32–3;
  eugenics 89–93; 'gross indecency' 96;
  homosexuality 95; legal aspects 94–7, 104–
  5; *see also* marriage
Sexual Offences Acts, 1956–76 94–6
Shared Action Planning 50
Sharpe, *Mr and Mrs* 123–4
Shaw, George Bernard 89
Short, Nigel 70
Shorter, Jan 29–30
short-term care 25, 26, 159, 175, 176, 179
siblings 19–21, 26; *see also* families
'sick role' 42–3
signing 177
Sinsheimer, R.L. 91–2
social attitudes 76–80, 237–45; abuse 15;
  'burden' 90, 241–2; 'children, permanent'
  11, 19, 100–107, 151, 152, 240–41; children
  of God 251; 'clients' 231–2; community
  living 19; 'deviancy' 47; fear, object of
  243–4; innocents 240; minority group 82–
  5, 151, 237–45, 253–60; 'packaged product'
  47; ridicule, object of 242; rights-denying
  29–33; 'right to be different' 224, 229, 258;
  role enhancement 211–18; 'same'/
  'different' 149–55; 'sick persons' 42–3, 239;
  stigma 147–55; 'surplus population' 79;
  'threat' 77–8, 79, 103, 239, 243; to be
  'normalised' 221, 224; to be protected 223;
  (un)consciousness 215, 233; value-
  changing 249–51
social construction theory 147–8, 154–5, 264,
  266
social expectation theory 249
social imagery 217
social role perceptions 237–45; *see also* social
  attitudes
social role valorisation (SRV) 47, 211; *see
  also* normalisation
social services: adulthood of handicapped
  104; Asian families 34–40; carers as victims
  234–5; clients as victims 231–2;
  handicapped representation 260; home
  aids 161; landlady scheme 162–3, 165;
  normalisation 221–2; *see also* professionals
social skills 13–14, 167–73, 180, 183–6, 190;
  behaviour-modification 29–30; role
  enhancement 212–16
social support 13–21
social workers: *as* interviewers 65–6; care
  role 202; family support 25–6, 28
South Western Regional Core Group 130–32
'spastic' (as term) 126
Spastics Society 241
special schools 84, 175
speech 37
SRV *see* social role valorisation

staffed homes/houses 55–61, 167–74, 176–9, 188–95; advocacy 195; individual 181; staff aims 194; staff as 'prosthesis' 168
statistical analysis 262–4
Steiner villages 258–9
stereotyping 43, 255–6; *see also* labelling
sterilisation 16, 184; nazism 89; unwilled 76, 105, 125
stigma 147–55
Stott, Arthur 70
Stowe, Harriet Beecher 240
structuralism 266–9
'stupid' (as term) 79
'subnormal' (as term) 104, 238
Survivors Speak Out organisation 230
symbolic interactionism 264–5, 266
Symington, Neville 145

Taylor, *Mr* 17
teachers 29–33, 44; *see also* professionals
Thomas 31–2
Thurnham, Peter, MP 90
Tongue-Tied (Deacon) 255
Tower Hamlets (London) Parent Adviser Scheme 34–40

Uncle Tom's Cabin (Stowe) 240

unemployment 15–17, 255; *compared with* mental handicap 100–107
United Nations Declaration on the Rights of Mentally Retarded Persons ('UN') 94–7
Universal History 238
'UN' *see* United Nations Declaration *etc.*

Variety Club of Great Britain 160
Vickers, Laura 68
Vicky 159–61

Walker, Ben 16
Walker, Enid *and* Ralph 70
Warnock, Mary 92
Watson, *Miss* 16
Wells Road (Bristol) service 188–96
West, Lucy 250
West, Mabel 68, 69
wheelchairs 160
White Papers *see* DHSS *etc.*
Whixley institution 121–4
Wilkinson, J. 265
Wise, Alice 69
women: *and* handicapped status 229–35; *as* carers 205, 229, 233–5; *see also* families
Woods, Joan 68, 69
'working alliance' 42–51; origin of term 50